Hunkin's Note

I'm flattered that people are still interested in the cartoons I drew for the *Observer* magazine over twenty years ago. I assumed this book would be intended as nostalgia for adults who remembered the originals, but am delighted to think it might also reach a new audience of young people.

The editor felt the random experiments needed a bit of explanation. I guess they are a little eccentric. I'm just not very good at reading for long periods. I get fidgety and want to get up and do something. So I felt that if people had the patience to read through a cartoon, they might then like to get up and do an experiment. Of course, any young people wishing to try the experiments will need some adult assistance.

This book is a selection of some of my favourite Rudiments of Wisdom cartoons, refreshed for the 21st century. I hope you enjoy them.

Hunkin's Research

Researching anything has become much easier since I did the cartoons. My washing machine went wrong earlier today, and after a few minutes on Google I found not only the most likely cause, but also a site to buy the spare part and even a video of how to replace it.

Twenty years ago, I had to find everything for my cartoons in books, in magazines, or by phoning experts. The difficulty of the research sometimes made it very satisfying and it was often fun talking to the experts. However, the internet is certainly a lot quicker. There is a lot of unreliable stuff online, but information can be unreliable wherever it comes from.

I still love books, even though they can be inaccurate too. I don't remember many of the facts in the cartoons but I often remember the books the facts came from. My books almost feel like extensions to my brain.

Anyway, whatever sources you use, researching things is always interesting. I hope the cartoons encourage you to start researching things for yourself!

P.S. (A day later.) The washing machine still doesn't work — the advice on Google didn't solve the problem. I'll have to do some more research...

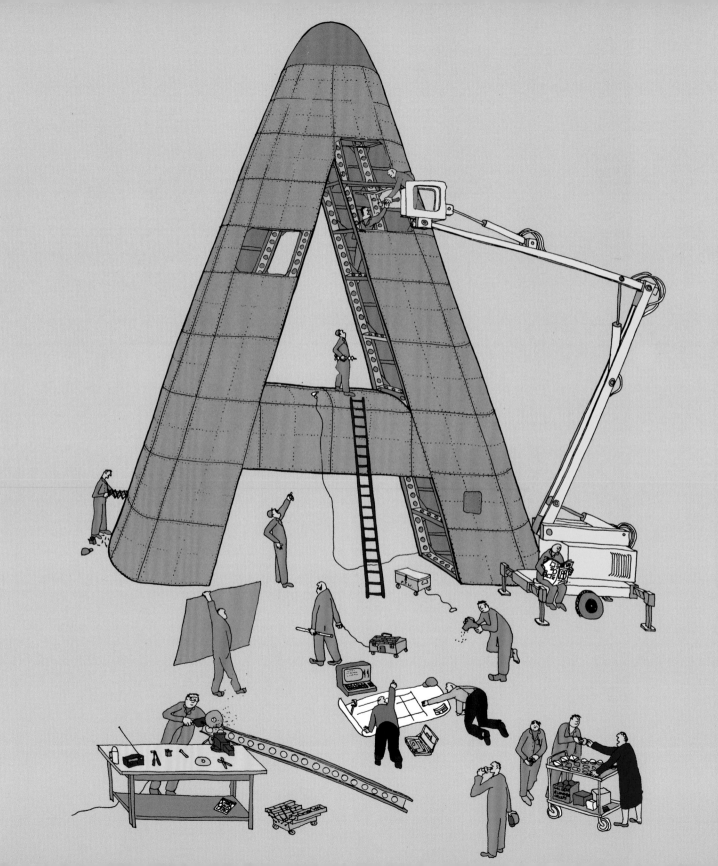

✩ ANAESTHETICS ✩
SUBSTANCES PRODUCING INSENSIBILITY

THE ORIGINAL ANAESTHETIC

THE EARLIEST REFERENCE TO AN ANAESTHETIC IS A 3RD-CENTURY CHINESE MANUSCRIPT DESCRIBING THE USE OF LARGE DOSES OF A WINE CALLED MA-FEI-SAN BY THE SURGEON HUA TO FOR RENDERING HIS PATIENTS INSENSIBLE TO PAIN.

VAN HELMONT, 1579-1644, WAS THE FIRST MAN TO REALIZE A CLASS OF GASEOUS SUBSTANCES EXISTED APART FROM AIR. HE MADE RATHER UNSUCCESSFUL ATTEMPTS TO COLLECT & CLASSIFY SAMPLES. BY THE 19TH CENTURY MANY GASES WERE BEING INHALED, SUPPOSEDLY CURING ALL SORTS OF DISEASES. IN 1794 BEDDOES'S PNEUMATIC INSTITUTE WAS FOUNDED TO INVESTIGATE THE PHYSIOLOGICAL EFFECTS OF GASES THOROUGHLY & THIS RESULTED IN THE DISCOVERY OF THE REMARKABLE PROPERTIES OF LAUGHING GAS (THE FIRST GASEOUS ANAESTHETIC)

GASES

THE LAUGHING-GAS SHOW

AN EXTRACT FROM AN 1844 POSTER FOR A LAUGHING GAS DEMONSTRATION. "THE EFFECT OF THE GAS IS TO MAKE THOSE WHO INHALE IT LAUGH, SING, SPEAK OR FIGHT ETC, ACCORDING TO THEIR LEADING TRAIT OF CHARACTER. N.B. THE GAS WILL ONLY BE ADMINISTERED TO GENTLEMEN OF THE FIRST RESPECTABILITY. THE OBJECT IS TO MAKE THE ENTERTAINMENT IN EVERY RESPECT A GENTEEL AFFAIR. MR COLTON WILL GIVE A PRIVATE ENTERTAINMENT FOR THOSE LADIES WHO DESIRE TO INHALE THE GAS." THE USE OF LARGER DOSES OF LAUGHING GAS AS AN ANAESTHETIC WAS FIRST TRIED IN 1846 BY AN AMERICAN DENTIST, HORACE WELLS, INSPIRED BY ONE OF MR COLTON'S SHOWS.

HEWITT'S APPARATUS

AN INGENIOUS PORTABLE DENTIST'S SET WITH A FOOT PUMP BUILT INTO THE CARRYING BAG

GUINEA PIGS

ETHER WAS FIRST ADMINISTERED TO CHICKENS TO TEST ITS EFFECTS OXYGEN WAS FIRST TESTED ON A MOUSE & LAUGHING GAS WAS FIRST TESTED ON ACTUAL GUINEA PIGS.

CLOVER'S APPARATUS

SIMPLY A LARGE SACK OF CHLOROFORM, PRE-MIXED WITH AIR IN THE CORRECT RATIO, SLUNG OVER THE DENTIST'S SHOULDER.

ALLIS'S APPARATUS 1875

THE FIRST CHLOROFORM INHALER NOT TO RESTRICT THE AIR-FLOW TO THE PATIENT. UNFORTUNATELY IT ALSO EXPOSED THE SURGEON & ALL HIS ASSISTANTS TO THE VAPOUR.

ANAESTHETICS & PRESSURE

ONE DISCOUNTED THEORY OF HOW ANAESTHETICS WORK DEPENDED ON THE OBSERVATION THAT INCREASED PRESSURES PREVENTED THEM FROM FUNCTIONING. IT IS NOW KNOWN THAT ANAESTHETICS AFFECT A NERVE'S TAKE UP OF IONS, BLOCKING MESSAGES OF PAIN TO THE BRAIN.

HOW TO MAKE YOUR ARMS RISE

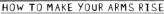

IN A DOORWAY, PUSH ARMS OUTWARDS AGAINST DOOR FRAME WITH CONSIDERABLE FORCE FOR 60 SECONDS. THEN RELAX & ARMS WILL MYSTERIOUSLY RISE AUTOMATICALLY.

ANAESTHETICS

ANIMAL EYES
ORGANS OF VISION OF LIFE FORMS

JELLYFISH EYES

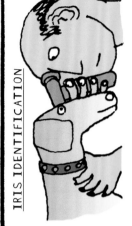

THE PORTUGUESE MAN-OF-WAR JELLYFISH HAS A PRIMITIVE EYE: A PIT WITH SOME LIGHT-SENSITIVE CELLS AT THE BOTTOM. UNFORTUNATELY, THIS JELLYFISH HAS NO DEFINITE BRAIN CAPABLE OF INTERPRETING ANY VISUAL INFORMATION.

IRIS IDENTIFICATION

THE IRIS OF THE DOG (& SOME OTHER MAMMALS) CARRIES A DISTINCTIVE PATTERN, UNIQUE TO EACH BEAST. ATTEMPTS HAVE BEEN MADE IN THE US TO USE THIS AS A METHOD OF IDENTIFICATION (IN A SIMILAR WAY TO FINGERPRINTS).

INVERTEBRATE EYES

SQUID, CUTTLEFISH & OCTOPUSES HAVE THE BEST SIGHT OF THE INVERTEBRATES. EXACTLY HOW MUCH THEIR LIMITED BRAINS CAN PROFIT FROM THEIR EYES IS UNCERTAIN.

HOW TO WRITE WITH A CALCULATOR

TURN YOUR CALCULATOR UPSIDE DOWN & PRESS EACH OF THE KEYS. YOU WILL FIND THAT YOU CAN MAKE SEVEN LETTERS OF THE ALPHABET.

SEE HOW MANY WORDS YOU CAN "WRITE" WITH THESE LETTERS.

COLOUR VISION

ANIMALS THAT CAN DISCRIMINATE COLOUR INCLUDE APES, BIRDS, MONKEYS, INSECTS & SOME FISHES. THOSE THAT CANNOT INCLUDE ELEPHANTS, CAMELS, HIPPOS, RHINOS & MOST BEASTS OF PREY.

THE THIRD EYE

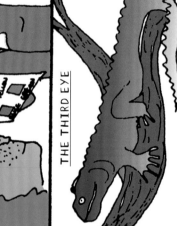

KING CRABS, LAMPREYS & THE TUATERA LIZARDS OF NEW ZEALAND HAVE A THIRD EYE CALLED THE PINEAL BODY. THE VESTIGIAL TRACES OF A THIRD EYE REMAIN ON TOP OF THE HEAD OF EVERY FISH, SOMETIMES ON A LONG STALK. THIRD EYES WERE ORIGINALLY USED AS PERISCOPES FOR SEEING ABOVE THE WATER SURFACE.

HARES' EYES

A HARE CAN SEE BEHIND ITSELF WHEN RUNNING & STILL KEEP A JUMP AHEAD OF A CHASING PREDATOR. UNFORTUNATELY, WHILE THUS OCCUPIED, IT SEES LITTLE OF WHAT LIES AHEAD & OFTEN COLLIDES WITH OBSTACLES.

MOLES' EYES

THE MOLE HAS THE SMALLEST EYE OF ANY VERTEBRATE ANIMAL. IT IS ONE MILLIMETRE IN DIAMETER.

SIDEWAYS VISION

HORSES, & MANY BREEDS OF DOG, CANNOT SEE DIRECTLY IN FRONT OF THEM. FOR THIS REASON IT IS IMPORTANT TO GIVE A HORSE A LOOSE REIN AFTER TAKING OFF ON A JUMP SO IT CAN MOVE ITS HEAD TO CALCULATE ITS LANDING.

ONE EYE

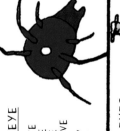

THE ONLY LIFE FORM TO HAVE A SINGLE EYE IS A PRIMITIVE FISH CALLED, PREDICTABLY, CYCLOPS.

BULLS' EYES

BULLS ARE COMPLETELY COLOUR-BLIND, SO THE TRADITIONAL RED BULLFIGHTER'S CLOAK COULD BE ANY COLOUR SO FAR AS THE BULL IS CONCERNED. IN ANY CASE, IT IS GENERALLY BELIEVED THAT BULLS CLOSE THEIR EYES WHEN CHARGING.

BIRDS' EYES

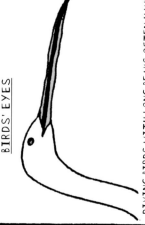

DIVING BIRDS WITH LONG BEAKS OFTEN HAVE COLOURED CHANNELS ALONG THE BEAK. THEY ARE THOUGHT TO USE THESE AS "SIGHTS" FOR AIMING THEIR DIVES TO CATCH PREY.

ARMOUR
DEFENCE DRESS FOR USE WHILE FIGHTING

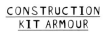

THE PROBLEMS WITH CHAIN MAIL

A CHAIN-MAIL SUIT IS VERY CLUMSY. ALMOST ALL ITS WEIGHT IS CARRIED BY THE SHOULDERS, UNLIKE A FITTED SUIT OF PLATE ARMOUR WHICH DISTRIBUTES THE WEIGHT OVER THE BODY. THE MAIL SUIT IS ALSO VERY STUFFY. TO PREVENT BONES FROM SHATTERING ON A SWORD IMPACT, A THICK QUILTED LAYER IS NEEDED AS UNDERWEAR. A FABRIC SURCOAT IS ALSO A NECESSITY TO PREVENT THE MAIL, OFTEN CLOGGED WITH ROTTEN GRASS & FOOD, FROM SMELLING. IT IS A MYSTERY HOW THE CRUSADERS MANAGED TO FIGHT WEARING MAIL SUITS IN THE MIDDLE EAST WHEN THE TEMPERATURE REACHED 32°C.

CONSTRUCTION KIT ARMOUR

IN 1548 THE ARCHDUKE MAXIMILIAN II OF AUSTRIA HAD A SUIT OF ARMOUR WITH 123 PIECES, ASSEMBLED IN 12 WAYS. THESE ADAPTED IT FOR WALKING, FOOT COMBAT, RIDING, JOUSTING & OTHER APPLICATIONS.

FASHIONABLE ARMOUR

THE DESIGN OF ARMOUR TENDED TO FOLLOW THE FASHION IN CLOTHES. WHEN SHOES WITH LONG POINTED TOES CAME INTO FASHION IN THE MID-15TH CENTURY THESE WERE COPIED BY ARMOURERS. THEY WERE SO CLUMSY THAT THEY WERE IMPRACTICAL WHEN THE WEARER WAS WALKING, SO THE TOE WAS MADE SEPARATELY & WAS SCREWED ON AFTER MOUNTING. LATER ARMOURERS COPIED IN METAL PUFFS & SASHES, IMITATION STITCHES & EVEN WIRE HAIR.

GLANCING BLOWS

IT IS OBVIOUSLY AN ADVANTAGE TO HAVE A HELMET THAT DEFLECTS BLOWS, ABSORBING THE IMPACT. IT IS THUS A MYSTERY WHY THE FLAT-TOPPED HELMET APPEARED IN THE 13TH CENTURY. IT WAS HIGHLY IMPRACTICAL NOT ONLY BECAUSE IT TRANSMITTED THE FULL IMPACT OF VERTICAL BLOWS BUT ALSO BECAUSE ITS MODE OF ATTACHMENT WAS INADEQUATE & HORIZONTAL BLOWS TENDED TO KNOCK IT OFF.

THE REVIVAL OF ARMOUR

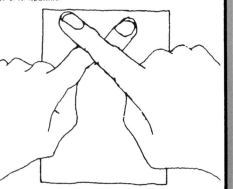

BY 1700 THE MAJORITY OF EUROPEAN TROOPS HAD DISCARDED ARMOUR BECAUSE OF ITS VULNERABILITY TO BULLETS. HOWEVER, ARMOUR WAS REINTRODUCED IN 1915 WHEN IT WAS FOUND THAT THE TROOPS IN THE TRENCHES WERE SUFFERING A HIGH PERCENTAGE OF HEAD WOUNDS. TIN HATS WERE ISSUED TO ALL TROOPS & MACHINE-GUNNERS ALSO RECEIVED BREAST-PLATES.

HORSE ARMOUR

ALTHOUGH HORSE ARMOUR WAS USED IN PARADES AND TOURNAMENTS, A SATISFACTORY METHOD OF PROTECTING HORSES WAS NEVER DISCOVERED. PLATE ARMOUR EITHER DRASTICALLY REDUCED THEIR MOBILITY OR LEFT VITAL PARTS UNCOVERED. CHAIN-MAIL SUITS, FITTED TO 6,000 HORSES IN ONE DISASTROUS CAMPAIGN OF THE CRUSADES, WAS FOUND TO BE VIRTUALLY INSUPPORTABLE.

THE VOCABULARY

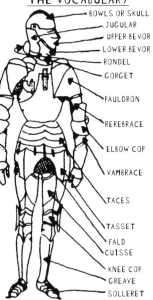

- BOWLS OR SKULL
- JUGULAR
- UPPER BEVOR
- LOWER BEVOR
- RONDEL
- GORGET
- PAULDRON
- REREBRACE
- ELBOW COP
- VAMBRACE
- TACES
- TASSET
- FALD
- CUISSE
- KNEE COP
- GREAVE
- SOLLERET

HOW TO BREAK A FINGER IN TWO WITHOUT DAMAGING IT

THIS EXPERIMENT WAS KINDLY SENT TO THE OBSERVER BY B. M. NESHAM.

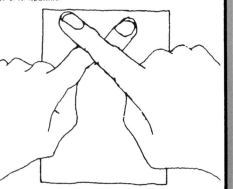

HOLD OUT BOTH INDEX FINGERS ABOUT 2CM APART & 5CM ABOVE A PIECE OF PAPER. FOCUS ON THE PAPER & THE BOTTOM FINGER WILL APPEAR TO BE DISJOINTED.

ASPIRIN
COMMON PAIN - RELIEVING DRUG

WILLOWS

ASPIRIN BELONGS TO A FAMILY OF DRUGS CALLED THE SALICYLATES, WHICH OCCUR NATURALLY IN MANY PLANTS, ESPECIALLY IN WILLOW TREES. HIPPOCRATES, THE ANCIENT GREEK PHYSICIAN, WAS USING WILLOW BARK FOR PAIN RELIEF IN 400 BC.

A PAINFUL REMEDY

SALICYLATE ACID, EXTRACTED FROM WILLOWS, BECAME A POPULAR CURE FOR FEVER PAIN & RHEUMATISM IN THE 19TH CENTURY BUT ITS SUCCESS WAS LIMITED BY THE DAMAGE IT CAUSED TO THE STOMACH LINING. ACETYLSALICYLATE ACID, A SIMILAR COMPOUND WITH LESS SERIOUS SIDE-EFFECTS, WAS INTRODUCED IN 1899 & NAMED ASPIRIN.

TRADE NAME

THE NAME ASPIRIN COMES FROM 'A' (FOR ACETYL) PLUS 'SPIR' (FOR SPIREA ULMARIA OR MEADOWSWEET, A FLOWER FROM WHICH SALICYLATE IS OBTAINED). IT WAS ORIGINALLY A TRADE NAME (REGISTERED BY BAYER IN 1906). IT STILL IS IN GERMANY & SCANDINAVIA.

OTHER USES

ASPIRIN IS NOT ONLY USEFUL FOR THE RELIEF OF PAIN & FEVER. IT IS ALSO USED IN THE TREATMENT OF ARTHRITIS, RHEUMATISM & SOME CANCERS & THROMBOSES.

BEAVERS

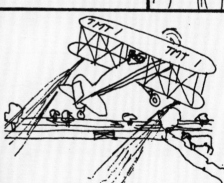

BEAVERS HAVE SECRETIONS OF ASPIRIN IN THEIR SKIN, BECAUSE THEY EAT SO MUCH WOOD & BARK.

WORLD CONSUMPTION

MORE THAN 100,000,000,000 ASPIRIN TABLETS ARE SWALLOWED IN THE WORLD EVERY YEAR.

100,000,000,000

FEMALE PREFERENCE

VARIOUS STUDIES IN AUSTRALIA HAVE FOUND THAT WOMEN CONSUME 60% MORE ASPIRIN THAN MEN. SCIENTISTS DON'T YET KNOW THE REASON.

SIDE-EFFECTS

ASPIRIN HAS VARIOUS SIDE-EFFECTS: IT CAUSES STOMACH ACHES IN ONE PERSON IN 20 & SKIN RASHES IN ONE PERSON IN 500. TAKEN TOO OFTEN, IT CAN CAUSE BLEEDING INSIDE THE STOMACH.

SPRAYING ASPIRIN

ASPIRIN HAS BEEN SPRAYED ON BEAN PLANTS IN MEXICO. IT REDUCES THEIR WATER CONSUMPTION & MAKES THEM MORE RESISTANT TO DROUGHT. IT MAY EVENTUALLY BE POSSIBLE TO BREED NATURAL ASPIRINS (FROM WILLOWS ETC.) INTO CROP PLANTS FOR GROWING IN ARID REGIONS.

OLD ASPIRINS

OLD ASPIRINS CAN MAKE HEADACHES WORSE BECAUSE THE CHEMICALS BREAK DOWN WITH TIME. MANUFACTURERS SAY THEY WILL LAST 2-3 YEARS IN DRY CONDITIONS, BUT IN HOT STEAMY BATHROOM CUPBOARDS THEY MAY LAST ONLY 4 MONTHS.

HOW TO KEEP CUT FLOWERS FRESH

A POPULAR WAY TO KEEP CUT FLOWERS FRESH IS TO DISSOLVE AN ASPIRIN IN THE WATER. RESEARCH SUGGESTS THAT THERE MAY WELL BE SOME VALUE IN DOING THIS.

☆ ATHLETICS ☆
COMBATS OF STRENGTH, SPEED, ENDURANCE & AGILITY

SPRINTING

IN A 100-METRE SPRINT, THE FEET TOUCH THE GROUND ONLY 40 TIMES & CONTACT LASTS FOR ONLY ABOUT A TENTH OF THE TIME TAKEN FOR EACH STRIDE. ALL THE SPRINTER'S ENERGY MUST BE PUT INTO THESE 0.025-SECOND CONTACTS.

TRAINING

IT HAS BEEN ESTABLISHED THAT A LONG PERIOD OF HIGH-ALTITUDE TRAINING IMPROVES THE PERFORMANCE OF ATHLETES IN SOME EVENTS (PARTICULARLY MIDDLE-DISTANCE RUNNING). HOWEVER, ALTITUDE TRAINING DOES NOT EQUAL THE ADVANTAGE OF BEING BORN & BRED IN A HIGH-ALTITUDE REGION, SUCH AS EAST AFRICA.

SHOT PUT

THERE ARE TWO MAIN SHOT-PUTTING STYLES. THE "SPIN" IS FAVOURED BY MOST TOP MALE PUTTERS. THE "GLIDE", HOWEVER, IS EASIER TO ATTAIN WITH CONSISTENCY, AND IS POPULAR AMONG WOMEN AND AMATEURS. THE BEST DISTANCE TO DATE (23.12M) WAS ACHIEVED USING THE SPIN, THE NEXT BEST (23.06M), USING THE GLIDE.

JAVELIN

THE CURRENT RECORD FOR JAVELIN-THROWING IS 98.48 METRES. ANY INCREASE IN RANGE WILL MAKE IT DIFFICULT TO CONTAIN THE EVENT IN A CONVENTIONAL STADIUM. STRINGENT SAFETY PRECAUTIONS HAVE TO BE OBSERVED. IN THE 1950S, THE SPANISH INVENTED A RUN-UP STYLE IN WHICH THE THROWER SPUN ROUND. THIS BROKE WORLD RECORDS BUT HAD TO BE BANNED BECAUSE THE FLIGHT PATH WAS UNPREDICTABLE.

MARATHON

MARATHON RUNNERS OFTEN WEAR SPECIAL METALLICIZED STRING VESTS WHICH HELP TO KEEP THEIR BODIES COOL. THEY ALSO EMPLOY AN UNUSUAL PRE-RACE DIET CALLED THE CARBOHYDRATE LOADING SYSTEM: CARBOHYDRATE STARVATION FOR A PERIOD PRIOR TO THE RACE, FOLLOWED BY CARBOHYDRATE SATURATION DIRECTLY BEFORE.

LONG JUMP

THE RANGE OF THE LONG JUMP COULD BE INCREASED IF THE ATHLETES CARRIED HAND WEIGHTS & RELEASED THEM IN MID-AIR (AS DID THE ANCIENT GREEKS), BUT MODERN RULES PROHIBIT THIS. THE RANGE CAN ALSO BE INCREASED IF THE JUMPER SOMERSAULTS IN MID-AIR. THIS HAS ALSO BEEN BANNED FOR THE ATHLETES' SAFETY.

POLE VAULT

THE POLE VAULT USED TO BE PERFORMED WITH A RIGID WOODEN POLE. IN THE 1880S IT WAS FOUND POSSIBLE TO CLIMB UP THE POLE WHILE IN MID-AIR. THE RULES BANNED THIS, AND THE HEIGHT HAS NOW INCREASED DRAMATICALLY WITH THE INTRODUCTION OF THE SPRINGY GLASS-FIBRE POLE.

HOW TO DO A COIN TRICK

YOU CAN TRANSFER A PILE OF COINS RESTING ON YOUR ELBOW (SEE ABOVE) TO YOUR HAND BY SIMPLY THROWING YOUR ARM FORWARD & CATCHING THEM. PRACTISE FIRST WITH A SINGLE COIN.

BEASTS
IRRATIONAL ANIMALS

CATCHING A UNICORN

THE UNICORN IS SAID TO HAVE BEEN VERY FAST & DIFFICULT TO HUNT. HOWEVER, ONE STRATAGEM THAT NEVER FAILED WAS TO SEND A VIRGIN GIRL INTO A WOOD BY HERSELF. ANY UNICORN THERE WOULD SOON "LEAP INTO HER LAP & EMBRACE HER, WHEN IT MIGHT EASILY BE CAUGHT". UNFORTUNATELY, IF SOME AUTHORITIES ARE CORRECT IN THINKING THAT THE UNICORN AROSE FROM MISINTERPRETED DESCRIPTIONS OF THE RHINO, THE POOR GIRL WOULD CERTAINLY BE FATALLY CRUSHED.

THE AMPHISBENA

THE AMPHISBENA WAS AN ENDEARING MEDIEVAL REPTILE WITH TWO HEADS. WITH ONE HEAD HOLDING THE OTHER IT WAS SAID TO BOWL ALONG IN EITHER DIRECTION LIKE A HOOP. THE STORY PROBABLY REFERS TO THE INDIAN SAND BOA WHICH HAS A LUMP IN ITS TAIL AND IS OFTEN CALLED THE TWO-HEADED SNAKE.

CYCLOPS & MERMAIDS

TALES OF ONE-EYED GIANTS & MERMAIDS MAY HAVE STEMMED FROM GENETICALLY DEFORMED BABIES THE LACK OF AN EYE AND THE FUSION OF THE FEET OCCUR OCCASIONALLY & HAVE THE MEDICAL NAMES CYCLOPIA AND SYMPODIA.

THE CALDRICUS

THIS BIRD IS SAID TO HAVE POSSESSED THE USEFUL ABILITY TO TELL IF VERY ILL PEOPLE WERE GOING TO SURVIVE. IF THE BIRD FACES THE PATIENT, THE MAN WILL LIVE, BUT IF THE BIRD TURNS ITS BACK ON THE PATIENT, HE WILL DIE. THE DIFFICULTY IN IDENTIFYING THIS BIRD IS PARTLY DUE TO THE FACT THAT PEOPLE DID NOT ACTUALLY HAVE TO BUY ONE TO RECEIVE A DIAGNOSIS, SO DEALERS WERE RELUCTANT TO DISPLAY THEM.

THE ECHENIS

THE ECHENIS IS AN ODD CREATURE, ONLY 6 INCHES LONG BUT REPUTED TO HOLD A SHIP MOTIONLESS BY CLINGING TO IT. THE CREATURE'S ORIGIN IS OBSCURE.

THE PHOENIX

MANY IDENTITIES HAVE BEEN SUGGESTED FOR THE PHOENIX, INCLUDING A BIRD OF PARADISE, A FLAMINGO, A STORK & AN EGRET. ONE LIKELY THEORY IS THAT IT WAS REALLY A PURPLE HERON, NAMED AFTER THE PHOENICIANS WHO USED PURPLE DYE. ANOTHER THEORY IS THAT IT WAS NOT A BIRD BUT THE SUN, AS THIS WOULD EXPLAIN HOW IT DIED IN ITS OWN FIRES & THEN ROSE AFRESH.

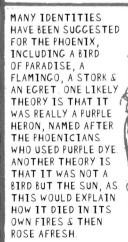

THE BASILISK

THE BASILISK IS ONE OF THE MOST TERRIFYING MEDIEVAL BEASTS. IT WAS SAID TO KILL PEOPLE MERELY BY ITS BREATH, AND A BIRD FLYING PAST IT, EVEN IF FAR FROM ITS MOUTH, WOULD FRIZZLE UP & BE DEVOURED. FORTUNATELY, THE BASILISK COULD BE CONQUERED BY WEASELS.

HOW TO GET AN ENEMY'S FEET WET

PUNCH LOTS OF HOLES IN THE BOTTOM OF A PLASTIC BOTTLE WITH A SCREW TOP. FILL WITH WATER BY IMMERSING BOTTLE COMPLETELY & SCREW ON CAP WHILE IT'S STILL IMMERSED. REMOVE BOTTLE FROM WATER & BET YOUR ENEMY HE IS NOT STRONG ENOUGH TO UNSCREW TOP. WATER WILL NOT FALL THROUGH HOLES TILL TOP IS OFF.

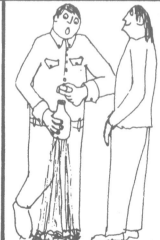

BEDS
PIECES OF FURNITURE FOR SLEEPING ON

BEDS BEDS BEDS BEDS BEDS BEDS

DRAUGHTY BEDS
UNTIL THE INTRODUCTION OF GLASS WINDOWS (FROM ABOUT 1500 ONWARDS), BEDROOMS WERE DRAUGHTY. BEDS FITTED WITH HEAVY CURTAINS (FOUR-POSTERS) WERE AN ATTEMPT TO CUT OUT DRAUGHTS.

BEDSIDE LIGHTS
MEDIEVAL BEDROOMS WERE SO DRAUGHTY THAT CANDLES KEPT BLOWING OUT. THIS LED TO CANDLES BEING PLACED INSIDE THIN BITS OF HORN CALLED LANT-HORNS (THE ORIGIN OF THE WORD LANTERN).

MAKING THE BED
IN SAXON TIMES, VISITORS WERE GIVEN A SACK & SOME STRAW & HAD TO LITERALLY "MAKE THEIR BED".

MOVING BEDS
15TH CENTURY ENGLISH NOBLEMEN REGARDED THEIR BEDDING WITH MUCH GREATER RESPECT THAN THEIR BEDSTEADS. WHEN TRAVELLING, THE BEDDING WOULD BE PACKED & MOVED IN ADVANCE FROM ONE BEDSTEAD TO ANOTHER BY 'YEOMAN HANGERS' OR 'BEDGOERS'.

BED-WARMERS
EARTHENWARE HOT-WATER BOTTLE. GLADSTONE IS SAID TO HAVE FILLED HIS WITH TEA.

DUTCH WIFE (FULL OF FEATHERS) USED TO KEEP BEDS COOL IN SUMMER.

EARTHENWARE BOTTLE SHAPED TO FIT ON CHEST

WARMING PAN FILLED WITH HOT COALS. EMPTY PANS WERE SOMETIMES USED BY NOBILITY TO SECRETLY SWAP BABIES.

HOT COALS ON TRAY OR ELECTRIC LIGHT BULB IN WICKER CAGE

WHEELED BEDS
A WHEELED BED, CALLED A TRUCKLE, WHICH PULLED OUT FROM UNDER THE MAIN BED, BECAME COMMON IN THE 16TH CENTURY FOR VISITORS & HONOURED SERVANTS.

IN PARTS OF CHINA, PEOPLE USED TO SLEEP IN COMMUNAL BRICK BEDS WITH FIRES UNDERNEATH.

NUPTIAL BEDS
IN MANY PARTS OF BRITAIN, IT WAS TRADITIONAL FOR WEDDING GUESTS TO ACCOMPANY THE BRIDE & GROOM TO THEIR BEDROOM. HERE THEY WOULD SING & DANCE UNTIL THE BED HAD BEEN BLESSED BY A PRIEST.

LEONARDO'S BED
LEONARDO DA VINCI DID NOT LIKE FEATHER MATTRESSES BECAUSE HE OBJECTED TO LYING ON THE SPOILS OF DEAD ANIMALS.

DANGEROUS BEDS
IN VARIOUS PARTS OF ASIA, A CIRCULAR COMMUNAL BEDSPREAD WAS USED WITH A SUNKEN CHARCOAL FIRE IN THE MIDDLE. HEADACHES & SUFFOCATION FROM THE FUMES WERE SAID TO HAVE BEEN A PROBLEM.

PUBLIC BEDS
LOUIS XIV HELD COURT IN HIS BEDROOM AT VERSAILLES. GETTING UP BECAME SUCH A FORMAL CEREMONY THAT HE TOOK TO SLEEPING IN AN ADJOINING ROOM. HERE HE HELD A "PETITE LEVÉE" (A MORE INTIMATE GETTING-UP CEREMONY) BEFORE MOVING TO HIS "GRANDE LEVÉE".

LUXURIOUS BEDS
LOUIS XIV HAD 353 BEDS. RESENTFUL THAT ORDINARY MORTALS SHOULD "SLEEP IN GLORY", HE FORBADE ANY COMMONER TO OWN A BED EMBODYING GOLD OR SILVER.

THE BED OF NAILS
LYING ON A BED OF NAILS IS NOT AS PAINFUL AS OFTEN SUPPOSED. A PERSON CAN PRESS THEIR HAND ON THE POINT OF A NAIL WITH A FORCE OF ABOUT 0.5KG WITHOUT EXCESSIVE PAIN. THUS A BED OF 10 X 40 NAILS SHOULD COMFORTABLY SUPPORT THE DISTRIBUTED WEIGHT OF AN AVERAGE PERSON. (NOT ONE TO TRY AT HOME!)

THE BODY
OMNIVEROUS BIPED ORGANISM

JAWS
CAPABLE OF EXERTING 200 KG CRUSHING FORCE

REPRODUCTION
THE MOST CHILDREN EVER PRODUCED BY ONE MOTHER IS 69

MUSCLES
GLUTEUS MAXIMUS (THE BUTTOCK MUSCLE) IS THE LARGEST OF YOUR 637 MUSCLES

TOES
THE LARGEST NUMBER OF TOES RECORDED IS 12 ON EACH FOOT

SNEEZING
THE HIGHEST SPEED OF THE EXPELLED PARTICLE HAS BEEN MEASURED AS 165 KM/H. THE LONGEST RECORDED SNEEZING FIT LASTED 977 DAYS.

YOU SHRINK 1CM EVERY DAY
THE FIBRO CARTILAGES BETWEEN THE VERTEBRAE ACT AS SHOCK-ABSORBERS GETTING SQUASHED THROUGH THE DAY & RECOVERING AT NIGHT.

CONSUMPTION
THE AVERAGE WEIGHT OF FOOD EATEN THROUGH A LIFETIME IS 30 TONS, EQUAL TO 6 ELEPHANTS OR 30 COWS.

FINGERNAILS
THE LONGEST FINGERNAIL EVER RECORDED MEASURED 88CM

WHAT THE BODY IS MADE FROM

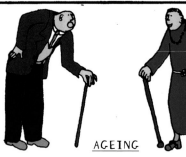

THE RAW MATERIALS OF WHICH THE BODY IS COMPOSED WERE EXPRESSED BY A POLITICIAN, SIR W. GRENFELL, AS:

IRON: ENOUGH FOR A MEDIUM NAIL.

LIME: ENOUGH TO WHITEWASH A CHICKEN HOUSE.

SULPHUR: ENOUGH TO RID A DOG OF FLEAS.

SUGAR: ENOUGH TO FILL A JAM JAR.

POTASSIUM: ENOUGH TO EXPLODE A TOY CANNON.

FAT: ENOUGH TO MAKE 7 BARS OF SOAP.

SAMUEL BUTLER, A SATIRIST, WAS EVEN MORE RUDE ABOUT THE BODY, DESCRIBING IT AS A PAIR OF PINCERS SET OVER A BELLOWS & A STEWPAN & THE WHOLE THING MOUNTED ON STILTS.

AGEING

THE LONGEST AUTHENTICATED LIFE IN THE UK WAS 111 YEARS 339 DAYS, RECORDED BY A MRS ROWE. OTHER COUNTRIES CLAIM AS MUCH AS 256 YEARS. THESE CLAIMS MAY BE TRUE BUT ARE MORE LIKELY DUE TO MISTAKES ARISING FROM INADEQUATE RECORDS. WOMEN LIVE 7 YEARS LONGER THAN MEN ON AVERAGE.

HAIR

THE LONGEST KNOWN HAIR MEASURED 7.9M, RECORDED BY SWAMI PANDARASANNADI, HEAD OF THE THERAVADA THURAI MONASTERY IN INDIA. THE RECORD LENGTHS FOR BEARDS ARE 5M FOR MEN & 35CM FOR WOMEN. BLONDS HAVE AN AVERAGE OF 150,000 HAIRS ON THEIR HEAD, NEARLY TWICE AS MANY AS REDHEADS (BRUNETTES ARE SOMEWHERE IN BETWEEN).

THE VOICE
THE RANGE OF NOTES POSSIBLE FOR A HUMAN HAS BEEN GREATLY EXTENDED BY A NEW TRAINING TECHNIQUE. FRL. MARITA GUNTHER HAS COVERED THE WHOLE RANGE OF THE PIANO (7 OCTAVES, OF WHICH 6 ARE CONSIDERED TO BE "OF MUSICAL VALUE").

THE CONTENTS OF THE BRAIN

OUR BRAIN CELLS ARE DYING AT THE RATE OF 100 PER MINUTE. SOME AMERICAN RESEARCH ON RATS HAS REVEALED THAT THE AMOUNT OF SPACE BETWEEN BRAIN CELLS DECREASES FROM 26% TO 4% DURING THEIR LIFE & SUGGESTS THAT SENILITY IS CAUSED BY THE SPACES GETTING CLOGGED WITH DEAD CELLS. PERHAPS IT IS A COMPLIMENT TO BE CALLED EMPTY-HEADED.

IMPROVING YOUR EARS WITH 2 UMBRELLAS

ARRANGE UMBRELLAS AND CLOCK AS SHOWN. PLACE EAR IN FRONT OF THE FAR UMBRELLA. THE INCREASED VOLUME OF THE TICK IS TRULY AMAZING.

✦ BONE ✦
HARD SUBSTANCE FORMING SKELETONS OF HIGHER ANIMALS

THE FIRST BONES

SEAWATER CONTAINS LOTS OF DISSOLVED CALCIUM SALTS. THESE SALTS ACCUMULATED IN THE CIRCULATION OF PREHISTORIC BONELESS ANIMALS. AS THE CONCENTRATION INCREASED, SOME OF THE SALTS CRYSTALLIZED UNDER THEIR SKINS. THE RESULTING CRYSTALS EVENTUALLY DEVELOPED INTO RIGID CASINGS (SHELLS) &, LATER, INTERNAL BONES.

BONE STRUCTURE

BONE IS COMPOSED OF CRYSTALS OF CALCIUM PHOSPHATE & COLLAGEN. COLLAGEN IS AN ORGANIC FIBROUS PROTEIN WHICH ALSO FORMS OUR TENDONS & LIGAMENTS. IN BONES IT ACTS AS A SEED BED, CRYSTALLIZING CALCIUM PHOSPHATE OUT FROM THE BODY FLUIDS. THE TOUGH, BUT FLEXIBLE, COLLAGEN & THE RIGID, BUT BRITTLE, CALCIUM PHOSPHATE COMBINE TO GIVE A TOUGH RIGID MATERIAL (SIMILAR TO THE COMBINATION OF RESIN & GLASS THAT FORMS FIBREGLASS).

BONE SIZE

LARGE ANIMALS REQUIRE PROPORTIONATELY THICKER BONES THAN SMALL ANIMALS TO SUPPORT THEIR WEIGHT. ANY ANIMAL LARGER THAN AN ELEPHANT WOULD THUS BE IMPOSSIBLY CLUMSY.

BONY GROWTHS

CALCIUM PHOSPHATE READILY CRYSTALLIZES IN OUR BODIES, BUT, UNFORTUNATELY, NOT ALWAYS AS BONE. GALL STONES & KIDNEY STONES ARE LAYERS OF CALCIUM PHOSPHATE THAT HAVE GROWN ROUND FOREIGN BODIES. THE LARGEST GALL STONE ON RECORD MEASURES 70X38MM. IT WAS REMOVED FROM JOHN CHARLES MATTHEW BULLOCK OF TASMANIA, AUSTRALIA, IN 2009.

THE HERO SHREW

THE BACKBONE OF THE HERO SHREW HAS EVOLVED TO PREVENT IT FROM BEING CRUSHED WHILE BURROWING. IT NOW HAS THE STRONGEST BACKBONE, IN PROPORTION TO ITS SIZE, OF ANY ANIMAL & IS CLAIMED TO BE CAPABLE OF BEARING THE WEIGHT OF A 75KG MAN.

ODD SKULLS

BONELESS

DURING LONG SPACE MISSIONS, ASTRONAUTS BEGIN TO LOSE THEIR SKELETONS BECAUSE BONES BECOME SLIGHTLY SMALLER IN WEIGHTLESS CONDITIONS.

BONES ARE SURPRISINGLY FLEXIBLE AT BIRTH, PARTICULARLY THE SKULL. THE NAVAJO TRIBE, ARIZONA, TRADITIONALLY FLATTENED THE BACKS OF THEIR BABIES' HEADS BY STRAPPING THEM TO BOARDS. MORE SPECTACULAR SKULL DEFORMITIES RESULT FROM BANDAGING THE HEAD, A FORMER PRACTICE IN PARTS OF AFRICA & PERU. OUR HEADS ARE CONSIDERABLY SHAPED BY THE PRESSURES EXERTED DURING CHILDBIRTH. (BABIES DELIVERED BY CAESAREAN SECTION OFTEN HAVE DOMED HEADS.)

HOW TO CUT THE CARD WITHOUT CUTTING THE RIBBON

YOU WILL NEED A RIBBON, AN UNWANTED PLAYING CARD & A VERY BLUNT PAIR OF SCISSORS. PREPARE THE TRICK BY PUTTING THE CARD IN A HOT OVEN FOR A FEW MINUTES. YOU SHOULD THEN FIND THAT THE CARD IS BRITTLE ENOUGH FOR THE SCISSORS TO "CRACK" IT IN TWO WITHOUT HARMING THE RIBBON.

BUMBLE-BEES

NOISE

BUMBLE-BEES WERE CALLED HUMBLE-BEES (BECAUSE OF THE HUMMING OF THEIR WINGS) UNTIL THE 1600S. "BUMBLE" WAS PROBABLY A NURSERY WORD AT FIRST, POSSIBLY CONNECTING BUZZ & HUM.

NESTS

BUMBLE-BEES NEST IN HOLES IN THE GROUND, OFTEN IN DESERTED MOUSE NESTS. THEY BUILD AN IRREGULAR ARRANGEMENT OF BROOD CELLS & FOOD POTS OUT OF PLANT RESINS & WAX.

CUCKOO-BEES

CUCKOO-BEES LOOK SIMILAR TO BUMBLE-BEES BUT ARE PARASITES & HAVE NO WORKER CASTE. THEIR FEMALES INVADE TRUE BUMBLE-BEE NESTS TO LAY EGGS WHICH AFTER HATCHING ARE REARED BY BUMBLE-BEE WORKERS.

SEASONS

SPRING

IN THE SPRING YOUNG FERTILIZED QUEENS START NEW COLONIES.

SUMMER

IN THE SUMMER MORE & MORE WORKER BEES MATURE UNTIL THE COLONY CONTAINS 100-500 BEES.

AUTUMN

IN THE AUTUMN THE QUEEN WATCHES FERTILE MALES & FEMALES & THESE LEAVE THE COLONY & MATE.

WINTER

IN THE WINTER THE COLONY DIES & ONLY THE FERTILIZED QUEENS SURVIVE.

INCUBATION

BUMBLE-BEES INCUBATE THEIR BROODS BY SITTING ON THEM, JUST AS BIRDS SIT ON THEIR EGGS.

SOCIAL & SOLITARY BEES

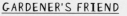

THE SIZE OF COLONY & DEGREE OF SOCIALIZATION OF DIFFERENT SPECIES OF BEE MAY BE RELATED TO THEIR NEST-BUILDING TECHNIQUES. SOLITARY BEES USE MOSTLY MUD FOR THEIR NESTS. ONLY BEES THAT USE WAX OR WOOD PULP CAN MAKE NESTS STRONG ENOUGH TO SUPPORT LARGE COLONIES.

GARDENER'S FRIEND

BUMBLE-BEES ARE VALUABLE POLLINATORS. THEIR LONG TONGUES CAN REACH THE POLLEN OF MANY FLOWER SPECIES THAT HONEY-BEES CANNOT REACH.

HOW TO ESCAPE FROM A BEE WHEN CYCLING

AS BUMBLE-BEES FLY AT 18KM/H MAXIMUM (FASTER THAN MOST OTHER BEES & WASPS), IT IS USUALLY POSSIBLE SIMPLY TO OUTSPRINT THEM, OR ANY OTHER BEE OR WASP, WHEN CYCLING.

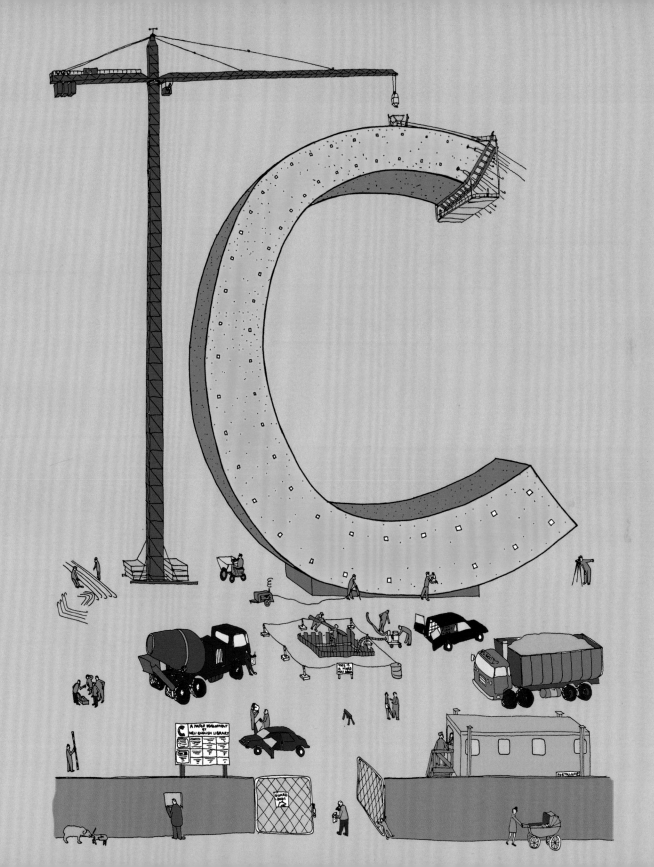

CANNIBALISM

LIVING THINGS EATING THE FLESH OF THEIR OWN KIND

DISCOVERY

THE WORD CANNIBAL COMES FROM THE SOUTH AMERICAN CARIB TRIBE. 16TH-CENTURY SPANISH EXPLORERS BELIEVED THAT THEY ATE HUMAN FLESH.

NORMAL BEHAVIOUR

CANNIBALISM IS A NORMAL PHENOMENON IN HUNDREDS OF DIFFERENT ANIMAL SPECIES, MOSTLY INVERTEBRATES.

OVERCROWDING

POPULATION EXPLOSIONS OFTEN LEAD TO CANNIBALISM AMONG ANIMALS INCLUDING MICE, DAMSELFLIES, PIKE, BUTTERFLIES & SEA SLUGS.

GENETIC CANNIBALISM

THE TENDENCY TO CANNIBALISM IS PARTLY DETERMINED GENETICALLY. DIFFERENT STRAINS OF FLOUR BEETLE SHOW INHERITED DIFFERENCES IN APPETITE.

GULLS

HERRING GULLS OFTEN EAT THE EGGS OF THEIR NEIGHBOURS, ESPECIALLY WHEN LOTS OF GULLS NEST CLOSE TOGETHER.

FEMALE CANNIBALISM

FEMALE INSECTS ARE GENERALLY MORE CANNIBALISTIC. EATING THE MALE AFTER MATING, TO PROVIDE EXTRA FOOD DURING PREGNANCY, IS ALSO COMMON AMONG SPIDERS.

WALLEYE FISH

WALLEYE FISH EAT EACH OTHER, TAIL FIRST. "CHAINS" OF CANNIBALISM ARE SOMETIMES SEEN.

BONY FISH

SOME BONY FISH TAKE TO CANNIBALISM AS A WAY OF GETTING EXTRA FOOD. THEY EAT ALL THEIR YOUNG OR SOME OF THEIR EGGS.

EXAGGERATION

MANY TALES OF HUMAN CANNIBALISM, INCLUDING THE MASS RITUAL ORGIES OF THE AZTECS & THE FATTENING OF PRISONERS PRIOR TO COOKING IN THE CONGO, ARE NOW THOUGHT TO BE FALSE. THE TALES WERE INVENTED OR GREATLY EXAGGERATED BY EARLY EXPLORERS TO JUSTIFY THEIR OWN ATROCITIES.

LIONS

A MALE LION TAKING OVER A PRIDE WILL SOMETIMES EAT ANY CUBS OF THE PREVIOUS MALE. THIS MEANS HE CAN MATE WITH THE LIONESSES VERY SOON AND FATHER HIS OWN CUBS, WHICH ARE BROUGHT UP BY THE PRIDE.

RESPECTFUL CANNIBALISM

THE PRACTICE OF EATING DEAD RELATIVES, AS THE MOST RESPECTFUL METHOD OF DISPOSING OF THEIR REMAINS, WAS KNOWN TO OCCUR IN TRIBES IN AFRICA, AUSTRALIA & SOUTH AMERICA.

INNOCENT CANNIBALISM

IN 1978, AFTER A GANGLAND KILLING IN TOKYO, THE HANDS OF THE VICTIM ENDED UP IN A LARGE POT OF SOUP ON A STREET STALL. AT LEAST 50 PEOPLE UNWITTINGLY BECAME CANNIBALS.

CARBON DATING

RADIOACTIVE ATMOSPHERE

THE CARBON CONTENT OF ALL LIVING MATTER IS SLIGHTLY RADIOACTIVE (CURRENTLY ABOUT ONE ATOM IN A BILLION). THE RADIOACTIVE FORM (CALLED CARBON 14) IS CREATED BY THE REACTIONS OF COSMIC RAYS IN THE UPPER ATMOSPHERE.

RADIOACTIVE REMAINS

WHEN LIVING THINGS DIE, THEY CEASE TO ABSORB CARBON & THE UNSTABLE RADIOACTIVE FORM SLOWLY DECAYS. BY MEASURING THE AMOUNT OF CARBON 14 LEFT IN ARCHAEOLOGICAL SAMPLES, SCIENTISTS CAN WORK OUT THEIR DATES.

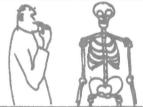

DISCOVERY

RADIOCARBON DATING WAS DISCOVERED BY A PROFESSOR LIBBY AS A BY-PRODUCT OF NUCLEAR RESEARCH IN CHICAGO IN THE EARLY 1940S.

INACCURACY

IN THE LATE 1950S CARBON DATING WAS TRIED ON VARIOUS OBJECTS PREVIOUSLY DATED BY OTHER METHODS (TREE RINGS) & FOUND TO BE WILDLY INACCURATE. IT WAS THEN REALIZED THAT THE RADIOACTIVITY OF ATMOSPHERIC CARBON VARIES.

COMPARISONS

SCIENTISTS MEASURE THE AMOUNT OF CARBON 14 IN A SAMPLE BY COUNTING THE PULSES OF RADIATION EMITTED AS EACH ATOM DECAYS. THIS IS COMPARED WITH A SAMPLE OF COAL (VERY OLD ORGANIC MATERIAL) & A SAMPLE OF 1950 OXALIC ACID (RECENT ORGANIC MATERIAL) KEPT BY THE US BUREAU OF STANDARDS.

CORRECTIONS

TO ALLOW FOR THE VARIATION OF RADIOACTIVE CARBON IN THE ATMOSPHERE, SCIENTISTS NOW MAKE CORRECTIONS BASED ON OBJECTS DATED BY OTHER METHODS. BUT THE CORRECTIONS USED BY DIFFERENT AUTHORITIES VARY CONSIDERABLY & THERE ARE NO RELIABLY DATED OBJECTS MORE THAN 8,000 YEARS OLD.

BONES

CARBON DATING WORKS ONLY ON ORGANIC MATERIAL (WOOD, CLOTH, BONE, ETC.) UNDER ABOUT 70,000 YEARS OLD.

DESTRUCTION

ONE PROBLEM WITH CARBON DATING IS THAT IT NEEDS QUITE A LARGE SAMPLE (A WHOLE BONE) WHICH IS DESTROYED IN THE PROCESS (THE CARBON HAS TO BE CONVERTED TO A LIQUID OR GAS).

POTS

POTTERY CAN BE DATED BY "THERMOLUMINESCENCE". THE OLDER THE POT, THE BRIGHTER THE FRAGMENTS WILL GLOW WHEN REHEATED (AGAIN BECAUSE OF RADIOACTIVE REACTIONS).

HIGH SPEED

A NEW METHOD OF CARBON DATING HAS RECENTLY BEEN INTRODUCED. THE SAMPLE IS PUT IN A PHYSICIST'S MASS SPECTROMETER WHICH CAN COUNT THE CARBON 14 ATOMS. IT IS QUICKER & NEEDS A SAMPLE 100 TIMES SMALLER THAN CONVENTIONAL METHODS.

HIGH SPEED DATING

ROCKS

SOME ROCKS CAN ALSO BE DATED BY RADIOACTIVE DECAY, MEASURING MUCH SLOWER REACTIONS THAN CARBON DECAY. THE OLDEST ROCKS KNOWN ARE 4,600 MILLION-YEAR-OLD METEORITES.

SEEDS

HIGH SPEED DATING

ANALYSING SEEDS WITH THE MASS SPECTROMETER HAS PRODUCED SOME SURPRISING RESULTS SEEDS FROM AN EGYPTIAN SITE, ESTIMATED BY ARCHAEOLOGISTS TO BE 20,000 YEARS OLD, TURNED OUT TO BE ONLY 200 YEARS OLD.

CARBON DATING

MIAOWWWW!

☆ CATS ☆

SMALL DOMESTICATED CARNIVORES

CAT FERTILISER

AN EGYPTIAN TEMPLE AT BENIHASSAN, EXCAVATED IN THE 19TH CENTURY, YIELDED 300,000 MUMMIFIED CATS, THEY WERE SHIPPED TO LIVERPOOL & SOLD AS FERTILIZER AT £4 A TONNE

ISLAMIC CATS

THE ANCIENT EGYPTIAN FEELING FOR CATS HAS CONTINUED IN THE ISLAMIC WORLD. CATS ARE SAID TO HAVE BEEN MUHAMMAD'S FAVOURITE ANIMALS. SOME TABBY CATS ARE BELIEVED TO BE HOLY. FOUR STRIPES BETWEEN THE EARS INDICATE WHERE THEY HAVE BEEN STROKED BY THE PROPHET.

CATS' EYES

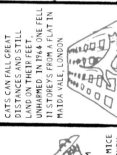

CATS HAVE LIMITED COLOUR VISION. IT HAS RECENTLY BEEN FOUND THAT THEY CAN DISTINGUISH THE COLOUR ONLY OF VERY LARGE OR CLOSE OBJECTS (COVERING AN ANGLE OF OVER 45°)

CAT FALLS

CATS CAN FALL GREAT DISTANCES AND STILL LAND ON THEIR FEET, UNHARMED. IN 1964 ONE FELL 11 STOREYS FROM A FLAT IN MAIDA VALE, LONDON

CAT EXPORT

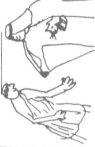

THE ANCIENT EGYPTIANS FORBADE THE EXPORT OF CATS, SO THE GREEKS & ROMANS REMAINED WITHOUT THEM UNTIL ABOUT 100 AD. MICE IN GRANARIES WERE CONTROLLED BY FERRETS & WEASELS WHICH OFTEN ATE CHICKENS & DUCKS AS WELL.

CAT POPULATION

6,000,000

BRITAIN'S CAT POPULATION IS ESTIMATED TO BE 6,000,000. 100,000 ARE USED ON GOVERNMENT PROPERTY, CONTROLLING MICE.

CAT DIET

THE DIET OF FARM CATS IS HIGHLY VARIED. BESIDES MICE & YOUNG BIRDS, THEY EAT MOLES, SLOW WORMS, WEASELS & INSECTS (MAINLY GRASSHOPPERS)

CAT ATTACK

THE ANCIENT EGYPTIAN VENERATION OF CATS WAS USED TO GOOD EFFECT BY THEIR ENEMIES, THE PERSIANS, IN 500 BC. THE EGYPTIANS, BESIEGED IN THE TOWN OF PELUSIUM, RESISTED SUCCESSFULLY UNTIL THE PERSIANS ATTACKED, EACH CARRYING A CAT, AND WITH HUNDREDS OF CATS RUNNING AHEAD. THE EGYPTIANS WOULD NOT THROW THEIR SPEARS FOR FEAR OF KILLING THE CATS & SURRENDERED

CAT PUNISHMENT

AN ANCIENT ICELANDIC PUNISHMENT ENTAILED DROPPING A WOMAN, TIED IN A SACK WITH A CAT, INTO A POND FOR SEVERAL MINUTES

CAT SCARES

DEAD CATS, WITH MICE IN THEIR TEETH, WERE BUILT INTO THE FOUNDATIONS OF SOME ENGLISH 14TH–18TH–CENTURY HOUSES TO SCARE AWAY RATS

CAT SCREAMS

AN ANCIENT SCOTTISH METHOD OF RAISING THE DEVIL WAS TO ROAST A SUCCESSION OF LIVE CATS FOR 4 DAYS. ONLY THE MOST CALLOUS COULD SURVIVE THE APPALLING SCREAMS

☆ CELLULOSE ☆
LONG UNBRANCHED CHAINS OF GLUCOSE MOLECULES

CELLULOID

THE AMERICANS STARTED EXPERIMENTS WITH PARKESINE INDUCED BY AN OFFER OF $10,000 FROM A BILLIARD-BALL MANUFACTURER WHO WAS BADLY IN NEED OF A SUBSTITUTE FOR IVORY. IT WAS FOUND THAT CAMPHOR WORKED BETTER THAN VEGETABLE OILS & THE NEW VERSION WAS NAMED "CELLULOID".

CELLOPHANE

CELLOPHANE IS MADE OF CELLULOSE MIXED WITH A SOLVENT WHICH IS EVAPORATED TO LEAVE A THIN, TRANSPARENT FILM. IT IS THINLY COATED WITH LACQUER (VARNISH) ON BOTH SIDES BECAUSE PURE CELLOPHANE IS SOLUBLE IN WATER.

RAYON

THE FIRST NON-FLAMMABLE PLASTIC WAS CELLULOSE ACETATE (MADE WITH VINEGAR INSTEAD OF NITRIC ACID IN THE CELLULOID PROCESS). THIS WAS DRAWN INTO FILAMENTS & SPUN TO MAKE RAYON.

ENERGY

SOME EXPERTS BELIEVE THAT THE MOST PROMISING RENEWABLE ENERGY SOURCE IS CELLULOSE. IT CAN BE CONVERTED TO SUGAR OR METHANE OR BURNED AS FUEL. ACCORDING TO ONE ESTIMATE, A 250-MILE SQUARE OF HYBRID, FAST-GROWING POPLAR TREES COULD PROVIDE ENOUGH FUEL TO POWER EVERY US ELECTRICITY-GENERATING STATION.

FIRE

CELLULOID IS HIGHLY FLAMMABLE. EARLY DETACHABLE COLLARS MADE OF IT WERE SOMETIMES IGNITED BY CIGARETTES, CAUSING SERIOUS BURNS. IT IS NOW USED ONLY FOR PING-PONG BALLS, GUITAR PLECTRUMS & DRUM TRIM – FOR WHICH NO SUBSTITUTES HAVE BEEN FOUND.

DRIP-DRY CLOTHES

CELLULOSE TRIACETATE WAS FIRST USED FOR WATERPROOFING THE CANVAS ON WORLD WAR I AIRCRAFT. BY THE END OF THE WAR THERE WERE HUGE STOCKS OF IT. EXPERIMENTS WITH THE SURPLUS LED TO THE INVENTION OF "CELANESE" FIBRES & THE FIRST "DRIP-DRY" CLOTHING.

HOW TO MAKE A PENCIL CHANGE COLOUR

WRAP A COLOURED PIECE OF PAPER NEATLY ROUND A PENCIL & SECURE WITH A THIN STRIP OF SELLOTAPE. SHOW PENCIL TO AUDIENCE – THEN PULL IT THROUGH A HANKERCHIEF IN YOUR HAND, LEAVING THE PAPER COVER BEHIND.

SUGAR

CELLULOSE CONSISTS OF LONG CHAIN MOLECULES OF SUGAR (GLUCOSE). PLANTS CONVERT THE SUGARS IN THEIR SAP TO CELLULOSE. SOME ANIMALS, SUCH AS SHEEP & COWS, CAN BREAK CELLULOSE DOWN AGAIN INTO SUGARS IN THEIR STOMACHS.

PARKESINE

PARKESINE, THE EARLIEST PLASTIC (C.1860), WAS MADE BY PEOPLE DISSOLVING CELLULOSE (AS SAWDUST) IN NITRIC ACID & MIXING IT WITH VEGETABLE OILS. THIS MADE A DOUGH WHICH COULD BE PRESSED INTO MOULDS & HEATED TO SET IT.

ABUNDANCE

CELLULOSE IS THE MOST ABUNDANT BIOLOGICAL CHEMICAL IN THE WORLD. THE WALLS OF ALL PLANT CELLS ARE MADE OF IT. PLANTS & TREES MAKE 100 BILLION TONNES OF IT A YEAR.

COTTON WOOL

NATURAL COTTON WOOL IS ONE OF THE PUREST FORMS OF CELLULOSE.

CHOCOLATE

A PASTE BASED ON GROUND COCOA BEANS

EATING CHOCOLATE

CHOCOLATE WAS REGARDED EXCLUSIVELY AS A DRINK UNTIL THE 19TH CENTURY. ONLY WHEN ADDITIONAL BUTTER OR OIL IS ADDED DOES THE CONSISTENCY OF THE COCOA BECOME SUITABLE FOR EATING. THE FIRST ADVERTISEMENT FOR EATING CHOCOLATE APPEARED IN BUTLER'S "MEDICINE CHEST DICTIONARY" IN 1826. FRY'S CHOCOLATE LOZENGES WERE DESCRIBED AS "A PLEASANT & NUTRITIOUS SUBSTITUTE FOR FOOD WHEN TRAVELLING OR WHEN UNUSUAL FASTING IS CAUSED BY IRREGULAR PERIODS OF EATING".

CONCHING

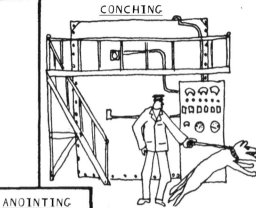

CHOCOLATE FACTORIES FIRST ROAST THE BEANS & REMOVE THEIR SHELLS. THEY THEN CRUSH & MELT THE BEANS INTO LUMPS CALLED "NIBS". THE NIBS ARE THEN HEATED, KNEADED & AERATED (A PROCESS CALLED CONCHING) TO MAKE THEM SMOOTH & CREAMY. THE EARLY CONCHING MACHINES CONSISTED OF CHOCOLATE BATHS WITH HEAVY GRANITE ROLLERS INSIDE MOVING BACK & FORTH ON FLAT GRANITE BEDS. THE PROCESS CONTINUES FOR UP TO 24 HOURS. MANUFACTURERS ALL USE SLIGHTLY DIFFERENT CONCHING PROCESSES & GUARD THE DETAILS WITH STRICT SECURITY.

ANOINTING

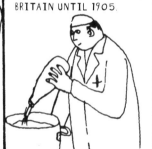

KING HENRI CHRISTOPHE (1767-1820) OF HAITI HAD HIMSELF ANOINTED WITH CHOCOLATE SYRUP AT HIS CORONATION, AS A SYMBOL OF THE IMPORTANCE OF COCOA TO THE ECONOMY.

MILK CHOCOLATE

MILK CHOCOLATE (MADE BY THE ADDITION OF CREAM TO A PLAIN-CHOCOLATE MIX) WAS INVENTED IN SWITZERLAND IN 1875. IT WAS NOT MANUFACTURED IN BRITAIN UNTIL 1905.

HOW TO LEVITATE

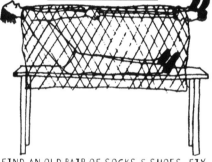

FIND AN OLD PAIR OF SOCKS & SHOES. FIX THEM TO TWO BROOMSTICKS AS ABOVE. LIE ON A TABLE COVERED BY A CLOTH WITH THE PRETEND FEET STICKING OUT. LIFT YOUR HEAD, ARMS & PRETEND FEET & THE AUDIENCE WILL THINK YOU ARE LEVITATING.

MYTHS

IN THE 1600S, THE CHOCOLATE DRINK BECAME FASHIONABLE THROUGHOUT EUROPE. SOME PEOPLE CLAIMED THAT DRINKING LARGE QUANTITIES WOULD CAUSE WHITE PEOPLE TO HAVE CHILDREN WITH DARK SKIN.

CACAO TREES

CHOCOLATE COMES FROM CACAO TREES. THESE ARE THE SIZE OF APPLE TREES WITH LARGE LEAVES & PODS. EACH POD IS 15-30CM LONG & CONTAINS 20-60 COCOA BEANS. ONE TREE YIELDS ENOUGH BEANS TO MAKE HALF A KILO OF COCOA.

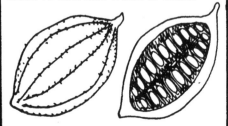

FERMENTATION

AFTER PICKING, THE BEANS ARE PILED IN DAMP HEAPS & ALLOWED TO FERMENT FOR A FEW DAYS. THEY ARE THEN SPREAD OUT TO DRY IN THE SUN BEFORE BEING SHIPPED TO CHOCOLATE FACTORIES.

SPANISH SECRETS

THE SPANISH EXPLORER CORTÉS DISCOVERED THE AZTECS DRINKING CHOCOLATE IN CENTRAL AMERICA IN 1519. IT WAS RATHER BITTER SO THE SPANISH ADDED SUGAR & THEN THEY BROUGHT IT HOME. THE SPANISH KEPT ITS PREPARATION A SECRET FROM OTHER EUROPEAN COUNTRIES FOR OVER 100 YEARS.

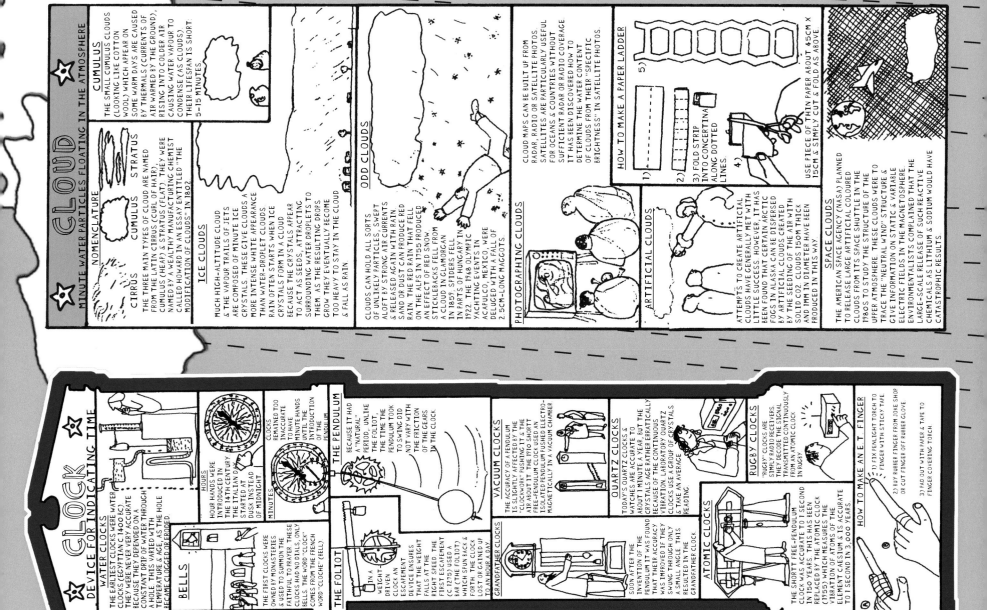

☆ CLOUD ☆
MINUTE WATER PARTICLES FLOATING IN THE ATMOSPHERE

NOMENCLATURE

CIRRUS   CUMULUS   STRATUS

THE THREE MAIN TYPES OF CLOUD ARE NAMED FROM THE LATIN CIRRUS (CURL OF HAIR), CUMULUS (HEAP) & STRATUS (FLAT). THEY WERE NAMED BY A WEALTHY MANUFACTURING CHEMIST CALLED HOWARD IN AN ESSAY ENTITLED "THE MODIFICATION OF CLOUDS" IN 1802.

CUMULUS

THE SMALL CUMULUS CLOUDS (LOOKING LIKE COTTON WOOL) WHICH APPEAR ON SOME WARM DAYS ARE CAUSED BY THERMALS (CURRENTS OF AIR WARMED BY THE GROUND), RISING INTO COLDER AIR CAUSING WATER VAPOUR TO CONDENSE (AS CLOUDS). THEIR LIFESPAN IS SHORT 5-15 MINUTES.

ICE CLOUDS

MUCH HIGH-ALTITUDE CLOUD & THE VAPOUR TRAILS OF JETS ARE COMPOSED OF MINUTE ICE CRYSTALS. THESE GIVE CLOUDS A MORE INTENSE WHITE APPEARANCE THAN WATER-DROPLET CLOUDS. RAIN OFTEN STARTS WHEN ICE CRYSTALS FORM IN A CLOUD BECAUSE THE CRYSTALS APPEAR TO ACT AS SEEDS, ATTRACTING SURROUNDING WATER DROPLETS TO THEM. AS THE RESULTING DROPS GROW THEY EVENTUALLY BECOME TOO HEAVY TO STAY IN THE CLOUD & FALL AS RAIN.

ODD CLOUDS

CLOUDS CAN HOLD ALL SORTS OF UNLIKELY PARTICLES, SWEPT ALOFT BY STRONG AIR CURRENTS & RELEASED AGAIN WITH RAIN. SAND OR DUST CAN PRODUCE RED RAIN. THE RED RAIN THAT FELL ON THE ALPS IN 1755 PRODUCED AN EFFECT OF RED SNOW. STICKLEBACKS FELL FROM A CLOUD IN GLAMORGAN IN 1859, SPIDERS FELL IN PARTS OF HUNGARY IN 1922. THE 1968 OLYMPIC YACHTING EVENTS IN ACAPULCO, MEXICO, WERE DELUGED WITH A FALL OF 2.5CM-LONG MAGGOTS.

PHOTOGRAPHING CLOUDS

CLOUD MAPS CAN BE BUILT UP FROM RADAR, RADIO OR SATELLITE PHOTOS. SATELLITES ARE PARTICULARLY USEFUL FOR OCEANS & COUNTRIES WITHOUT SUFFICIENT RADAR OR RADIO COVERAGE. IT HAS BEEN DISCOVERED HOW TO DETERMINE THE WATER CONTENT OF CLOUDS FROM THEIR "SPECIFIC BRIGHTNESS" IN SATELLITE PHOTOS.

ARTIFICIAL CLOUDS

ATTEMPTS TO CREATE ARTIFICIAL CLOUDS HAVE GENERALLY MET WITH LITTLE SUCCESS. HOWEVER, IT HAS BEEN FOUND THAT CERTAIN ARCTIC FOGS IN ALASKA CAN BE DISPERSED BY ARTIFICIAL CLOUDS CREATED BY THE SEEDING OF THE AIR WITH SOLID CO_2. CLOUDS 150M THICK AND 1MM IN DIAMETER HAVE BEEN PRODUCED IN THIS WAY.

HOW TO MAKE A PAPER LADDER

1) 2) 3) FOLD STRIP INTO CONCERTINA ALONG DOTTED LINES. 4) 5)

USE PIECE OF THIN PAPER ABOUT 45CM X 15CM & SIMPLY CUT & FOLD AS ABOVE.

SPACE CLOUDS

THE AMERICAN SPACE AGENCY (NASA) PLANNED TO RELEASE LARGE ARTIFICIAL COLOURED CLOUDS FROM ITS SPACE SHUTTLE IN THE 1980S TO STUDY THE STRUCTURE OF THE UPPER ATMOSPHERE. THESE CLOUDS WERE TO TRACE THE "NEUTRAL WIND" STATIC & VARIABLE ELECTRIC FIELDS IN THE MAGNETOSPHERE. ENVIRONMENTALISTS COMPLAINED THAT THE LARGE-SCALE RELEASE OF SUCH REACTIVE CHEMICALS AS LITHIUM & SODIUM WOULD HAVE CATASTROPHIC RESULTS.

☆ CLOCK ☆
DEVICE FOR INDICATING TIME

WATER CLOCKS

THE EARLIEST CLOCKS WERE WATER CLOCKS (EGYPTIAN C.1400 BC). THEY WERE NEVER VERY ACCURATE BECAUSE THEY DEPENDED ON A CONSTANT DRIP OF WATER THROUGH A HOLE. THIS VARIED WITH TEMPERATURE & AGE, AS THE HOLE BECAME CLOGGED OR ERODED.

HOURS

HOUR HANDS WERE INTRODUCED IN THE 14TH CENTURY. THE ITALIAN DAY STARTED AT DUSK INSTEAD OF MIDNIGHT.

MINUTES

CLOCKS REMAINED TOO INACCURATE TO HAVE MINUTE HANDS UNTIL THE INTRODUCTION OF THE PENDULUM.

BELLS

THE FIRST CLOCKS WERE OWNED BY MONASTERIES & USED TO SUMMON THE FAITHFUL TO PRAYER. THESE BELLS. THE WORD "CLOCK" COMES FROM THE FRENCH WORD "CLOCHE" (BELL).

THE FOLIOT

IN A WEIGHT-DRIVEN CLOCK AN ESCAPEMENT DEVICE ENSURES THAT THE WEIGHT FALLS AT THE RIGHT SPEED. THE FIRST ESCAPEMENT (C.1275) USED A BAR (THE FOLIOT) WHICH SPUN BACK & FORTH. THE CLOCK LOST OR GAINED UP TO AN HOUR A DAY.

THE PENDULUM

BECAUSE IT HAD A "NATURAL" PERIOD, UNLIKE THE FOLIOT, THE TIME THE PENDULUM TOOK TO SWING DID NOT VARY WITH THE FRICTION OF THE GEARS IN THE CLOCK.

GRANDFATHER CLOCKS

SOON AFTER THE INVENTION OF THE PENDULUM IT WAS FOUND THAT THEIR ACCURACY WAS IMPROVED IF THEY SWUNG THROUGH ONLY A SMALL ANGLE. THIS RESULTED IN THE GRANDFATHER CLOCK.

VACUUM CLOCKS

THE ACCURACY OF A PENDULUM IS SLIGHTLY AFFECTED BY THE "CLOCKWORK" PUSHING IT & THE AIR ABOUT IT. THE 1910 SHORT FREE-PENDULUM CLOCK USED AN ISOLATED PENDULUM PUSHED ELECTRO-MAGNETICALLY IN A VACUUM CHAMBER.

QUARTZ CLOCKS

TODAY'S QUARTZ CLOCKS & WATCHES ARE ACCURATE TO ABOUT 1 MINUTE A YEAR, BUT THE CRYSTALS AGE RATHER ERRATICALLY BECAUSE OF THE CONTINUOUS VIBRATION. LABORATORY QUARTZ CLOCKS USE A GROUP OF CRYSTALS & TAKE AN AVERAGE READING.

ATOMIC CLOCKS

THE SHORT FREE-PENDULUM CLOCK WAS ACCURATE TO 1 SECOND IN 150 YEARS. THIS HAS BEEN REPLACED BY THE ATOMIC CLOCK (1955) WHICH MEASURES THE VIBRATION OF ATOMS OF THE ELEMENT CAESIUM & IS ACCURATE TO 1 SECOND IN 3,000 YEARS.

RUGBY CLOCKS

"RUGBY" CLOCKS ARE SIMPLY RADIO RECEIVERS. THEY DECODE THE SIGNAL TRANSMITTED CONTINUOUSLY FROM AN ATOMIC CLOCK IN RUGBY.

HOW TO MAKE AN E.T. FINGER

1) FIX PENLIGHT TORCH TO FINGER WITH STICKY TAPE.
2) BUY RUBBER FINGER FROM JOKE SHOP OR CUT FINGER OFF RUBBER GLOVE.
3) PAD OUT WITH PAPER & TAPE TO FINGER COVERING TORCH.

CLOCK and CLOUD

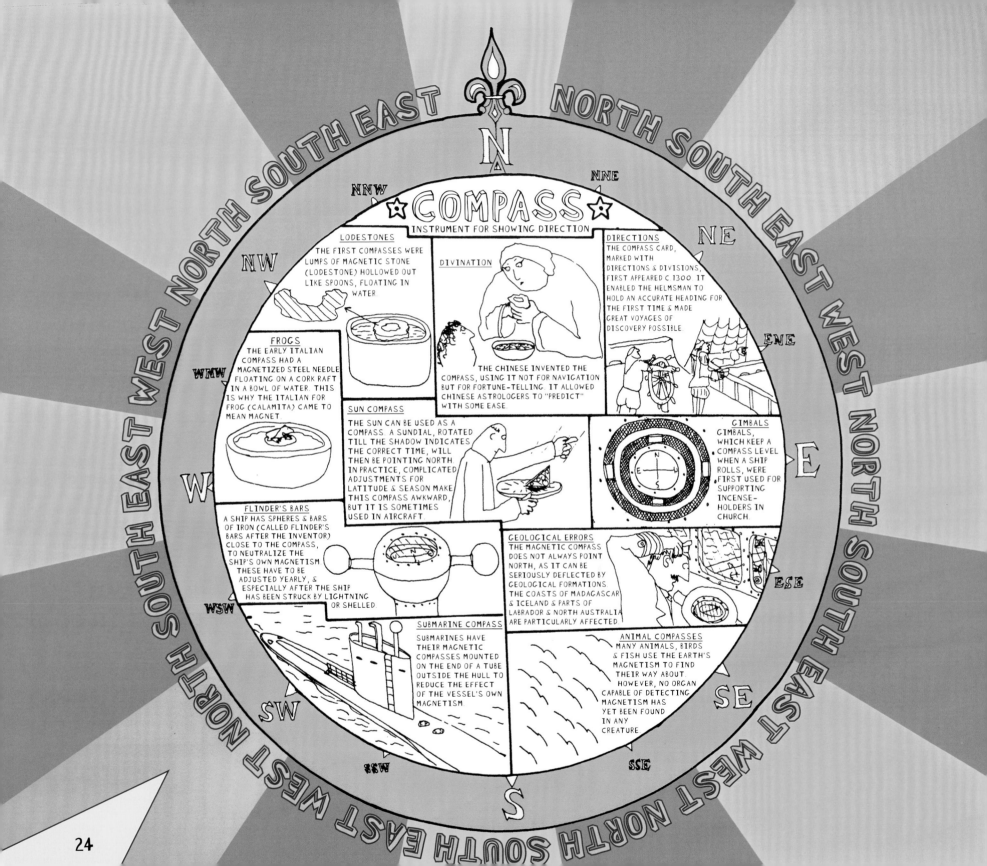

COMPASS
INSTRUMENT FOR SHOWING DIRECTION

LODESTONES
THE FIRST COMPASSES WERE LUMPS OF MAGNETIC STONE (LODESTONE) HOLLOWED OUT LIKE SPOONS, FLOATING IN WATER.

FROGS
THE EARLY ITALIAN COMPASS HAD A MAGNETIZED STEEL NEEDLE FLOATING ON A CORK RAFT IN A BOWL OF WATER. THIS IS WHY THE ITALIAN FOR FROG (CALAMITA) CAME TO MEAN MAGNET.

DIVINATION
THE CHINESE INVENTED THE COMPASS, USING IT NOT FOR NAVIGATION BUT FOR FORTUNE-TELLING. IT ALLOWED CHINESE ASTROLOGERS TO "PREDICT" WITH SOME EASE.

DIRECTIONS
THE COMPASS CARD, MARKED WITH DIRECTIONS & DIVISIONS, FIRST APPEARED C 1300. IT ENABLED THE HELMSMAN TO HOLD AN ACCURATE HEADING FOR THE FIRST TIME & MADE GREAT VOYAGES OF DISCOVERY POSSIBLE.

SUN COMPASS
THE SUN CAN BE USED AS A COMPASS. A SUNDIAL, ROTATED TILL THE SHADOW INDICATES THE CORRECT TIME, WILL THEN BE POINTING NORTH. IN PRACTICE, COMPLICATED ADJUSTMENTS FOR LATITUDE & SEASON MAKE THIS COMPASS AWKWARD, BUT IT IS SOMETIMES USED IN AIRCRAFT.

GIMBALS
GIMBALS, WHICH KEEP A COMPASS LEVEL WHEN A SHIP ROLLS, WERE FIRST USED FOR SUPPORTING INCENSE-HOLDERS IN CHURCH.

FLINDER'S BARS
A SHIP HAS SPHERES & BARS OF IRON (CALLED FLINDER'S BARS AFTER THE INVENTOR) CLOSE TO THE COMPASS, TO NEUTRALIZE THE SHIP'S OWN MAGNETISM. THESE HAVE TO BE ADJUSTED YEARLY, & ESPECIALLY AFTER THE SHIP HAS BEEN STRUCK BY LIGHTNING OR SHELLED.

GEOLOGICAL ERRORS
THE MAGNETIC COMPASS DOES NOT ALWAYS POINT NORTH, AS IT CAN BE SERIOUSLY DEFLECTED BY GEOLOGICAL FORMATIONS. THE COASTS OF MADAGASCAR & ICELAND & PARTS OF LABRADOR & NORTH AUSTRALIA ARE PARTICULARLY AFFECTED.

SUBMARINE COMPASS
SUBMARINES HAVE THEIR MAGNETIC COMPASSES MOUNTED ON THE END OF A TUBE OUTSIDE THE HULL TO REDUCE THE EFFECT OF THE VESSEL'S OWN MAGNETISM.

ANIMAL COMPASSES
MANY ANIMALS, BIRDS & FISH USE THE EARTH'S MAGNETISM TO FIND THEIR WAY ABOUT. HOWEVER, NO ORGAN CAPABLE OF DETECTING MAGNETISM HAS YET BEEN FOUND IN ANY CREATURE.

CRANE

CRANE
MACHINE FOR RAISING HEAVY WEIGHTS

★ THE LARGEST CRANE IN THE WORLD IS THE JAPANESE FLOATING CRANE, MUSAHI. IT WAS BUILT TO HANDLE 3,000-TONNE SECTIONS OF THE NANKO BRIDGE.

★ THE LARGEST CRANE ON WHEELS IS THE LIEBHERR LHM 600 S. IT WEIGHS 600 TONNES & CAN LIFT 208 TONNES TO A HEIGHT OF 45M.

PRE-CRANES

THE CRANE WAS INVENTED BY THE ROMANS. EARLIER CIVILIZATIONS USED TEMPORARY EARTH RAMPS INSTEAD. OBJECTS SUCH AS THE EGYPTIAN OBELISKS OR THE STONES OF STONEHENGE WERE PULLED UP THESE SLOPES ON ROLLERS & THEN LOWERED OVER THE EDGE INTO POSITION WITH ROPES & CROWBARS.

TREADMILLS

UNTIL THE ADVENT OF STEAM POWER, MOST CRANES DEPENDED ON HUMAN POWER. FOR HEAVY LOADS, CRANES WITH TREADMILLS FOR SEVERAL PEOPLE WERE QUITE COMMON ON MEDIEVAL BUILDING SITES.

MANPOWER

ONE MAN TURNING A HANDLE HAS THE POWER TO LIFT ONE TONNE AT ABOUT 70CM PER MINUTE - OR 10 TONNES AT 7CM PER MINUTE.

COUNTER-WEIGHT

THE FIRST TYPE OF CRANE TO HAVE A COUNTER-BALANCED JIB WAS PROBABLY THE "CROW", A MEDIEVAL SIEGE WEAPON. FITTED WITH A CLAW AT ONE END, IT WAS LOWERED OVER THE BATTLEMENTS TO SNATCH UP THE ENEMY. ALTERNATIVELY, IT COULD BE USED BY THE ATTACKING SIDE TO LOWER ASSAULT TOWERS INSIDE THE CITY.

DISASTER

PROBABLY THE BEST-KNOWN CRANE FAILURE OCCURRED DURING THE CONSTRUCTION OF THE QUEBEC BRIDGE IN 1916. A FAULTY CASTING CAUSED THE JIB TO BREAK, DROPPING A SPAN OF THE BRIDGE & KILLING 13 MEN.

MASS PRODUCTION

THE FIRST CRANE TO BE MASS-PRODUCED WAS THE COLES E.M.A. MOBILE CRANE. FIRST ORDERED BY THE AIR MINISTRY IN 1937, THIS BECAME THE STANDARD MILITARY CRANE. MOUNTED ON A VARIETY OF CHASSIS, IT WAS USED THROUGHOUT WORLD WAR II. IT REMAINED IN VERY WIDE USE UNTIL THE INTRODUCTION OF TELESCOPIC & HYDRAULIC CRANES IN THE 1960S.

CROCODILE
AMPHIBIOUS CARNIVEROUS REPTILE

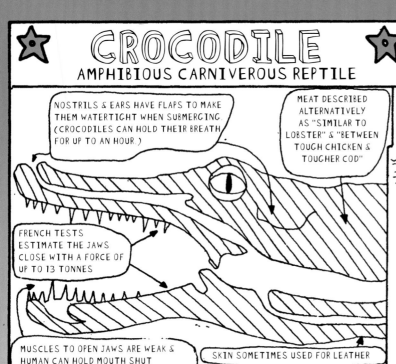

NOSTRILS & EARS HAVE FLAPS TO MAKE THEM WATERTIGHT WHEN SUBMERGING. (CROCODILES CAN HOLD THEIR BREATH FOR UP TO AN HOUR.)

MEAT DESCRIBED ALTERNATIVELY AS "SIMILAR TO LOBSTER" & "BETWEEN TOUGH CHICKEN & TOUGHER COD"

FRENCH TESTS ESTIMATE THE JAWS CLOSE WITH A FORCE OF UP TO 13 TONNES

MUSCLES TO OPEN JAWS ARE WEAK & HUMAN CAN HOLD MOUTH SHUT

SKIN SOMETIMES USED FOR LEATHER

UNSCRUPULOUS ALLIES

THE ESTUARINE CROCODILE EATS MORE PEOPLE THAN ANY OTHER CARNIVORE (2,000 PER YEAR). IN 1945 1,000 JAPANESE INFANTRY WERE CORNERED BY THE ENGLISH IN A MANGROVE SWAMP IN THE BAY OF BENGAL. BOTH SIDES SETTLED DOWN FOR THE NIGHT BUT THE BRITISH WERE PUZZLED BY SHOTS, SCREAMS & GROANS COMING FROM THE SWAMP. THE LOCAL CROCODILES HAD OBVIOUSLY BEEN ATTRACTED BY THE SMELL & NOISE OF THE BATTLE BECAUSE ONLY 20 JAPANESE WERE LEFT UNEATEN BY MORNING.

THE CROCODILE'S CAPACITY

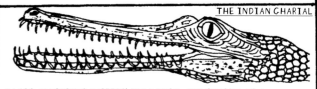

THE SALT-WATER CROCODILE (ESTUARINE) IS THE WORLD'S LARGEST REPTILE (UP TO 8M LONG). THE NILE CROC, THOUGH SMALLER (6M), HAS A LARGE APPETITE. THE STOMACH OF ONE SHOT IN BOTSWANA IN 1969 CONTAINED THE REMAINS OF A ZEBRA, A DONKEY, 2 GOATS & A WOMAN WHO HAD BEEN MISSING FOR 17 DAYS.

THE MYSTERY OF A MUGGER'S STOMACH

STONES & PEBBLES WEIGHING AS MUCH AS 13KG ARE FREQUENTLY FOUND IN THE STOMACHS OF MATURE ADULT CROCS. IT HAS BEEN SUGGESTED THAT THEY AID THE DIGESTION, GRINDING TOUGHER MORSELS SUCH AS HIPPO BONES. A MORE LIKELY REASON IS THAT THE CUNNING REPTILES EAT ENOUGH TO ADJUST THEIR BUOYANCY SO THEY CAN JUST FLOAT WITH ONLY THEIR SNOUTS SHOWING ABOVE THE SURFACE. THIS THEORY IS SUPPORTED BY THE FACT THAT YOUNG ADULTS, WHO DO NOT EAT STONES, ARE MUCH MORE CLUMSY IN WATER.

THE INDIAN GHARIAL

A LESS DANGEROUS VARIETY THAN MOST, THE GHARIAL IS A LONG-NOSED, WEB-FOOTED, FISH-EATING CROCODILE WITH SOME ENDEARING HABITS. IT IS SHY & TICKLISH & HAS AN ELEGANT WAY OF CATCHING FISH, FLIPPING THEM UNCONSCIOUS INTO THE AIR WITH ITS TAIL & CATCHING THEM IN ITS MOUTH.

CROCODILE CULTS

THE EGYPTIANS VENERATED THE CROCODILE. RECORDS SUGGEST IT WAS CUSTOMARY IN 10 BC TO VISIT A CROC TAMED BY PRIESTS AT LAKE MOERIS (THEY CALLED IT SUCHOS) & TO FEED IT CAKES & HONEY WINE. IN PARTS OF AFRICA IT IS BELIEVED THAT CROCODILES EAT ONLY HUMANS WHO ARE POSSESSED BY WITCHES, AND THAT THESE INDIVIDUALS MUST BE FOUND & EXECUTED. ONE TRIBE LEAVES THE UNLUCKY "WITCHES" IN CROCODILE TRAPS AS BAIT.

HOW TO FIND WATER IN A DESERT

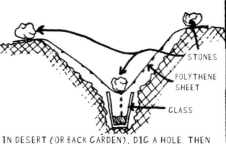

STONES

POLYTHENE SHEET

GLASS

IN DESERT (OR BACK GARDEN), DIG A HOLE. THEN PUT GLASS IN BOTTOM & COVER WITH POLYTHENE SHEET. HOLD DOWN SHEET WITH STONES OVER GLASS, AS ABOVE, & LEAVE. WATER WILL CONDENSE UNDER SHEET & FILL GLASS.

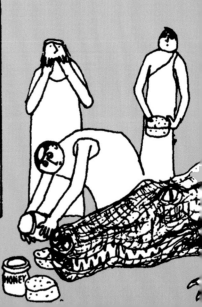

DIVING

★ WORKING & EXPLORING UNDER WATER ★

ANCIENT AQUALUNG

THE ANCIENT ASSYRIANS (C.900 BC) SWAM UNDER WATER FOR UP TO 20 MINUTES BY BREATHING FROM GOAT SKINS FULL OF AIR

THE DIVING BELL

THE ASTRONOMER SIR EDMUND HALLEY PERFECTED THE DIVING BELL IN 1670

HALLEY'S CAP OF MAINTENANCE, THE PREDECESSOR OF THE HELMET

LEAD-LINED BARRELS OF AIR DROPPED FROM THE SURFACE TO REPLENISH AIR IN BELL

A NATURAL DIVING BELL

THE WATER SPIDER CREATES A BELL-SHAPED CHAMBER OF SILK ANCHORED TO WATER-WEEDS. IT TRAPS AIR FROM THE SURFACE IN ITS BODY HAIR AND CARRIES IT DOWN TO FILL THE UNDERWATER CHAMBER.

STEALING AIR

A BEETLE LARVA LIVING UNDER WATER STEALS ITS AIR SUPPLY FROM AIR POCKETS IN THE ROOTS OR STEMS OF WATER LILY-PLANTS.

DEEP-SEA BREATHING

DIVERS CAN GO MUCH DEEPER BY BREATHING A MIXTURE OF HELIUM, NITROGEN & OXYGEN THAN BY BREATHING AIR. HELIUM DOES NOT DISSOLVE SO READILY IN THE BLOOD &, BEING LIGHTER, DIFFUSES OUT FASTER – MAKING THE BENDS LESS LIKELY

THE BENDS

AS A DIVER DESCENDS, THE PRESSURE INSIDE HIS BODY INCREASES, & HIS BLOOD TAKES UP MORE & MORE NITROGEN FROM THE AIR

FIZZO
FIZZO
FIZZO

WHEN THE DIVER RISES TOO FAST, NITROGEN BUBBLES APPEAR IN THE BLOOD (JUST LIKE THE BUBBLES THAT FORM WHEN A FIZZY-DRINK BOTTLE IS OPENED & PRESSURE IS REDUCED). THE NITROGEN BUBBLES CAUSE "THE BENDS", WITH SYMPTOMS SUCH AS CRAMPS, PARALYSIS & EVEN DEATH

THE DIVER

THE EARLIEST HELMETS WERE NOT SEALED TO A SUIT AT THE NECK & FILLED WITH WATER IF THE DIVER FELL

THE DIVER ADJUSTS AN EXHAUST VALVE TO ALTER THE VOLUME OF AIR IN HIS SUIT – & HENCE HIS BUOYANCY.

DRYSUITS

DRYSUITS ARE SEALED AT WRISTS & ANKLES TO KEEP THE DIVER DRY & CAN BE WORN WITH WARM UNDERWEAR.

AS THE DIVER DESCENDS, ANY RESIDUAL AIR IN THE SUIT IS COMPRESSED & CREASES BECOME RIGID, PINCHING THE SKIN & HAMPERING MOVEMENT. THESE SUITS ARE WORN ONLY FOR WORK IN POLLUTED OR VERY COLD WATER

HOW TO STOP WRITING FROM RUNNING WHEN WET

SIMPLY RUB A CANDLE THOROUGHLY OVER THE WRITING

WETSUITS

WETSUITS ARE CLOSE-FITTING BUT NOT WATERTIGHT. WATER SEEPS IN, BECOMES TRAPPED & QUICKLY WARMS UP. THE AIR BUBBLES IN THE FOAM MATERIAL ACT AS AN INSULATOR.

AS THE DIVER DESCENDS, THE FOAM BUBBLES ARE COMPRESSED, REDUCING HIS BUOYANCY. A DIVER WHO FLOATS AT SURFACE LEVEL MAY SINK AT 50M BELOW

LUXURY SUITS

SOME EXPENSIVE WETSUITS USE MILLIONS OF TINY SEALED BUBBLES OF GLASS INSTEAD OF FOAM. THESE ARE INCOMPRESSIBLE & KEEP THE BUOYANCY CONSTANT

DIVING

DOLPHINS

AQUATIC MAMMALS OF THE DELPHINIDAE FAMILY

DOLPHINS AS MINESWEEPERS

THE US NAVY IS TESTING A CLAW ATTACHED TO A MOUTHPIECE WHICH IS GRASPED BY A DOLPHIN. THE ANIMAL IS TRAINED TO LOCATE A TORPEDO & PRESS THE CLAW AGAINST IT. THIS ACTION RELEASES THE MOUTHPIECE & FILLS A BALLOON WITH GAS, LIFTING THE TORPEDO TO THE SURFACE. IT HAS ALSO BEEN CLAIMED THAT DOLPHINS ARE TO BE USED IN A MORE SINISTER MANNER (AT THE COST OF THEIR OWN LIVES), DETONATING THE HARD-TO-REMOVE MINES IN HAIPHONG HARBOUR.

MATTRESSES

THERE ARE MANY FANTASTIC STORIES OF DROWNING PEOPLE BEING LIFTED & CARRIED SAFELY TO THE SHORE BY DOLPHINS. THIS BEHAVIOUR IS NOT AS IMPROBABLE AS IT SOUNDS. A DOLPHIN WAS ONCE OBSERVED ESCORTING A MATTRESS IN EXACTLY THE SAME MANNER, SO IT MAY BE AN INSTINCTIVE REACTION TO ANY ROUGHLY DOLPHIN-SHAPED SINKING OBJECT.

DOLPHINS & HUMANS

DOLPHINS ARE MAMMALS QUITE SIMILAR TO HUMANS. IF DOLPHINS COULD SHORTEN THEIR NECKS, LOWER SPINE & COCCYX, LENGTHEN THEIR ARMS, LOSE THE SKIN BETWEEN THEIR FINGERS, GROW BACK LEGS, ENLARGE THEIR PELVIS, GROW HAIR & EXTERNAL EARS, REDUCE THE SIZE OF THEIR UPPER LIPS & MOVE THEIR NOSTRILS FROM THE TOP OF THEIR HEAD TO THE FRONT, WE MIGHT BE COMPLETELY INDISTINGUISHABLE

TALKING TO DOLPHINS

MANY SCIENTISTS HAVE ATTEMPTED TO UNDERSTAND THE DOLPHIN'S ELABORATE COMMUNICATION LANGUAGE, THOUGH WITHOUT MUCH SUCCESS. ONE THEORY FOR THIS FAILURE IS THAT DOLPHINS USE THEIR ECHO-LOCATING SONAR TO CONVEY EMOTION, RATHER AS WE USE FACIAL EXPRESSIONS.

HIGH-SPEED DOLPHINS

THE SPEED OF MOST ANIMALS CAN BE WELL PREDICTED FROM A CALCULATION OF THE POWER OUTPUT CAPABLE FROM A GIVEN MASS OF MUSCLE. HOWEVER THIS GIVES THE DOLPHIN'S MAX SPEED AS 11 KNOTS WHEREAS ACTUALLY IT CAN EASILY REACH 25 KNOTS. THE REASON FOR THIS IS NOT KNOWN BUT IS THE SUBJECT OF INTENSIVE RESEARCH IN THE HOPE OF FINDING A WAY TO DOUBLE THE SPEED OF SUBMARINES.

DOLPHINS & SCIENCE

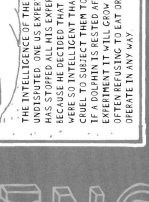

THE INTELLIGENCE OF THE DOLPHIN IS UNDISPUTED. ONE US EXPERT, DR J. LILLY, HAS STOPPED ALL HIS EXPERIMENTS BECAUSE HE DECIDED THAT DOLPHINS WERE SO INTELLIGENT THAT IT WAS CRUEL TO SUBJECT THEM TO CAPTIVITY. IF A DOLPHIN IS RESTED AFTER AN EXPERIMENT IT WILL GROW BORED, OFTEN REFUSING TO EAT OR CO-OPERATE IN ANY WAY.

HOW TO MAKE A MICROSCOPE

PUT OBJECT TO BE EXAMINED ON A TABLE (A HUMAN HAIR WORKS WELL). STICK PIECE OF SELLOTAPE ACROSS 2 PENCILS & PLACE DROP OF WATER ON SELLOTAPE ABOVE OBJECT. NOW LOOK AT OBJECT UNDER WATER-DROP THROUGH A MAGNIFYING GLASS.

DOLPHINS

DRAGONS
MYTHICAL FIRE-BREATHING REPTILIAN MONSTERS

ANATOMY OF A DRAGON
THE CHINESE DESCRIBE THE DRAGON AS BEING MADE UP OF 9 COMPONENTS OF OTHER ANIMALS (WITH A LUMP ON THE BACK OF ITS HEAD, WITHOUT WHICH IT CANNOT FLY).

HORNS OF A STAG

LUMP ON HEAD (WITHOUT WHICH IT CANNOT FLY)

EARS OF A COW

EYES OF A DEMON

HEAD OF A TIGER

CLAWS OF AN EAGLE

SCALES OF A CARP

BELLY OF A CLAM

NECK OF A SNAKE

FEET OF A TIGER

ST GEORGE'S DRAGON
ST GEORGE'S DRAGON CAN BE TRACED TO THE GREEK LEGEND OF A SEA MONSTER SLAIN BY PERSEUS AT JOPPA, ISRAEL. WITH THE SPREAD OF CHRISTIANITY, THE CREDIT FOR THE SLAYING WAS TRANSFERRED TO ST GEORGE

HURRICANE DRAGON
THE WEST INDIANS BELIEVED THAT EARTHQUAKES & HURRICANES WERE CAUSED BY A DRAGON CALLED HURACAN. HE USUALLY WALKED ABOUT ON ONE LEG, IN THE FORM OF A TORNADO

AERIAL DRAGONS
THE CHINESE BELIEVE THAT DRAGONS DIVIDE THE SKY INTO TERRITORIES. CLOUDS ARE THEIR BREATH, IN WHICH THEY HIDE

DRAGON BOATS
THE JAPANESE STILL MAKE DRAGON BOATS AS PLEASURE CRUISERS

HORSE DRAGONS
THE JAPANESE SAY THAT, IN HEAVEN, A HORSE IS MADE INTO A DRAGON. AMONG MEN, A DRAGON IS MADE INTO A HORSE.

NICE DRAGONS
IN THE WESTERN WORLD, DRAGONS HAVE ALWAYS BEEN REGARDED AS EVIL. IN THE EAST, THIS IS NOT THE CASE. BUDDHA IS SAID TO HAVE TAMED ONE, & CHINESE EMPERORS ARE SAID TO HAVE KEPT THEM AS PETS.

ST MARGARET'S DRAGON
ST MARGARET BECAME THE PATRON SAINT OF CHILDBIRTH BECAUSE OF HER ENCOUNTER WITH A DRAGON. AFTER BEING DEVOURED, SHE MIRACULOUSLY REAPPEARED OUT OF ITS STOMACH

THE MOUTH OF HELL
THE ENTRANCE TO HELL WAS OFTEN DEPICTED AS A DRAGONS MOUTH IN MEDIEVAL CHRISTIAN ART.

THE CAVERNOUS MOUTH
THE HINDU GOD KRISHNA RASHLY TOOK SHELTER IN A DRAGON'S MOUTH, MISTAKING IT FOR A MOUNTAIN CAVE. FORTUNATELY, HE ESCAPED BY MAKING HIMSELF VERY LARGE & BURSTING THE BEAST APART

HOW TO PULL A STRING RIGHT THROUGH YOUR NECK

(1) BRING THUMBS TOGETHER

(2) MOVE LEFT LOOP FROM THUMB TO FIRST FINGER

(3) SLIP LEFT THUMB INTO RIGHT LOOP

(4) RELEASE LEFT LOOP & PULL HANDS APART

ELEPHANTS

LARGE PACHYDERMS WITH PROBOSCES

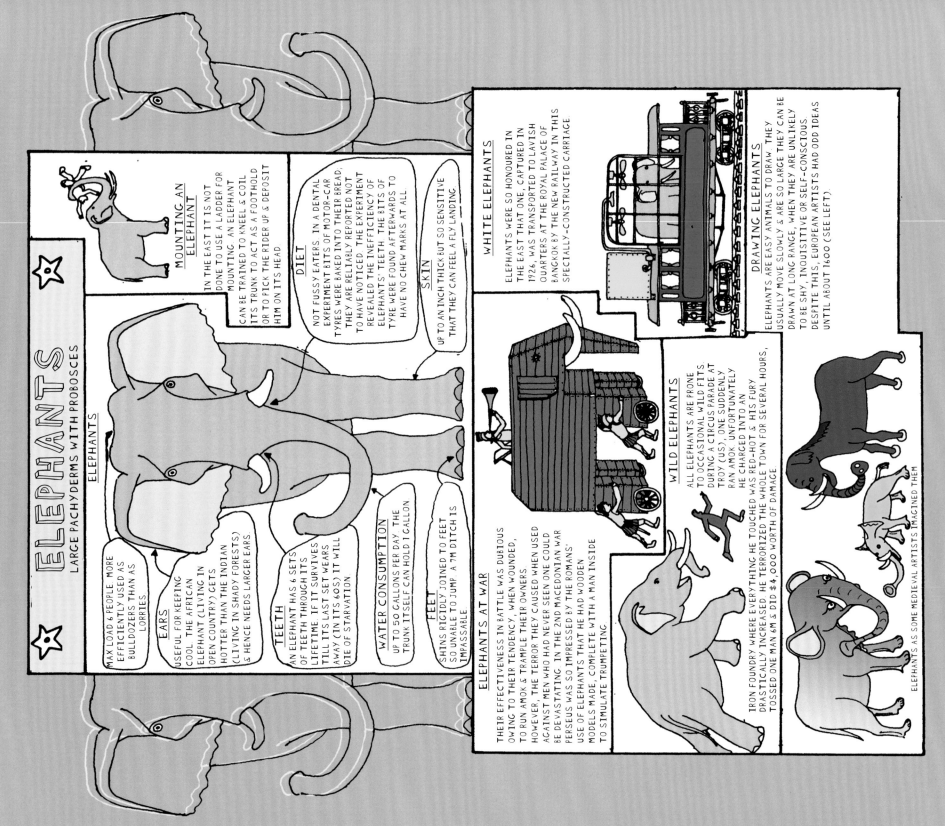

ELEPHANTS

MAX LOAD 6 PEOPLE MORE EFFICIENTLY USED AS BULLDOZERS THAN AS LORRIES

EARS

USEFUL FOR KEEPING COOL. THE AFRICAN ELEPHANT (LIVING IN OPEN COUNTRY) GETS HOTTER THAN THE INDIAN (LIVING IN SHADY FORESTS) & HENCE NEEDS LARGER EARS.

TEETH

AN ELEPHANT HAS 6 SETS OF TEETH THROUGH ITS LIFETIME. IF IT SURVIVES TILL ITS LAST SET WEARS AWAY (IN ITS 60S) IT WILL DIE OF STARVATION.

WATER CONSUMPTION

UP TO 50 GALLONS PER DAY. THE TRUNK ITSELF CAN HOLD 1 GALLON

FEET

SHINS RIGIDLY JOINED TO FEET SO UNABLE TO JUMP A 7M DITCH IS IMPASSABLE

MOUNTING AN ELEPHANT

IN THE EAST IT IS NOT DONE TO USE A LADDER FOR MOUNTING. AN ELEPHANT CAN BE TRAINED TO KNEEL & COIL ITS TRUNK TO ACT AS A FOOTHOLD OR TO PICK THE RIDER UP & DEPOSIT HIM ON ITS HEAD.

DIET

NOT FUSSY EATERS. IN A DENTAL EXPERIMENT BITS OF MOTOR-CAR TYRES WERE BAKED INTO THEIR BREAD. THEY ARE RELIABLY REPORTED NOT TO HAVE NOTICED. THE EXPERIMENT REVEALED THE INEFFICIENCY OF ELEPHANTS' TEETH. THE BITS OF TYRE WERE FOUND AFTERWARDS TO HAVE NO CHEW MARKS AT ALL.

SKIN

UP TO AN INCH THICK BUT SO SENSITIVE THAT THEY CAN FEEL A FLY LANDING.

ELEPHANTS AT WAR

THEIR EFFECTIVENESS IN BATTLE WAS DUBIOUS OWING TO THEIR TENDENCY, WHEN WOUNDED, TO RUN AMOK & TRAMPLE THEIR OWNERS. HOWEVER, THE TERROR THEY CAUSED WHEN USED AGAINST MEN WHO HAD NEVER SEEN ONE COULD BE DEVASTATING. IN THE 2ND MACEDONIAN WAR PERSEUS WAS SO IMPRESSED BY THE ROMANS' USE OF ELEPHANTS THAT HE HAD WOODEN MODELS MADE, COMPLETE WITH A MAN INSIDE TO SIMULATE TRUMPETING.

WHITE ELEPHANTS

ELEPHANTS WERE SO HONOURED IN THE EAST THAT ONE, CAPTURED IN 1926, WAS TRANSPORTED TO LAVISH QUARTERS AT THE ROYAL PALACE OF BANGKOK BY THE NEW RAILWAY IN THIS SPECIALLY-CONSTRUCTED CARRIAGE

WILD ELEPHANTS

ALL ELEPHANTS ARE PRONE TO OCCASIONAL WILD FITS. DURING A CIRCUS PARADE AT TROY (US), ONE SUDDENLY RAN AMOK. UNFORTUNATELY HE CHARGED INTO AN IRON FOUNDRY WHERE EVERYTHING HE TOUCHED WAS RED-HOT & HIS FURY DRASTICALLY INCREASED. HE TERRORIZED THE WHOLE TOWN FOR SEVERAL HOURS, TOSSED ONE MAN 6M & DID $4,000 WORTH OF DAMAGE

DRAWING ELEPHANTS

ELEPHANTS ARE EASY ANIMALS TO DRAW. THEY USUALLY MOVE SLOWLY & ARE SO LARGE THEY CAN BE DRAWN AT LONG RANGE, WHEN THEY ARE UNLIKELY TO BE SHY, INQUISITIVE OR SELF-CONSCIOUS. DESPITE THIS, EUROPEAN ARTISTS HAD ODD IDEAS UNTIL ABOUT 1600 (SEE LEFT).

ELEPHANTS AS SOME MEDIEVAL ARTISTS IMAGINED THEM

UP ↗ ↙ DOWN

ESCALATORS

REVOLVING STAIRS
THE IDEA OF AN ESCALATOR WAS FIRST PATENTED IN 1859. IT WAS REFERRED TO AS A "REVOLVING STAIR", BUT THE DESIGN WAS CRUDE & DANGEROUS & NEVER BUILT.

MOVING RAMPS
THE FIRST PRACTICAL ESCALATOR (A MOVING RAMP WITHOUT STEPS) WAS BUILT BY A US ENGINEER CALLED JESSE W. RENO IN 1894. ALTHOUGH INTENDED AS A FUNCTIONAL ALTERNATIVE TO THE LIFT, THE FIRST ONE WAS SOLD TO CONEY ISLAND PIER AS A FUNFAIR RIDE.

COMBS
THE RAMP WAS MADE OF WOODEN SLATS WHICH PASSED BETWEEN COMB-LIKE DEVICES AT EACH END. THIS ENSURED THAT PEOPLE WERE CARRIED SAFELY OFF THE MOVING PARTS & PREVENTED OBJECTS FROM JAMMING.

HARRODS' ESCALATOR
BRITAIN'S FIRST ESCALATOR WAS INSTALLED IN HARRODS IN 1898. AN ATTENDANT AT THE TOP DISPENSED BRANDY TO THOSE OVERCOME BY THE RIDE.

1921
THE OTIS LIFT COMPANY BOUGHT ALL THE PRACTICAL ESCALATOR PATENTS IN 1910 & COMBINED THEIR BEST FEATURES. SINCE THE INTRODUCTION OF THE OTIS "L" TYPE IN 1921, THERE HAVE BEEN NO FUNDAMENTAL DESIGN CHANGES.

RIDE THE ESCALATOR 5c

OTIS

LENGTH
THE ONE AT LENINGRAD UNDERGROUND IS ABOUT 120M LONG. THE LONGEST ON THE LONDON UNDERGROUND IS ON THE PICCADILLY LINE AT LEICESTER SQUARE (50M).

ESCALATORS FOR TROLLEYS
ESCALATORS WITH RAMPS INSTEAD OF STEPS HAVE RETURNED TO FAVOUR IN SOME SHOPS. THE RAMP IS DESIGNED TO LOCK ONTO SUPERMARKET TROLLEYS TO ALLOW SHOPPERS TO TAKE THEM FROM ONE FLOOR TO ANOTHER.

CONFIDENCE
PLEASE DO NOT SIT ON THE STAIRS STEP OFF WITH LEFT FOOT FIRST

LONDON TRANSPORT'S FIRST ESCALATOR WAS INSTALLED AT EARLS COURT STATION IN 1911. A MAN WITH A WOODEN LEG WAS EMPLOYED TO RIDE UP & DOWN ALL DAY TO INSPIRE CONFIDENCE.

SLOW SPEED
ESCALATORS IN DEPARTMENT STORES ARE SLOWER THAN OTHER ESCALATORS. TRANSPORTATION IS SECONDARY TO THEIR FUNCTION AS SALES AIDS – GIVING THE CUSTOMERS PANORAMIC VIEWS OF THE SHOP.

THE SPEED OF AN ESCALATOR
IT IS POSSIBLE TO MEASURE THE SPEED OF AN (EMPTY) ESCALATOR BY WALKING IN THE WRONG DIRECTION SO YOU ARE JUST REMAINING STATIONARY. COUNT HOW MANY STEPS YOU HAVE TO TAKE IN 10 SECONDS. THEN MEASURE THE DISTANCE BETWEEN STEPS.

$$SPEED = \frac{DISTANCE}{TIME}$$

$$\frac{(NUMBER\ OF\ STEPS) \times (HEIGHT\ OF\ STEP)}{10\ SECONDS}$$

SAFETY
COMB PLATES HAVE PRESSURE SWITCHES WHICH SENSE IF ANYTHING IS CAUGHT BETWEEN COMB & STEPS.

SIZE OF GAPS BETWEEN MOVING & STATIONARY PARTS IS CRITICAL FOR SAFETY.

ALL ESCALATORS HAVE A BRAKE WHICH COMES ON AUTOMATICALLY IN THE EVENT OF A POWER CUT.

EVOLUTION
THE DEVELOPMENT OF ORGANISMS

EVOLUTION & SURVIVAL

DARWIN'S THEORY OF EVOLUTION IS OFTEN CALLED THE SURVIVAL OF THE FITTEST. THIS IS BECAUSE ANY CHANCE GENETIC VARIATION THAT HELPS A PLANT OR ANIMAL TO SURVIVE & REPRODUCE SHOULD LEAD TO THE SPREAD OF THAT VARIATION IN SUCCESSIVE GENERATIONS.

EVOLUTION ARMS RACE

DARWIN'S THEORY OF EVOLUTION CAN BE SEEN AS AN ARMS RACE. FOR EXAMPLE CHEETAHS THAT RUN FASTER ARE MORE LIKELY TO CATCH GAZELLES, SO THE SPECIES IS UNDER PRESSURE TO BECOME FASTER. GAZELLES THAT RUN FASTER ARE MORE LIKELY TO ESCAPE, SO THEIR SPECIES ALSO BECOMES FASTER.

NO EVOLUTION

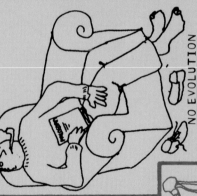

THE PHILOSOPHER BERTRAND RUSSELL SAID "IT IS QUITE POSSIBLE TO CONJECTURE A WORLD THAT CAME INTO EXISTENCE FIVE MINUTES AGO, COMPLETE WITH MY MEMORIES & THE HOLES IN MY SOCKS."

SCIENCE OR NOT?

SCIENTIFIC THEORIES ARE FOUNDED ON EXPERIMENTS WHICH CAN BE REPEATED AT ANY TIME AS CONFIRMATION. SOME PEOPLE CLAIM THAT EVOLUTION IS NOT A SCIENTIFIC THEORY BECAUSE IT DEALS WITH HISTORICAL EVENTS THAT CANNOT BE RE-TESTED.

TWO LEGS BETTER?

WALKING ON TWO LEGS WAS A KEY STAGE IN THE EVOLUTION OF HUMANS. IT TOOK LESS ENERGY THAN GETTING AROUND ON ALL FOURS, WHICH WAS USEFUL AT A TIME WHEN OUR APE-LIKE ANCESTORS HAD TO WALK FURTHER AND FURTHER BETWEEN PATCHES OF FOOD. FREEING UP THE HANDS WAS ALSO HANDY FOR HUNTING, CARRYING FOOD AND MAKING SIMPLE TOOLS.

THE EVOLUTION OF THE HAND

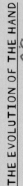

OPOSSUM   TREE SHREW   CALAGO   TARSIER

DARWIN'S RIVAL

DARWIN'S RIVAL, LAMARCK, CLAIMED THAT ANIMALS & PLANTS PASS ON TO THEIR DESCENDANTS CHARACTERISTICS ACQUIRED IN THEIR OWN LIFETIME. LAMARCK DIED 30 YEARS BEFORE DARWIN PUBLISHED HIS IDEAS.

CHIMPANZEES TO HUMANS

THE DIFFERENCE BETWEEN CHIMPANZEE & HUMAN DNA (THE GENETIC CODE) IS ABOUT ONE PER CENT. THIS IS LESS THAN THE DIFFERENCE BETWEEN SPECIES OF FROGS.

HOW TO CALCULATE A FRIEND'S AGE & THE CHANGE IN THEIR POCKET

- AGE (EG. 12)   12
- DOUBLE IT   24
- ADD 5   29
- MULTIPLY BY 50   1,450
- SUBTRACT 365   1,085
- ADD CHANGE IN POCKET (EG. 25P)   1110

ASK FRIEND TO PERFORM ABOVE SUM. ADD 115 TO THE TOTAL. THE FIRST TWO FIGURES WILL BE HIS OR HER AGE, THE LAST TWO, THE AMOUNT OF CHANGE.

EVOLUTION FROM SPACE

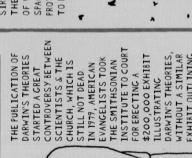

BABOON   ORANG-UTAN   MAN

SIR FRED HOYLE, THE ASTRONOMER, PROPOSED THE THEORY THAT EVOLUTION HAS OCCURRED BECAUSE OF VIRUSES WHICH REACH EARTH FROM OUTER SPACE. THESE COLLECT ON COMETS COVERED IN A PROTECTIVE LAYER OF ICE & OCCASIONALLY FALL TO EARTH.

EVOLUTION & THE CHURCH

THE PUBLICATION OF DARWIN'S THEORIES STARTED A GREAT CONTROVERSY BETWEEN SCIENTISTS & THE CHURCH, WHICH IS STILL NOT DEAD. IN 1979, AMERICAN EVANGELISTS TOOK THE SMITHSONIAN INSTITUTE TO COURT FOR ERECTING A $200,000 EXHIBIT ILLUSTRATING DARWIN'S THEORIES, WITHOUT A SIMILAR EXHIBIT OUTLINING THE BIBLICAL VERSION.

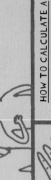

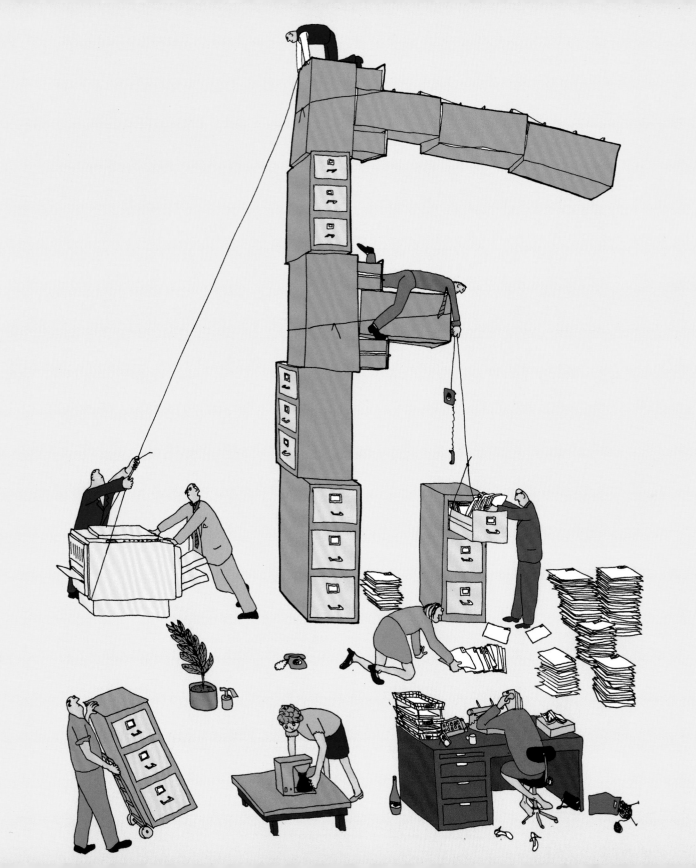

FACES

VITAL COMPONENTS OF HUMAN APPEARANCE

SUPPORT

THE FACE IS SUPPORTED BY 144 BONES & MORE THAN 100 MUSCLES.

SIZE

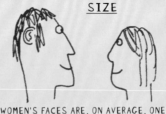

WOMEN'S FACES ARE, ON AVERAGE, ONE FIFTH SMALLER THAN MEN'S FACES.

WRINKLES

THE FACE WRINKLES WITH AGE BECAUSE SKIN BECOMES LESS ELASTIC, ALTHOUGH THE SKIN CELLS ARE CONTINUALLY RENEWED. IT MAY BE BECAUSE THE CELLS ARE REPLACED LESS FREQUENTLY OR BECAUSE THE REPLACEMENT CELLS ARE WEAKER.

GREEK BEAUTY

THE GREEKS BELIEVED THAT THE PERFECT FACE HAD THE RATIO OF X TO Y EQUALLING Y TO Z.

MEDIEVAL BEAUTY

MEDIEVAL ARTISTS THOUGHT THAT THE PERFECT FACE SHOULD DIVIDE INTO SEVENTHS.

BABY CHEEKS

BABIES HAVE PLUMP CHEEKS TO ACT AS SUCKING PADS. THEY ARE CLEARLY IMPORTANT, AS STARVING BABIES RETAIN THEIR CHEEK FAT.

PLUMPERS

A STRANGE DEVICE FOR CONCEALING FACIAL DEFECTS WAS THE PLUMPER: A PAD OF COTTON & CORK WORN INSIDE THE MOUTH TO SWELL THE CAVITIES LEFT BY LOSS OF TEETH. IT WAS POPULAR FROM ABOUT 1660 TO 1800.

FACE-FLATTENING

FRENCH PEASANTS, NORTH AMERICAN INDIANS, AFRICANS, ARISTOCRATIC ANCIENT GREEKS & ROMANS HAVE ALL PRACTISED THE ART OF FLATTENING THE FOREHEADS OF THEIR CHILDREN. THE SKULL OF A NEWBORN BABY IS FLEXIBLE & THE PLATES, KEPT TIGHTLY TIED TO IT FOR THE FIRST 5 WEEKS, HAVE NO APPARENT ILL-EFFECTS.

SPECTACLES

AMERICAN EXPERIMENTS SUPPORT THE IDEA THAT WEARING SPECTACLES MAKES OTHERS THINK YOU ARE MORE INTELLIGENT.

FEMALE PERCEPTION

AMERICAN EXPERIMENTS HAVE SHOWN THAT WOMEN LOOK AT THE FACES OF PEOPLE THEY ARE TALKING TO MORE THAN MEN DO.

GUESSING FACES

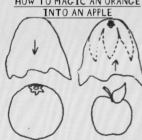

PEOPLE ARE MUCH BETTER AT GUESSING "SIMULATED" EXPRESSIONS OF ACTORS THAN AT READING GENUINE ONES OF ORDINARY PEOPLE. THIS IS PROBABLY BECAUSE ACTORS' EXPRESSIONS ARE LARGER THAN LIFE & MORE STEREOTYPED.

HOW TO MAGIC AN ORANGE INTO AN APPLE

CUT THE PEEL OF AN ORANGE INTO 4 SEGMENTS – LEAVING THEM JOINED AT THE TOP – & SCOOP OUT FLESH. ARRANGE "HOLLOW" PEEL ON TABLE WITH APPLE INSIDE. PLACE HANKY OVER ORANGE & LIFT OFF, CARRYING PEEL WITH IT.

FACES & ILLNESS

EXOPHTHALMIC GOITRE CAUSES WILDLY STARING EYES.

ACROMEGALY CAUSES AN ENLARGEMENT OF NOSE & CHIN.

CONGENITAL SYPHILIS CAN CAUSE A SADDLE NOSE.

CUSHING'S DISEASE CAUSES A MOON-SHAPED FACE.

FEET

THE PARTS OF THE VERTEBRATE BODY NORMALLY IN CONTACT WITH THE GROUND

FOSSILS

FOSSILIZED FOOTPRINTS HELP TO DATE THE ORIGINS OF MAN, BECAUSE OUR FEET ARE SO UNLIKE THOSE OF ANY FOUR-LEGGED ANIMAL. PROTO-HUMAN PRINTS IN TANZANIA (PRESERVED BY BEING COVERED IN VOLCANIC DUST) ARE 3 MILLION YEARS OLD.

BONES

OUR FEET ARE SURPRISINGLY INTRICATE, EACH ONE CONTAINING 26 BONES.

MONKEY FEET

MONKEYS HAVE BIG TOES WHICH POINT SIDEWAYS (TO GRIP BRANCHES) & FLAT FEET (WITHOUT AN ARCH). THE ARCH ON HUMAN FEET MAKES THEM STRONGER & BETTER AT BALANCING.

USE

THE AVERAGE PERSON IN A WESTERN COUNTRY WALKS ABOUT 80,000 KM IN A LIFETIME.

ANGLE

OUR FEET ARE ANGLED OUTWARDS AT ABOUT 7°. A SMALLER ANGLE CAUSES INSTABILITY & A WIDER ANGLE ADDS TO THE EFFORT OF WALKING OR RUNNING.

HEAVY RIGHT FEET

A SURVEY BY THE GOODYEAR RUBBER COMPANY HAS FOUND THAT SHOES ON RIGHT FEET USUALLY WEAR OUT FASTER THAN SHOES ON LEFT FEET. THE REASON IS UNKNOWN.

FUNGI

THE FUNGUS TRICHOPHYTON MENTAGRAPHYTES IS PRESENT ON EVERYBODY'S FEET, LIVING OFF THE DEAD OUTER LAYERS OF SKIN. IN THE WARM, DAMP ENVIRONMENT OF SOCKS & SHOES IT CAN MULTIPLY TOO FAST & ATTACK LIVE SKIN. THIS IS KNOWN AS "ATHLETE'S FOOT".

PERMANENT BOOTS

IF SHOES ARE LEFT ON FOR LONG PERIODS, THE SKIN OF THE FOOT CAN BECOME FUSED TO THE LEATHER TO FORM A SINGLE TISSUE. THIS HAPPENED TO SOLDIERS IN WORLD WAR I TRENCHES & PROBABLY EXPLAINS WHY MANY COWBOYS WERE BURIED IN THEIR BOOTS.

TWO-TOED TRIBE

SOME OF THE KALANGA TRIBE OF ZIMBABWE AND BOTSWANA HAVE ONLY 2 TOES. THIS "LOBSTER CLAW" SYNDROME IS HEREDITARY.

FIRE! FIRE!

FIRE ENGINES
MACHINES FOR EXTINGUISHING FIRE

SQUIRTS

THE FIRST FIRE PUMPS WERE SIMPLY BIG SYRINGES CALLED FIRE SQUIRTS, INTRODUCED BY THE PORTUGUESE AROUND 1550.

FIRE & GIN

LONDON HAD SEVERAL PRIVATE FIRE BRIGADES IN THE 1800S. THE MOST FAMOUS WAS THAT OWNED BY HODGES DISTILLERY, LAMBETH. THEIR ENGINES EACH CARRIED A BARREL OF GIN INSCRIBED: "IF FIRE YOU WANT TO PUT IN, TRY HODGES CORDIAL & GIN. IF FIRE YOU WANT TO PUT OUT, TRY HODGES ENGINES & SPOUT"

LACK OF HOSE

UNTIL FLEXIBLE HOSES WERE INVENTED (C.1690) FIRE ENGINES HAD TO BE POSITIONED VERY CLOSE TO THE FIRE. THE RESULT WAS THAT THEY OFTEN CAUGHT FIRE THEMSELVES.

THE FIRST SELF-PROPELLED STEAM FIRE ENGINE (1859) WAS CALLED THE STEAM ELEPHANT.

STOKING-UP TIME

A DISADVANTAGE OF THE STEAM-PROPELLED ENGINE WAS THE TIME TAKEN TO STOKE UP THE FIRE BEFORE IT COULD MOVE. THE BOILER WAS KEPT HOT IN THE FIRE STATION WITH A GAS RING UNDERNEATH, BUT AT LEAST 2 MINUTES' DELAY WAS NEEDED TO BUILD UP PRESSURE.

HIGH-SPEED GETAWAY

HORSE-DRAWN FIRE ENGINES COULD TURN OUT WITHIN 5 SECONDS OF RECEIVING AN ALARM CALL. THE TRAINED HORSES RUSHED, UNGUIDED, FROM THEIR STABLES TO THE QUICK-HITCH HARNESS SUSPENDED ABOVE THE ENGINE.

PEDAL POWER

VARIOUS PEDAL-POWERED FIRE ENGINES APPEARED IN THE 1890S. MOST CARRIED HOSE TO BE COUPLED TO THE MAINS, BUT ONE INCORPORATED A PEDAL-POWERED PUMP.

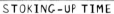

SAFE INSIDE

AS THE SPEED OF PETROL FIRE ENGINES INCREASED, THE TRADITIONAL ARRANGEMENT, SEATING THE CREW ALONG THE SIDES, BECAME HIGHLY DANGEROUS. FINALLY, IN 1928, A FIREMAN IN CHIPPENHAM FELL OFF & WAS KILLED. ALL FIRE ENGINES SINCE HAVE SEATED THE CREW SAFELY INSIDE.

SUPER JETS

WATER JETS CAN GO NEARLY TWICE AS FAR IF A SMALL AMOUNT OF POLYETHYLENE OXIDE IS ADDED TO THE WATER. THIS REDUCES THE FRICTION BETWEEN THE HOSE & THE WATER BY UP TO 50%.

HOW TO MAKE STRUCTURES FROM PEAS & TOOTHPICKS

USE DRIED PEAS, SOFTENED BY SOAKING OVERNIGHT. JOIN TOOTHPICKS WITH PEAS TO MAKE DOMES, BRIDGES, TOWERS ETC. HOLD COMPETITIONS FOR HIGHEST TOWER, STRONGEST BRIDGE, USING ONLY A GIVEN QUANTITY OF BITS.

FLAGS
IDENTIFYING SYMBOLS

THE FIRST FLAGS

THE CHINESE WERE THE FIRST TO USE FLAGS – REFERENCES DATE BACK TO 1122 BC. THE ROMAN LEGIONS CARRIED BANNERS (VEXILLA) BUT THE FIRST TRUE FLAGS IN THE WESTERN WORLD WERE PROBABLY THE VIKINGS' RAVEN FLAGS & SOME EARLY ARAB ONES.

IMPERIAL CHINA

A DRAGON EATING THE SUN WAS THE FLAG USED THROUGHOUT IMPERIAL CHINA. DIFFERENT OFFICIALS HAD DIFFERENT TYPES OF DRAGON.

COMMUNIST CHINA

THE BIG STAR REPRESENTS THE "COMMON PROGRAMME" OF THE PARTY & THE 4 SMALL STARS THE GREAT UNITY OF THE CHINESE PEOPLE.

NO FLAG

GREENLAND (PART OF DENMARK) HAD NO FLAG OF ITS OWN UNTIL 1985.

THE UNITED STATES

THE US FLAG ORIGINALLY HAD A STAR & A STRIPE FOR EACH OF ITS STATES. AS MORE STATES JOINED, THE FLAG BECAME INCREASINGLY FIDDLY, UNTIL 1818, WHEN THE STRIPES WERE PERMANENTLY REDUCED TO THE ORIGINAL 13. THE NUMBER OF STARS IS NOW 50. THE MOST RECENT ADDITIONS WERE ALASKA (1959) & HAWAII (1960).

CANADA

CANADA'S NATIONAL FLAG WAS ADOPTED IN 1965. PREVIOUSLY, IT HAD USED A BRITISH RED ENSIGN WITH A CANADIAN COAT OF ARMS IN ONE CORNER.

NORWAY

NORWAY WAS RULED BY DENMARK UNTIL 1814, THEN BY SWEDEN UNTIL 1905, THEN BECAME A SEPARATE NATION. ITS FLAG REMAINS A COMBINATION OF THE SWEDISH & DANISH FLAGS.

SWEDEN

DENMARK

ISLE OF MAN

THE ORIGIN OF THE ISLE OF MAN'S 3-LEGGED DESIGN IS UNKNOWN BUT A SIMILAR SYMBOL ALSO APPEARS IN SICILY. IT MAY HAVE BEEN BROUGHT TO BOTH PLACES BY THE VIKINGS.

THE SKULL & CROSSBONES WAS FIRST USED BY A FRENCH PIRATE, EMMANUEL WYNNE, IN ABOUT 1700.

BATTLE FLAGS

BRITISH WARSHIPS HAVE TO FLY TWO NATIONAL FLAGS (WHITE ENSIGNS) WHEN IN ACTION. IF ONE IS SHOT OFF, THERE IS NO CHANCE OF THE SHIP BEING REGARDED AS HAVING SURRENDERED.

SIGNAL FLAGS

EVERY WARSHIP STILL CARRIES 70 SIGNAL FLAGS. THESE REPRESENT COMMONLY USED WORDS, PHRASES & LETTERS OF THE ALPHABET. NELSON'S FAMOUS COMMAND BEFORE THE BATTLE OF TRAFALGAR WAS ORIGINALLY "NELSON CONFIDES EVERY MAN WILL DO HIS DUTY", BUT THERE WERE NO FLAGS FOR "NELSON" OR "CONFIDES", SO, INSTEAD OF SPELLING THEM OUT LETTER BY LETTER, THE FLAGS FOR THE WORDS "ENGLAND" & "EXPECTS" WERE SUBSTITUTED.

NEPAL

NEPAL IS THE ONLY COUNTRY IN THE WORLD WHOSE NATIONAL FLAG IS NOT RECTANGULAR. UNTIL 1962, BOTH SUNS HAD FACES.

THE TRICOLOUR

THE STRIPES IN THE FRENCH TRICOLOUR ARE OF UNEQUAL THICKNESS (IN THE RATIO OF 30:33:37). THIS IS DELIBERATE, TO MAKE THEM APPEAR EQUAL FROM A DISTANCE.

REVOLUTIONARY SPIRIT

IRELAND   ITALY   ROMANIA

VARIOUS EUROPEAN COUNTRIES ADOPTED TRICOLOURS IN SYMPATHY WITH THE FRENCH REVOLUTION.

FURNITURE

CONTAINERS FOR POSSESSIONS & PEOPLE

THE CABINETMAKER

IN THE 17TH CENTURY VARIOUS FURNITURE MAKERS CAME TO ENGLAND FROM FRANCE & ITALY BRINGING A RANGE OF NEW TECHNIQUES FOR PRODUCING VENEER, INLAY & DOVETAIL JOINTS. THEY WERE KNOWN AS CABINETMAKERS & THEIR WORK QUICKLY BECAME FASHIONABLE, FORCING THE JOINERS TO MOVE TO MORE BACKWARD RURAL AREAS.

POSTHUMOUS FAME

CHIPPENDALE, HEPPLEWHITE & SHERATON EACH PRODUCED A HIGHLY INFLUENTIAL PATTERN BOOK WHICH FORMED THE BASIS OF 18TH-CENTURY ENGLISH FURNITURE DESIGN. CHIPPENDALE & HEPPLEWHITE WERE CABINETMAKERS WHO USED THEIR PATTERN BOOKS AS CATALOGUES. SHERATON WAS A RATHER UNSUCCESSFUL WRITER, PUBLISHER & TEACHER WHO DIED IN OBSCURITY.

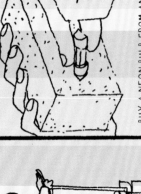

HOW TO MAKE A NEON LIGHT UP

BUY A NEON BULB FROM AN ELECTRICAL SHOP (THE SORT USED IN MAINS-TESTING ELECTRICAL SCREWDRIVERS). FIND A PIECE OF EXPANDED POLYSTYRENE FOAM (USED FOR CEILING TILES, INSULATION & PACKAGING). HOLD ONE END OF THE BULB & RUB THE OTHER AGAINST THE POLYSTYRENE. THE NEON WILL GLOW.

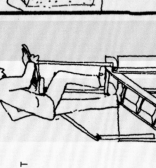

ADJUSTABLE FURNITURE

THE VICTORIANS PATENTED SEVERAL HUNDRED DESIGNS OF DUAL-PURPOSE FURNITURE, BUT THE CONCEPT WAS NOT NEW. IN THE 1780S SHERATON DESIGNED VARIOUS PIECES INCLUDING THE LIBRARY TABLE, RIGHT, WHICH CONVERTED INTO A STEPLADDER. PERHAPS THE EARLIEST EXISTING PIECE IS A MEDIEVAL BENCH WITH A SWING BACK, ABOVE. THIS ENABLED PEOPLE TO SIT ON EITHER SIDE WITHOUT MOVING THE WHOLE BENCH (WHICH WAS EXCEEDINGLY HEAVY).

BODGING

BODGERS WERE SPECIALIST CRAFTSMEN WHO MADE THE ROUND LEGS & STRETCHERS OF MOST SIMPLE CHAIRS. THEY BOUGHT A BEECH COPPICE AT AUCTION & MOVED IN, BUILDING SMALL PRIMITIVE HUTS. THEY FELLED THE TREES, SAWED THEM INTO SECTIONS THE LENGTH OF A CHAIR LEG, SPLIT THE SECTIONS INTO STICKS & TURNED THE STICKS TO FINISHED LEGS ON PRIMITIVE HOME-MADE POLE LATHES. WHEN ALL TREES HAD BEEN USED, THE BODGERS MOVED OUT, SELLING THE LAND & THE FINISHED LEGS.

THE CARPENTER & THE JOINER

JOINERS TOOK OVER MAKING FURNITURE FROM CARPENTERS WHO MADE SHIPS & WOODEN BUILDINGS, DURING THE 14TH & 15TH CENTURIES. THE MAIN TECHNIQUE, OR MYSTERY, OF THE JOINERS' GUILD WAS THE SYSTEM OF PANELLING & FRAMING WHICH OVERCAME THE TENDENCY OF EARLIER FURNITURE TO SPLIT & WARP.

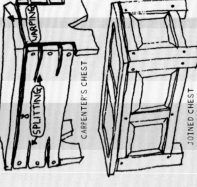

WARPING

SPLITTING

CARPENTER'S CHEST

JOINED CHEST

FARTHINGALE CHAIRS

THE FIRST PADDED CHAIRS WITHOUT ARMS WERE PRODUCED IN RESPONSE TO AN URGENT NEED. IN ABOUT 1570 FARTHINGALE SKIRTS SUDDENLY BECAME FASHIONABLE & LADIES FOUND THEMSELVES UNABLE TO SIT IN ANY ARMCHAIR.

GEARS

SYSTEMS OF PARTS FOR TRANSMITTING MOTION

ROMAN GEARS

THE ROMANS KNEW ABOUT GEARS BUT GENERALLY REGARDED THEM AS CURIOSITIES RATHER THAN AS USEFUL DEVICES. HERO'S MOST COMPLEX DESIGN WAS THE FIRST MILEOMETER (WHICH HE CALLED A BODOMETER). THIS WAS A LONG TRAIN OF GEARS ATTACHED TO THE WHEEL OF A CART ENABLING THE DISTANCE TRAVELLED TO BE READ OFF.

WOODEN GEARS

THE WOODEN-TOOTHED WHEEL WAS THE PREDECESSOR OF THE METAL GEAR. IT WAS MUCH BETTER SUITED TO PRIMITIVE CONSTRUCTION TECHNIQUES AS PRECISE ALIGNMENT WAS LESS CRITICAL. WOODEN TEETH CONTINUED TO BE FITTED TO GEARING IN SOME RURAL DEVICES (MILLS & THRESHING MACHINES) UNTIL RECENTLY AS THEY WERE QUIETER & EASIER TO REPLACE WHEN BROKEN.

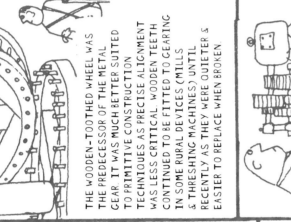

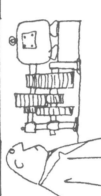

LOSING POWER

THE MAXIMUM EFFICIENCY OF A PAIR OF GEARS IS ABOUT 95%. THIS MEANS THAT 5% OF THE POWER PRODUCED BY AN ENGINE IS LOST WITH EACH PAIR OF GEARS IT RUNS THROUGH.

HIGH-SPEED MACHINING

MACHINE TOOLS WERE ALL DRIVEN BY BELTS & PULLEYS UNTIL ABOUT 1900. GEARS BECAME NECESSARY ONLY WITH THE INTRODUCTION OF ELECTRIC MOTORS & HIGH-SPEED STEEL. (HIGH-SPEED STEEL WAS SO CALLED BECAUSE THE WORKING LIFE OF A CUTTING TOOL IS DETERMINED BY THE SPEED AT WHICH IT IS MADE TO CUT). TOOLS WERE LIMITED TO ABOUT 12M/MINUTE UNTIL THE ARRIVAL OF HIGH SPEED STEEL (ALLOYED WITH CHROMIUM & VANADIUM) – THIS CUT AT 37M/MINUTE

CUTTING GEARS

ONE INGENIOUS GEAR-CUTTING MACHINE HAS A CUTTING TOOL THE SHAPE OF A SMALL GEAR. THIS ROTATES ALONGSIDE THE UNCUT GEAR WHILE GOING BACK & FORTH ALONG ITS SHAFT. AS THE DISTANCE BETWEEN THE SHAFTS OF THE CUTTER & THE GEAR IS SLOWLY REDUCED THE RECIPROCATING CUTTER PROGRESSIVELY SCRAPES OUT THE TEETH IN THE BLANK.

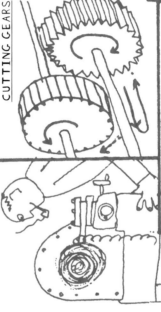

CUTTING WORM GEARS

THE TEETH ON WORM GEARS HAVE TO BE CUT AT A SLIGHT ANGLE. THEY ARE CUT ON AN INGENIOUS MACHINE CALLED A HOB. THE CUTTER IS THE SHAPE OF A FAT BOLT WITH LONGITUDINAL GROOVES CUT IN IT. THIS ROTATES FAST ALONGSIDE THE EDGE OF THE UNCUT GEAR WHICH ROTATES SLOWLY. THE DISTANCE BETWEEN THE CUTTER & THE GEAR IS SLOWLY REDUCED, AND THUS THE TEETH ARE SCRAPED OUT.

IMPRACTICAL GEARING

THE USEFULNESS OF TRAINS OF GEARS WAS VERY LIMITED UNTIL THE 1700S BECAUSE OF THE BIG POWER LOSSES RESULTING FROM PRIMITIVE BEARINGS. THE PRACTICAL LIMITATIONS DID NOT, HOWEVER, DETER INVENTORS. THIS DESIGN FOR UPROOTING TREES BY WINDPOWER DATES FROM ABOUT 1680

HOW TO MAKE A SPACESHIP POWERED BY A BALLOON

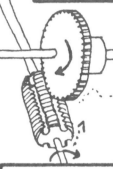
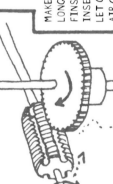

MAKE A CYLINDER OF STRONG PAPER ABOUT 25CM LONG & 8CM IN DIAMETER. GLUE ON THIN CARD FINS & BASE (WITH HOLE CUT IN MIDDLE). INSERT BALLOON THROUGH THIS HOLE & INFLATE. LET GO & THE SPACESHIP WILL SHOOT INTO THE AIR (HAS BEEN KNOWN TO REACH A HEIGHT OF 6M).

GIANT PANDAS

LARGE BLACK AND WHITE HERBIVOROUS MAMMALS

PÈRE DAVID'S SKINS

THE WESTERN WORLD FIRST LEARNED OF THE EXISTENCE OF THE GIANT PANDA IN 1869, WHEN SOME SKINS ARRIVED IN PARIS FROM CHINA, SENT BY THE MISSIONARY & NATURALIST PÈRE DAVID.

NAMES

CHINESE NAMES FOR THE GIANT PANDA INCLUDE WHITE BEAR, SPECKLED BEAR & MONK AMONG BEARS.

IGNORED PANDAS

CHINESE RECORDS OF GIANT PANDAS DATE FROM ABOUT AD 650. THE FUR WAS COARSER THAN MOST BEARS' & THE MEAT WAS NOT A DELICACY. LIVING IN INACCESSIBLE FORESTS, THEY WERE ALMOST TOTALLY UNHUNTED.

PANDA SHOOTS

PRESIDENT ROOSEVELT'S SONS, AMONG OTHERS, SET OUT TO SHOOT GIANT PANDAS IN CHINA IN THE 1920s. THEY HAD POPULAR SUPPORT (CONSERVATION HAD NOT YET BECOME AN ISSUE) BUT, BECAUSE PANDAS LIVE IN SUCH REMOTE PLACES, MOST HUNTERS RETURNED EMPTY-HANDED.

TOUGH FOOD

THE PANDA'S STAPLE FOOD IS BAMBOO. IN THE WILD, PANDAS SPEND MUCH OF THEIR TIME EATING BECAUSE BAMBOO IS NOT VERY NUTRITIOUS & IS HARD TO DIGEST (ONLY ABOUT 50% OF ITS ENERGY VALUE IS EXTRACTED).

TOUGH STOMACHS

THE PANDA'S GULLET & STOMACH HAVE TO BE EXCEPTIONALLY TOUGH TO DIGEST THE SHARP SLIVERS OF BAMBOO.

HANDS

GIANT PANDAS GRIP THEIR FOOD BETWEEN 5 FINGERS & A PSEUDO THUMB. THEIR REAL THUMB IS ONE OF THE FINGERS & THEIR PSEUDO THUMB IS A HORNY EXTENSION OF THEIR HAND.

EASY FOOD

GIVEN A CHOICE OF FOODS, PANDAS IN ZOOS READILY ABANDON BAMBOO IN FAVOUR OF MORE EASILY DIGESTIBLE FOOD LIKE PORRIDGE.

DEFENCE

LITTLE IS KNOWN ABOUT THE PANDA'S LIFE IN THE WILD. PANDAS HAVE A POWERFUL BITE BUT CANNOT RUN FAST. IT IS NOT KNOWN WHETHER THE BLACK & WHITE COLOURING SERVES AS CAMOUFLAGE (AS IN THE ZEBRA) OR AS A WARNING (AS IN THE SKUNK).

BEAR OR RACOON?

IT IS STILL UNCERTAIN WHETHER THE PANDA IS A GIANT OF THE RACOON FAMILY OR A HERBIVOROUS BEAR.

BABIES

ONE REASON PANDAS ARE HARD TO REAR IN CAPTIVITY IS THAT THEY ARE BORN VERY SMALL (ABOUT 15CM LONG) & CANNOT EVEN CRAWL FOR 3-4 MONTHS.

MOTHERING

FEMALE PANDAS DO NOT MAKE GOOD MOTHERS. VARIOUS CASES OF MOTHERS INADVERTENTLY ROLLING OVER & CRUSHING THEIR OFFSPRING HAVE BEEN KNOWN. THEY NEVER REAR MORE THAN ONE CUB. IF THEY HAVE TWINS, ONE IS SIMPLY IGNORED.

GOATS

HOLLOW-HORNED RUMINANTS OF THE BOVIDAE FAMILY

SCOTTISH WILD GOATS

SOME SCOTSMEN CLAIM THAT THE WILD GOATS ON THE WESTERN ISLES ARE DESCENDED FROM ONES THAT ESCAPED THE WRECKS OF THE SPANISH ARMADA. IT IS KNOWN THAT THE SPANISH CARRIED GOATS ON THEIR SHIPS (TO PROVIDE FRESH MILK FOR THE OFFICERS) BUT IT IS DOUBTFUL THAT ANY GOATS COULD HAVE SURVIVED SINCE THEY HAVE A STRONG AVERSION TO WATER. IT IS MORE PROBABLE THAT GOATS WERE ORIGINALLY IMPORTED BY THE VIKINGS, WHO WANTED TO USE THE ISLANDS AS PROVISION STATIONS.

GOATS & ECOLOGY

GOATS CAN CAUSE DISASTROUS CHANGES TO THE ECOLOGY OF A REGION BECAUSE THEY "BROWSE" (EAT FOOD AT EYE LEVEL) INSTEAD OF GRAZING LIKE OTHER HERBIVORES. IF KEPT IN INAPPROPRIATE HABITATS, THEY WILL CHEW YOUNG TREES TO BITS & STRIP BARK OFF LARGER TREES. WITHOUT TREE ROOTS, ARID LAND IS VERY LIABLE TO EROSION; THIS HAS CAUSED THE DEFOLIATION OF ST HELENA'S ISLAND & MAY HAVE PLAYED A MAJOR ROLE IN THE CREATION OF THE SAHARA DESERT.

GOATS & DEER

DEER HAVE AN AVERSION TO GOATS, POSSIBLY BECAUSE THE SMELL OF A GOAT IS SO STRONG THAT IT OVERPOWERS ALL OTHER SCENTS & CAUSES THE SENSITIVE DEER TO FEEL INSECURE.

GOATS?

THE PLURAL OF GOAT HAS NOT ALWAYS BEEN GOATS. THE OXFORD ENGLISH DICTIONARY RECORDS THE USE OF GETE, GEET, GEETE, GEATES, GOATES, GAIT, GOETE, GOTES & GAYTE.

GOATS & COWS

FARMERS HAVE ALWAYS CLAIMED THAT IT IMPROVES THE HEALTH OF CATTLE TO KEEP A GOAT WITH EACH HERD. THIS IS NOW BELIEVED BY SCIENTISTS, WHO HAVE FOUND THAT ERGOT & RYE, EATEN EAGERLY & SAFELY BY GOATS, CAN CAUSE VARIOUS DISEASES AMONG CATTLE.

GOATS & HORSES

GOATS ARE OFTEN KEPT WITH HORSES. THEY HELP TO CALM HIGHLY-STRUNG RACEHORSES & ARE SAID TO STOP ANY HORSE PANICKING IN THE EVENT OF FIRE. THIS CLAIM IS SOMEWHAT SUSPECT. WHEN WATNEYS BREWERY WAS BOMBED IN 1943 THE 85 HORSES WERE LED AWAY CALMLY BUT THE GOATS PANICKED & COULD BE RESCUED ONLY WITH GREAT DIFFICULTY.

GOATS & MOUNTAINS

JUDAS GOATS

ONE GRISLY USE OF GOATS IS FOR LEADING RELUCTANT CATTLE & LIVESTOCK INTO THE SLAUGHTERHOUSE.

GOATS CAN SEPARATE THE TWO TOES ON EACH HOOF & PRESS THEM STRONGLY TOGETHER, ENABLING THEM TO GRIP SMALL PROJECTIONS & ASCEND ALMOST VERTICAL ROCK FACES. IN PARTS OF NORTH AMERICA, SOME LIVE A LARGELY ARBOREAL EXISTENCE 3-6M ABOVE THE GROUND IN ACACIA SHRUBS.

HOW TO FIND YOUR WALKING SPEED

WIND A BALL OF STRING ROUND A CARDBOARD TUBE, TYING A KNOT EVERY 4M. TIE A STONE TO THE END OF THE STRING. WITH A FRIEND WHO OWNS A GOOD WATCH, START WALKING. THEN DROP THE STONE & COUNT THE NUMBER OF KNOTS YOU UNREEL IN 30 SECONDS. DIVIDE THIS NUMBER BY 2 TO FIND YOUR APPROXIMATE WALKING SPEED IN KM/H.

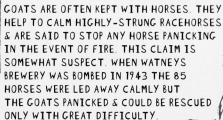

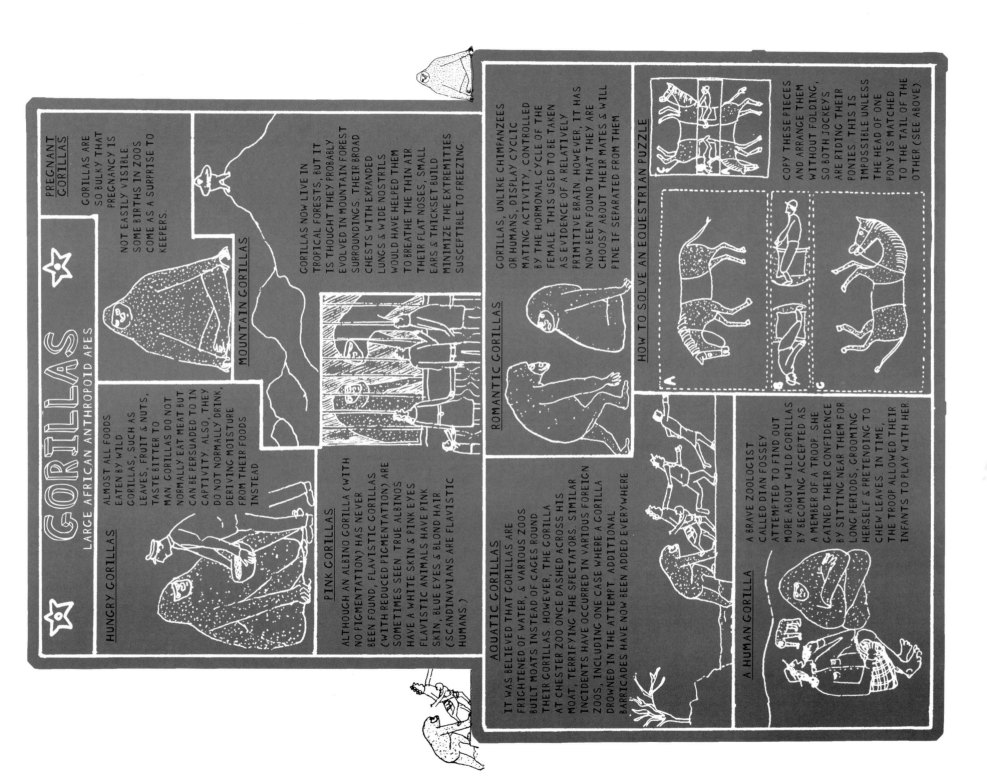

GORILLAS
LARGE AFRICAN ANTHROPOID APES

PREGNANT GORILLAS

GORILLAS ARE SO BULKY THAT PREGNANCY IS NOT EASILY VISIBLE SOME BIRTHS IN ZOOS COME AS A SURPRISE TO KEEPERS.

MOUNTAIN GORILLAS

GORILLAS NOW LIVE IN TROPICAL FORESTS, BUT IT IS THOUGHT THEY PROBABLY EVOLVED IN MOUNTAIN FOREST SURROUNDINGS. THEIR BROAD CHESTS WITH EXPANDED LUNGS & WIDE NOSTRILS WOULD HAVE HELPED THEM TO BREATHE THE THIN AIR. THEIR FLAT NOSES, SMALL EARS & THICKSET BUILD MINIMIZE THE EXTREMITIES SUSCEPTIBLE TO FREEZING.

HUNGRY GORILLAS

ALMOST ALL FOODS EATEN BY WILD GORILLAS, SUCH AS LEAVES, FRUIT & NUTS, TASTE BITTER TO MAN. GORILLAS DO NOT NORMALLY EAT MEAT BUT CAN BE PERSUADED TO IN CAPTIVITY. ALSO, THEY DO NOT NORMALLY DRINK, DERIVING MOISTURE FROM THEIR FOODS INSTEAD

PINK GORILLAS

ALTHOUGH AN ALBINO GORILLA (WITH NO PIGMENTATION) HAS NEVER BEEN FOUND, FLAVISTIC GORILLAS (WITH REDUCED PIGMENTATION) ARE SOMETIMES SEEN. TRUE ALBINOS HAVE A WHITE SKIN & PINK EYES. FLAVISTIC ANIMALS HAVE PINK SKIN, BLUE EYES & BLOND HAIR (SCANDINAVIANS ARE FLAVISTIC HUMANS.)

AQUATIC GORILLAS

IT WAS BELIEVED THAT GORILLAS ARE FRIGHTENED OF WATER, & VARIOUS ZOOS BUILT MOATS INSTEAD OF CAGES ROUND THEIR GORILLAS. HOWEVER, THE GORILLA AT CHESTER ZOO ONCE DASHED ACROSS HIS MOAT, TERRIFYING THE SPECTATORS. SIMILAR INCIDENTS HAVE OCCURRED IN VARIOUS FOREIGN ZOOS, INCLUDING ONE CASE WHERE A GORILLA DROWNED IN THE ATTEMPT. ADDITIONAL BARRICADES HAVE NOW BEEN ADDED EVERYWHERE

ROMANTIC GORILLAS

GORILLAS, UNLIKE CHIMPANZEES OR HUMANS, DISPLAY CYCLIC MATING ACTIVITY, CONTROLLED BY THE HORMONAL CYCLE OF THE FEMALE. THIS USED TO BE TAKEN AS EVIDENCE OF A RELATIVELY PRIMITIVE BRAIN. HOWEVER, IT HAS NOW BEEN FOUND THAT THEY ARE CHOOSY ABOUT THEIR MATES & WILL PINE IF SEPARATED FROM THEM

HOW TO SOLVE AN EQUESTRIAN PUZZLE

COPY THESE PIECES AND ARRANGE THEM WITHOUT FOLDING, SO BOTH JOCKEYS ARE RIDING THEIR PONIES. THIS IS IMPOSSIBLE UNLESS THE HEAD OF ONE PONY IS MATCHED TO THE TAIL OF THE OTHER (SEE ABOVE)

A HUMAN GORILLA

A BRAVE ZOOLOGIST CALLED DIAN FOSSEY ATTEMPTED TO FIND OUT MORE ABOUT WILD GORILLAS BY BECOMING ACCEPTED AS A MEMBER OF A TROOP. SHE GAINED THEIR CONFIDENCE BY SITTING NEAR THEM FOR LONG PERIODS, GROOMING HERSELF & PRETENDING TO CHEW LEAVES. IN TIME, THE TROOP ALLOWED THEIR INFANTS TO PLAY WITH HER

☆GUITARS☆

ORIGINS

THE FIRST GUITARS APPEARED IN SPAIN IN THE 15TH CENTURY, WITH SMALL BODIES & 4 DOUBLE STRINGS. THEY WERE USED BY PEASANTS & COURTESANS ALIKE TO PROVIDE ACCOMPANIMENT FOR SONGS, BUT NEVER BECAME RESPECTABLE ORCHESTRAL INSTRUMENTS.

AMPLIFICATION

SOUND HOLE — BRIDGE

SOUNDBOARD

THE VOLUME OF A SOUND DEPENDS ON HOW MUCH AIR IS MOVED. THE ACOUSTIC GUITAR AMPLIFIES THE SOUND OF THE STRINGS BY MAKING THE BRIDGE & WHOLE SOUNDBOARD VIBRATE UP & DOWN. THIS "PUMPS" ALL THE AIR INSIDE THE GUITAR BODY & PROJECTS THE MAGNIFIED VIBRATIONS OUT OF THE HOLE.

WASTAGE

MAKING A CLASSICAL GUITAR USES A LOT OF WOOD. SAWING ALL THE PARTS WITH THE GRAIN IN THE BEST DIRECTION FOR SOUND & STRENGTH INVOLVES 80-90% WASTAGE.

THE SOUNDBOARD

THE SOUNDBOARD IS THE PART OF THE GUITAR THAT MOST AFFECTS THE QUALITY OF NOTES PRODUCED. IT HAS TO BE BRACED TO MAKE IT STRONG ENOUGH TO RESIST THE TENSION OF THE STRINGS BUT FLEXIBLE ENOUGH TO ALLOW THE BRIDGE TO VIBRATE.

GUITAR MAKERS TAP THEIR SOUNDBOARDS DURING CONSTRUCTION & GO TO GREAT TROUBLE TO OBTAIN A PARTICULAR RESONANCE.

19TH-CENTURY — MODERN CLASSICAL

12-STRING — GIBSON ELECTRIC

DIFFERENT TYPES OF GUITAR HAVE DIFFERENT TYPES OF BRACING (GLUED TO SOUNDBOARD INSIDE GUITAR BODY).

GUT STRINGS

TRADITIONAL GUT STRINGS OFTEN SUFFERED FROM FALSE VIBRATIONS CAUSED BY INCONSISTENCIES IN THEIR DIAMETER & COMPOSITION. THEY ALSO FRAYED & WENT OUT OF TUNE EASILY.

NYLON STRINGS

NYLON MONOFILAMENT, DEVELOPED IN THE 1950S FOR FISHING LINES, HAS BEEN ADOPTED BY GUITAR MAKERS & IS NOW GENERALLY USED INSTEAD OF GUT. NYLON IS "FLABBIER" THAN GUT WHICH MAKES THE SOUND SLIGHTLY LESS BRILLIANT.

STEEL STRINGS

STEEL STRINGS, FIRST USED IN AMERICA (1900), PRODUCE A LOUDER SOUND WITH MORE OVERTONES. THE INTERFERENCE OF THE HIGHER OVERTONES GIVES STEEL STRINGS THEIR "TWANG".

WOLF NOTES

BOTH THE SOUNDBOARD & THE VOLUME OF AIR INSIDE THE BODY HAVE CERTAIN NATURAL FREQUENCIES AT WHICH THEY RESONATE. GUITAR MAKERS TRY TO PREVENT THESE COINCIDING AS TOGETHER THEY CAN PRODUCE ONE NOTE MUCH LOUDER THAN ALL THE REST (KNOWN AS A WOLF NOTE).

ELECTRIC PURITY

SOLID ELECTRIC GUITARS PRODUCE PURE STRING TONES, VIRTUALLY UNAFFECTED BY THE GUITAR BODY. SOME EARLY EXPERIMENTS IN THE 1930S USED RAILWAY SLEEPERS AS "SOLID" GUITAR BODIES.

SUSTAIN

THE BODY OF THE SOLID ELECTRIC GUITAR DOES NOT VIBRATE WITH THE STRINGS SO IT DOES NOT ABSORB ANY ENERGY, AND A STRING WILL CONTINUE TO VIBRATE FOR A LONG TIME.

ELECTRIC PICK-UPS

THE PICK-UPS ON ELECTRIC GUITARS ARE SMALL COILS OF WIRE WOUND ROUND MAGNETS. AS A STEEL STRING VIBRATES IT INTERFERES WITH THE MAGNET'S FIELD & INDUCES SMALL CURRENTS IN THE COIL. WHEN AMPLIFIED & FED TO A LOUD SPEAKER THESE CURRENTS REPRODUCE THE SOUND OF THE STRING.

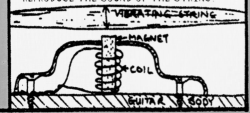

VIBRATING STRING

MAGNET

COIL

GUITAR BODY

HEARTS

HOLLOW MUSCULAR ORGANS PROPELLING BLOOD

GALEN'S FURNACE

GALEN'S THEORY OF THE HEART INVOLVED A SORT OF FURNACE IN WHICH BLOOD & AIR COMBINED. THIS CREATED THE HEAT WHICH WARMED THE BODY & ENRICHED THE BLOOD THAT WENT TO THE BRAIN.

HARVEY'S PUMP

WILLIAM HARVEY (1578-1657) FIRST REALIZED THAT THE HEART WAS A PUMP. MOST ANIMAL HEARTS BEAT TOO FAST FOR THE ACTION TO BE WATCHED CLEARLY, SO HE PERFORMED HIS EXPERIMENTS ON COLD REPTILES & DYING MAMMALS.

HEART STOP

THE LONGEST PERIOD FOR WHICH A HEART HAS STOPPED & YET RECOVERED IS 3 HOURS 32 MINUTES (WINNIPEG HOSPITAL, CANADA, 1977).

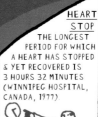

DIVING HEARTS

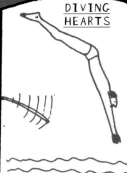

THE HEART OF EVERY VERTEBRATE AUTOMATICALLY SLOWS DOWN ON A DIVE INTO WATER. THIS SURVIVAL REFLEX SLOWS DOWN THE EFFECTS OF A LACK OF OXYGEN & ALLOWS US TO HOLD OUR BREATH FOR LONGER.

HEARTS & BRAINS

EXPERIMENTS AT OHIO UNIVERSITY HAVE SHOWN THAT PERFORMANCE IN INTELLIGENCE TESTS IS IMPROVED IF THE HEART RATE IS ARTIFICIALLY INCREASED.

CIRCULATION

HARVEY REALIZED THAT THE OUTPUT OF THE HEART WAS SO GREAT THAT IT WOULD PUMP THROUGH ALL THE BLOOD IN THE BODY IN LESS THAN AN HOUR. THIS LED TO HIS FAMOUS DISCOVERY OF THE CIRCULATION OF THE BLOOD.

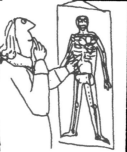

TRANSPLANTS

60-70% OF HUMAN HEART TRANSPLANTS ARE SUCCESSFUL.

HEARTS & MAGNESIUM

HEALTHY YOUNG PEOPLE WHO LIVE IN AREAS WITH SOFT WATER ARE 30% MORE LIKELY TO HAVE A HEART ATTACK. A NEW THEORY LINKS THIS WITH MAGNESIUM DEFICIENCY. THE STAGGERS, AS IT IS CALLED, IS KNOWN TO AFFECT ANIMALS WHO DROP DEAD UNEXPECTEDLY, BUT PEOPLE WERE THOUGHT TO BE UNAFFECTED.

BIG-HEARTED

THE BIGGEST HEART EVER WEIGHED WAS THAT OF A BLUE WHALE. IT WEIGHED 698.5KG, AS MUCH AS AN AVERAGE CAR.

FLYING HEARTS

BIRDS NEED BIG HEARTS BECAUSE THEY USE SO MUCH ENERGY WHEN FLYING. A SPARROW'S HEART IS 2.7 TIMES HEAVIER THAN THAT OF A MOUSE OF THE SAME SIZE.

SHOCKING HEARTS

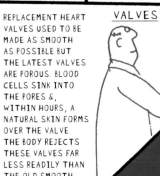

REPLACEMENT HEART VALVES USED TO BE MADE AS SMOOTH AS POSSIBLE BUT THE LATEST VALVES ARE POROUS. BLOOD CELLS SINK INTO THE PORES &, WITHIN HOURS, A NATURAL SKIN FORMS OVER THE VALVE. THE BODY REJECTS THESE VALVES FAR LESS READILY THAN THE OLD SMOOTH VALVES.

VALVES

HEART RHYTHMS THAT START FLUCTUATING VIOLENTLY CAN BE CURED BY THE HEART'S BEING MOMENTARILY STOPPED WITH AN ELECTRIC SHOCK. THE LATEST DEVICES, ENCASED IN TITANIUM & IMPLANTED UNDER THE SKIN, CAN BE SWITCHED ON BY THE PATIENT.

HERONS
LARGE SCREAMING WADING BIRDS

RELATIVES

MEMBERS OF THE HERON FAMILY (ARDEIDAE) INCLUDE THE EGRETS & BITTERNS. THEY ARE ALL WATER BIRDS LIVING MAINLY ON FISH & ARE FOUND EVERYWHERE IN THE WORLD (EXCEPT IN POLAR REGIONS).

NECKS

THE STRUCTURE OF THE HERON'S NECK VERTEBRAE ALLOWS THE NECK TO MOVE ONLY UP & DOWN; IT CANNOT MOVE FROM SIDE TO SIDE. NORMALLY THE NECK IS CURVED IN THE SHAPE OF AN "S" & THE HEAD IS DRAWN BETWEEN THE SHOULDERS. THE NECK IS EXTENDED ONLY TO SEIZE PREY WITH A STRONG & RAPID MUSCULAR ACTION WHICH CARRIES THE BEAK TO ITS TARGET. HERONS & THEIR RELATIVES ARE THE ONLY BIRDS THAT FLY WITH THEIR NECKS TUCKED BACK & HEADS BETWEEN THEIR SHOULDERS. THIS MAKES IT IMPOSSIBLE TO CONFUSE THEM, WHEN THEY ARE FLYING, WITH STORKS, CRANES, SWANS & SO ON.

CLEANING

HERONS HAVE A UNIQUE METHOD OF CLEANING THEIR FEATHERS. UNDER THEIR WINGS THEY HAVE THICK PATCHES OF POWDER DOWN WHICH RUBS OFF AS A FINE DUST. THIS IS APPLIED TO SOILED FEATHERS WHERE IT SOAKS UP SLIME & OIL. IT IS THEN SCRAPED OFF WITH THE COMB-LIKE EDGE OF THE BIRD'S MIDDLE CLAW.

EGRETS

EGRETS ARE NOTABLE FOR THEIR BEAUTY. THE DEMAND FOR THEIR FEATHERS (FOR HATS & SCARVES) NEARLY CAUSED THEIR EXTINCTION IN THE EARLY 1900S. SOUTH AMERICA ALONE USED TO EXPORT 15,000 KILOS OF FEATHERS & PLUMES EVERY YEAR. EACH KILO REPRESENTED A DEATH TOLL OF 300–1,000 BIRDS.

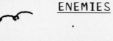

BITTERNS

THE MOST NOTABLE THING ABOUT A BITTERN IS THE EXTRAORDINARY BOOMING NOISE IT MAKES. THIS TERRITORIAL & MATING CALL IS AUDIBLE 3 MILES AWAY - USEFUL BECAUSE BITTERNS ARE UNSOCIABLE BIRDS.

NESTS

HERONS BUILD LARGE NESTS, ABOUT 1 METRE ACROSS & 0.7 METRES DEEP. THEY OCCASIONALLY NEST ON THE GROUND OR IN REEDS, BUT USUALLY IN TALL TREES. AS MANY AS 100 NESTS HAVE BEEN SEEN IN A SINGLE TREE.

ENEMIES

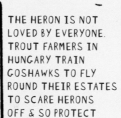

THE HERON IS NOT LOVED BY EVERYONE. TROUT FARMERS IN HUNGARY TRAIN GOSHAWKS TO FLY ROUND THEIR ESTATES TO SCARE HERONS OFF & SO PROTECT THEIR FISH.

COURTSHIP

THE COURTSHIP RITUAL OF THE HERON IS MOST APPEALING. AFTER VARIOUS DISPLAYS, THE MALE HOLDS OUT A BRANCH IN HIS BEAK. THE FEMALE TAKES IT & KEEPS IT TO START THE NEST. SUBSEQUENTLY, THE MALE BRINGS THE MATERIALS WHILE THE FEMALE BUILDS – SOMETIMES THEY FIGHT DURING THIS PROCESS.

HOW TO TURN YOURSELF INTO A FLEXIBLE GIANT

STICK TOGETHER SOME BITS OF EXPANDED POLYSTYRENE (FROM A BUILDERS' MERCHANT) & CARVE THEM INTO A HEAD SHAPE WITH A SERRATED KNIFE – BE CAREFUL. MAKE TUBE OF MATERIAL WITH WIRE RING STIFFENERS AS ABOVE. FIX BROOMSTICK IN HEAD & USE AS ABOVE.

HERONS

HIBERNATION
DORMANT WINTER CONDITION OF SOME MAMMALS

SNAILS

AN EGYPTIAN DESERT SNAIL, FIXED TO A CARD IN THE NATURAL HISTORY MUSEUM, LONDON, STARTED TO EXUDE SLIME AFTER 4 YEARS. IT WAS THEN IMMERSED IN WATER & THE SNAIL EMERGED FROM ITS SHELL.

ANTIFREEZE

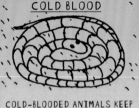

ANY ANIMAL WILL DIE IF THE WATER WITHIN ITS CELLS FREEZES. MANY INSECTS AVOID THIS BY HAVING GLYCEROL IN THEIR BODY FLUIDS, WHICH ACTS AS AN ANTIFREEZE.

PESTS

AMERICAN ENTOMOLOGISTS INVESTIGATING THE CORN BORER (A SERIOUS CROP PEST) HAVE FOUND THAT ITS HIBERNATION IN THE LARVAL STATE IS INDUCED BY A JUVENILE HORMONE. THEY HOPE EVENTUALLY TO EXTEND ITS HIBERNATION THROUGH THE SPRING – THUS ELIMINATING CROP DAMAGE.

COLD BLOOD

COLD-BLOODED ANIMALS KEEP THE SAME TEMPERATURE AS THEIR SURROUNDINGS. THEY WILL AUTOMATICALLY ENTER A STATE OF TORPOR AS THE TEMPERATURE FALLS.

WARM BLOOD

WARM-BLOODED ANIMALS MAINTAIN A CONSTANT TEMPERATURE. WHEN HIBERNATING THEY KEEP A LOWER CONSTANT TEMPERATURE (ABOUT 2°C LOWER). IF THIS DROPS THEY WAKE & WARM THEMSELVES UP.

DAMPNESS

ANIMALS MUST HIBERNATE IN A PLACE THAT IS RELATIVELY DAMP. HIBERNATORS THAT NORMALLY LIVE IN BURROWS BUILD SPECIAL DAMP CHAMBERS FOR THE WINTER.

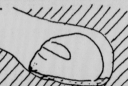

INSOMNIA

SOME HIBERNATING ANIMALS WAKE AT REGULAR INTERVALS. THE US GROUND SQUIRREL WAKES ABOUT ONCE EVERY 10 DAYS – USING UP AS MUCH ENERGY WHILE AWAKE AS DURING THE PREVIOUS 9 DAYS.

FISH

FISH DO NOT USUALLY HIBERNATE. YOUNG PLAICE ARE AN EXCEPTION, BURROWING IN THE SAND IN WINTER.

BIRDS

A FORM OF HIBERNATION OCCURS IN BIRDS. THEY SLEEP SO DEEPLY THAT THEIR BODY TEMPERATURE CAN DROP TO 6°C – THOUGH ONLY FOR A FEW HOURS AT A TIME. THIS IS NOT TRUE HIBERNATION. THEY DO NOT WAKE UP & IF THEIR TEMPERATURE FALLS BELOW 6°C THEY DIE.

"DEAD" DORMOUSE

THE HEART RATE OF A HIBERNATING DORMOUSE DROPS FROM 300 BEATS A MINUTE TO 8. NATURAL BODY REFLEXES (LIKE THE KNEE JERK IN HUMANS) & ELECTRICAL ACTIVITY IN THE BRAIN ARE SO LOW THAT THEY CANNOT BE DETECTED.

RIGID DORMOUSE

A HIBERNATING DORMOUSE IS SO COLD & RIGID THAT IT CAN BE ROLLED LIKE A BALL ACROSS A TABLE.

AESTIVATION

SOME ANIMALS HIBERNATE IN HOT, DRY CONDITIONS. THIS BEHAVIOUR IS CALLED AESTIVATION.

ERRATIC DORMOUSE

IN THE DAYS IMMEDIATELY BEFORE & AFTER HIBERNATION THE DORMOUSE'S BEHAVIOUR IS ERRATIC – ALTERNATING BETWEEN TORPOR & LIVELY ACTIVITY.

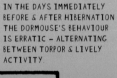

LUNGFISH

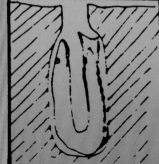

THE LUNGFISH, WHICH LIVES ON MUDFLATS, DIGS ITSELF A BURROW & SURROUNDS ITSELF IN A LEATHERY COCOON. IN A DROUGHT, IT CAN SURVIVE FOR MORE THAN A YEAR, CONSUMING MUSCLE TISSUE FROM ITS OWN TAIL.

FROGS

AUSTRALIAN DESERT FROGS AESTIVATE, FIRST FILLING THEMSELVES WITH WATER UNTIL THEY ARE ALMOST SPHERICAL.

CHEMICAL HIBERNATION

US GROUND SQUIRRELS, ISOLATED IN A LABORATORY, PERSIST IN THE HABIT OF HIBERNATION FOR ABOUT 2 YEARS & THEN STOP. IF SERUM FROM A WILD GROUND SQUIRREL IS THEN INJECTED, THE LABORATORY SQUIRREL WILL HIBERNATE AGAIN.

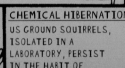

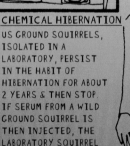

HIBERNATION

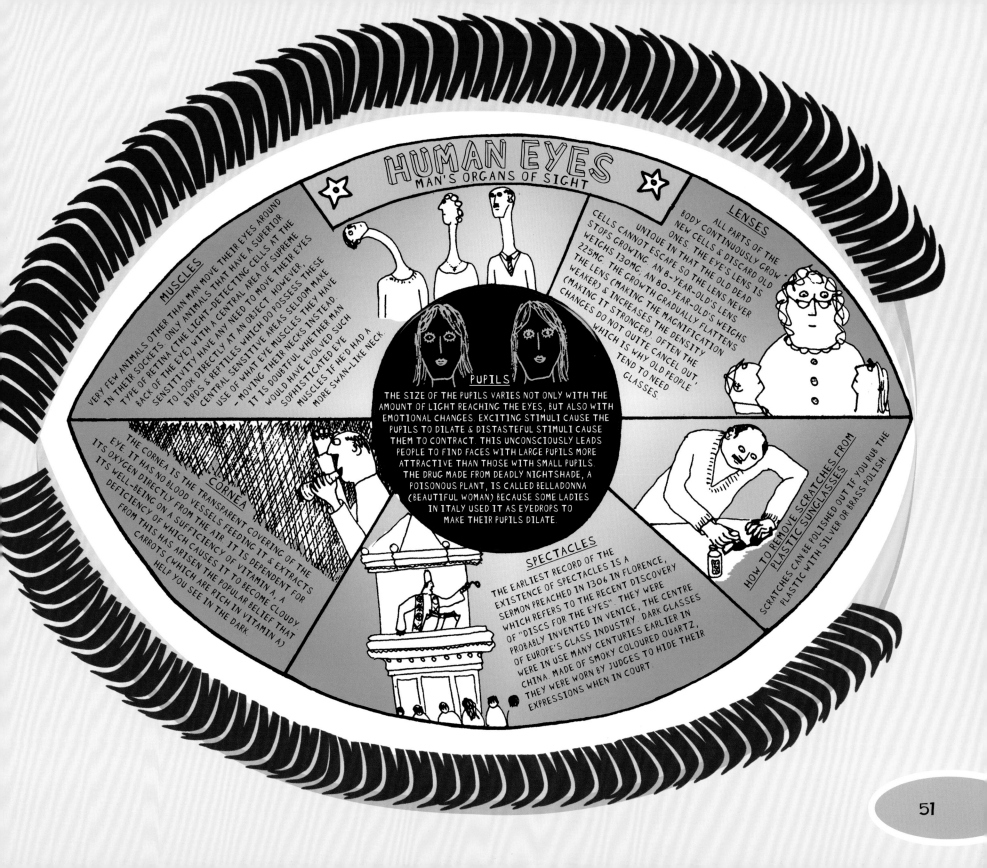

HUMAN EYES
MAN'S ORGANS OF SIGHT

MUSCLES

VERY FEW ANIMALS OTHER THAN MAN MOVE THEIR EYES AROUND IN THEIR SOCKETS. ONLY ANIMALS THAT HAVE A SUPERIOR TYPE OF RETINA (THE LIGHT-DETECTING CELLS AT THE BACK OF THE EYE) WITH A CENTRAL AREA OF SUPREME SENSITIVITY HAVE ANY NEED TO MOVE THEIR EYES TO LOOK DIRECTLY AT AN OBJECT. HOWEVER, BIRDS & REPTILES WHICH DO POSSESS THESE CENTRAL SENSITIVE AREAS SELDOM MAKE USE OF WHAT EYE MUSCLES THEY HAVE - MOVING THEIR NECKS INSTEAD. IT IS DOUBTFUL WHETHER MAN WOULD HAVE EVOLVED SUCH SOPHISTICATED EYE MUSCLES IF HE'D HAD A MORE SWAN-LIKE NECK.

LENSES

ALL PARTS OF THE BODY CONTINUOUSLY GROW NEW CELLS & DISCARD OLD ONES. THE EYE'S LENS IS UNIQUE IN THAT THE OLD DEAD CELLS CANNOT ESCAPE SO THE LENS NEVER STOPS GROWING. AN 8-YEAR-OLD'S LENS WEIGHS 130MG, AN 80-YEAR-OLD'S LENS WEIGHS 225MG. THE GROWTH GRADUALLY FLATTENS THE LENS (MAKING THE MAGNIFICATION WEAKER) & INCREASES THE DENSITY (MAKING IT STRONGER), OFTEN THE CHANGES DO NOT QUITE CANCEL OUT, WHICH IS WHY OLD PEOPLE TEND TO NEED GLASSES.

PUPILS

THE SIZE OF THE PUPILS VARIES NOT ONLY WITH THE AMOUNT OF LIGHT REACHING THE EYES, BUT ALSO WITH EMOTIONAL CHANGES. EXCITING STIMULI CAUSE THE PUPILS TO DILATE & DISTASTEFUL STIMULI CAUSE THEM TO CONTRACT. THIS UNCONSCIOUSLY LEADS PEOPLE TO FIND FACES WITH LARGE PUPILS MORE ATTRACTIVE THAN THOSE WITH SMALL PUPILS. THE DRUG MADE FROM DEADLY NIGHTSHADE, A POISONOUS PLANT, IS CALLED BELLADONNA (BEAUTIFUL WOMAN) BECAUSE SOME LADIES IN ITALY USED IT AS EYEDROPS TO MAKE THEIR PUPILS DILATE.

CORNEA

THE CORNEA IS THE TRANSPARENT COVERING OF THE EYE. IT HAS NO BLOOD VESSELS FEEDING IT & EXTRACTS ITS OXYGEN DIRECTLY FROM THE AIR. IT IS DEPENDENT FOR ITS WELL-BEING ON A SUFFICIENCY OF VITAMIN A, A DEFICIENCY OF WHICH CAUSES IT TO BECOME CLOUDY. FROM THIS HAS ARISEN THE POPULAR BELIEF THAT CARROTS (WHICH ARE RICH IN VITAMIN A) HELP YOU SEE IN THE DARK.

SPECTACLES

THE EARLIEST RECORD OF THE EXISTENCE OF SPECTACLES IS A SERMON PREACHED IN 1306 IN FLORENCE, WHICH REFERS TO THE RECENT DISCOVERY OF "DISCS FOR THE EYES". THEY WERE PROBABLY INVENTED IN VENICE, THE CENTRE OF EUROPE'S GLASS INDUSTRY. DARK GLASSES WERE IN USE MANY CENTURIES EARLIER IN CHINA. MADE OF SMOKY COLOURED QUARTZ, THEY WERE WORN BY JUDGES TO HIDE THEIR EXPRESSIONS WHEN IN COURT.

HOW TO REMOVE SCRATCHES FROM PLASTIC SUNGLASSES

SCRATCHES CAN BE POLISHED OUT IF YOU RUB THE PLASTIC WITH SILVER OR BRASS POLISH.

HYPNOSIS

MESMERISM

MESMER WAS AN INFLUENTIAL 18TH-CENTURY QUACK DOCTOR WHO BELIEVED IN ANIMAL MAGNETISM & INDUCED TRANCES IN HIS SUBJECTS (HENCE THE WORD MESMERIZE). THE WORD HYPNOTISM WAS COINED BY A SCOTTISH SURGEON, JAMES BRAID, IN 1843. HE WAS INVESTIGATING MESMER'S TRANCES TO SEE IF THEY COULD BE USED AS AN ANAESTHETIC.

HYPNOSIS & SLEEP

THE RUSSIAN PSYCHOLOGIST PAVLOV BELIEVED THAT THE HYPNOTIC TRANCE WAS A FORM OF SLEEP, SIMILAR TO SLEEPWALKING, IN WHICH THE SUBJECT REMAINS RESPONSIVE TO A NARROW RANGE OF STIMULI

STAGE HYPNOSIS

STAGE HYPNOSIS GENERALLY RELIES ON TRICKS, AS IT TAKES TOO LONG TO INITIATE A DEEP TRANCE. SUBJECTS, SELECTED FOR THEIR SUSCEPTIBILITY, WILL DO ALL SORTS OF THINGS WITHOUT THE NEED OF A TRANCE

FACTORY HYPNOSIS

THE CONSTANT "MUSIC WHILE YOU WORK", RHYTHMIC PROCESSES & SOUNDS IN MODERN FACTORIES INDUCE A STATE AKIN TO HYPNOSIS IN PEOPLE DOING REPETITIVE TASKS. THIS STATE REDUCES BOREDOM & FRUSTRATION & INCREASES PRODUCTIVITY.

HOW TO HYPNOTIZE A TROUT

SLOWLY SLIP HAND INTO POOL & ATTEMPT TO GET HAND BENEATH FISH. STROKE BELLY VERY GENTLY. THIS LULLS IT INTO IMMOBILITY SO THAT, WITH LUCK, IT MAY BE GRABBED. (ROCKING RESTLESS HUMAN BABIES HAS THE SAME IMMOBILIZING EFFECT.)

MEDICAL HYPNOSIS

THE MOST IMPORTANT MODERN MEDICAL USE OF HYPNOSIS IS AS AN ANAESTHETIC IN CASES WHERE DRUGS MIGHT BE DANGEROUS. THE EFFECT OF HYPNOTIC PAIN-KILLING IS VERY SIMILAR TO THAT PRODUCED BY ACUPUNCTURE

EYE HYPNOSIS

CHICKENS CAN BE IMMOBILIZED BY A PAIR OF GLASS EYES FIXED TO A STICK. THIS IMMOBILE STATE IN ANIMALS IS NORMALLY INDUCED BY FEAR, AS A WAY OF TRYING TO ESCAPE THE ATTENTION OF PREDATORS

UPSIDE-DOWN HYPNOSIS

IF A CHICKEN, RABBIT OR GUINEA PIG IS HELD UPSIDE-DOWN FOR ABOUT 30 SECONDS, IT WILL REMAIN FROZEN IN THIS POSITION FOR UP TO 3 HOURS. THE EFFECT HAS OCCASIONALLY BEEN PRODUCED FOR SHORT PERIODS IN HUMANS.

HYPNOTIC SUSCEPTIBILITY

CHILDREN ARE MORE SUSCEPTIBLE THAN ADULTS

PEOPLE WHO TELL LIES ARE LESS SUSCEPTIBLE

WOMEN ARE SLIGHTLY MORE SUSCEPTIBLE THAN MEN

PEOPLE TODAY ARE LESS SUSCEPTIBLE THAN 100 YEARS AGO

TV HYPNOSIS

FOR SOME YEARS, THE INDUCTION OF HYPNOSIS WAS NOT ALLOWED ON TELEVISION IN BRITAIN. EXPERIMENTS ON CLOSED-CIRCUIT TV SHOWED THAT SOME VIEWERS WENT INTO A TRANCE

SELF-HYPNOSIS

THE TRANCE STATES THAT YOGA & ZEN BUDDHIST MEDITATION CAN PRODUCE ARE VERY SIMILAR TO THE HYPNOTIC TRANCE

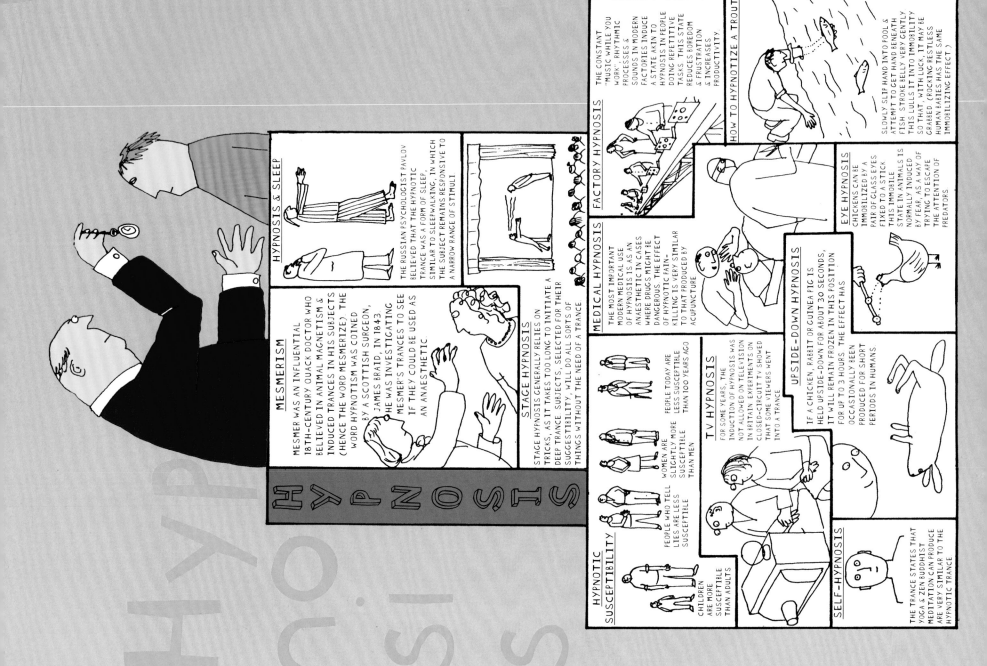

ICE
ABUNDANT SOLID COMPOUND OF HYDROGEN & OXYGEN

ICE CRYSTALS

IN SUB-ARCTIC INLAND LAKES FREEZING SOMETIMES TAKES PLACE ROUND A SINGLE NUCLEUS. THE WHOLE LAKE FREEZES INTO JUST ONE CRYSTAL, THOUGHT TO BE THE LARGEST SINGLE CRYSTAL OF ANY MATERIAL IN THE WORLD.

ICEFIELDS

THE DEMAND FOR ICE FOR PRESERVING FISH WAS SO GREAT IN THE 1830S THAT MANY FARMERS FLOODED THEIR FIELDS AT THE BEGINNING OF WINTER. WHEN THE WATER FROZE, THE ICE WAS RUSHED TO THE CITIES, WHERE THE FIRST TO ARRIVE FETCHED 15 SHILLINGS A CARTLOAD. THE ICE WAS THEN STORED IN LARGE UNDERGROUND ICE HOUSES WHERE, WITH LUCK, SOME OF IT LASTED TILL THE NEXT WINTER. THE PRACTICE CONTINUED UNTIL THE INTRODUCTION OF COMPRESSOR-DRIVEN ICE-MAKING MACHINES IN THE 1860S.

SNOW

(HIGH-CLOUD FLAKE)

(LOW-CLOUD FLAKE)

WATER DROPLETS WILL FREEZE AS SNOW (LARGE FLAKE CRYSTALS WITH HEXAGONAL SYMMETRY) IN COLD, RELATIVELY CALM AIR. INTENSELY COLD CLOUDS (USUALLY THE HIGHER CLOUDS) CONTAIN RELATIVELY LITTLE WATER VAPOUR & THEREFORE TEND TO PRODUCE SMALLER, SLOWER-GROWING & SOLID FLAKES. WARMER CLOUDS CONTAIN MUCH MORE MOISTURE & TEND TO PRODUCE LARGER, FASTER-GROWING, BRANCHING CRYSTALS.

INDIAN ICE

IN INDIA WATER IS FROZEN BY BEING LEFT IN POROUS VESSELS (CHATTI) ON CLEAR WINTER NIGHTS. THE EVAPORATION THROUGH THE PORES OF THE VESSEL ABSORBS SUFFICIENT HEAT FROM THE WATER ALTHOUGH THE AIR TEMPERATURE NEVER FALLS TO 0°C.

HAIL

ICE FORMS AS A HAILSTONE WHEN WATER DROPLETS COLLIDE WITH AN EXISTING ICE CRYSTAL. THIS REQUIRES THE TURBULENT ATMOSPHERIC CONDITIONS NORMALLY ASSOCIATED WITH THUNDERSTORMS. THE WORLD'S BIGGEST OFFICIALLY RECORDED HAILSTONE WAS 19CM IN DIAMETER, FOUND IN KANSAS, US, IN 1970. BRITAIN'S RECORD IS AN 11CM STONE WHICH FELL IN SUSSEX.

ICEBERGS

THREE-QUARTERS OF THE WORLD'S TOTAL FRESH-WATER SUPPLY IS LOCKED UP IN THE ICE SHEETS ROUND THE SOUTH POLE. SCHEMES TO LIBERATE THIS RESOURCE HAVE BEEN DEVELOPED IN THE PAST BY THE RAND CORPORATION IN AMERICA. THEY PROPOSED TOWING A TRAIN OF ICEBERGS 80KM LONG, 600M WIDE & 300M DEEP (FIRST CUTTING OFF ANY SHARP PROJECTIONS WITH A HUGE SAW) AT A SPEED OF ONE KNOT, BEHIND GIANT TUGS WITH AN OIL TANKER TO KEEP THEM FUELLED. SUCH A JOURNEY WOULD TAKE OVER A YEAR & EACH ICEBERG WOULD HAVE TO BE WRAPPED IN POLYTHENE TO PRESERVE THE FRESH WATER AS IT MELTED. DESPITE THE COMPLEXITY OF THE SYSTEM, RAND ESTIMATED THE WATER WOULD COST TWO-THIRDS LESS THAN WATER FROM CONVENTIONAL DESALINATION PLANTS (THOUGH LATER ESTIMATES HAVE BEEN MUCH LESS OPTIMISTIC).

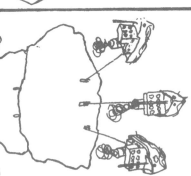

HOW TO BAFFLE WITH DOMINOES

SPREAD A SET OF DOMINOES ON A TABLE & ASK 2 FRIENDS TO PLAY EACH OTHER. AFTER FIRST BLINDFOLDING YOU. WHEN THEY HAVE FINISHED PLAYING YOU CAN MYSTERIOUSLY TELL THEM THE NUMBERS AT EACH END OF THE DOMINO LINE. THIS TRICK IS VERY SIMPLE. AS YOU SPREAD THE PIECES ON THE TABLE, SECRETLY PICK ONE UP, NOTE ITS NUMBERS, THEN SLIP IT IN YOUR POCKET. THESE NUMBERS WILL BE LEFT AT THE OPEN ENDS OF THE GAME.

GOAT BOATS

THE CHINESE HAVE USED INFLATED GOAT SKINS AS RAFTS FOR OVER 1,000, YEARS. UNTIL RECENTLY, LARGE 800-SKIN RAFTS WERE IN USE.

INFLATABLE BOATS

WELLINGTON'S PONTOON

THE DUKE OF WELLINGTON TRIED USING CANVAS IMPREGNATED WITH INDIA RUBBER TO MAKE AN INFLATABLE RAFT (DESIGNED TO SUPPORT A BRIDGE). TO TEST ITS STABILITY, 40 SOLDIERS WERE FLOATED OUT ON THE RAFT & COMMANDED TO STAND, SIT & LIE DOWN IN SEQUENCE.

PLEASURE BOATS

TODAY'S INFLATABLE BOATS ARE BASED ON THE DESIGNS OF THE BRITISH INVENTOR R. F. DAGNELL. HIS COMPANY SOLD A RANGE OF INFLATABLES IN THE 1930S. THEY CAME WITH TUBES TO CONNECT THEM TO CAR EXHAUST PIPES (THE EXHAUST GASES WERE USED TO INFLATE THE BOATS).

ROTTEN BOATS

SUNLIGHT ROTS NATURAL RUBBER, SO THE EARLY INFLATABLES WERE NEVER VERY DURABLE OR POPULAR. IN THE 1950S A CHEMICAL COATING CALLED HYPALON WAS DEVELOPED WHICH PREVENTED THE ROT.

LIFEBOATS

THE FIRST INFLATABLE INSHORE LIFEBOATS CAME INTO SERVICE IN 1963. THEIR FIRST RESCUE WAS AT ABERYSTWYTH WHEN 3 PEOPLE & A DOG WERE SAVED.

THE BOAT CLOAK

THE FIRST INFLATABLE BOAT WAS MADE BY A LT HALKETT IN 1844. IT WAS INCORPORATED INTO A CLOAK IN THE FORM OF AN INSET OVAL PANEL WHICH COULD BE INFLATED. THE BOAT CLOAK WAS USED ON SEVERAL ARCTIC EXPEDITIONS.

SURVIVAL BOATS

INFLATABLE BOATS WERE FIRST MASS-PRODUCED IN WORLD WAR II. BY 1941 ALL FIGHTER PILOTS HAD THEM FITTED TO THEIR PARACHUTE PACKS. THESE WERE ALSO THE FIRST CRAFT TO INFLATE AUTOMATICALLY FROM A GAS CYLINDER. THEY SAVED OVER 7,000 AIRMEN DURING THE WAR.

UNSINKABLE BOATS

INFLATABLE BOATS ARE TOO FLEXIBLE TO TRAVEL FAST IN ROUGH SEAS. HOWEVER, BY THE ADDITION OF A RIGID BOTTOM THEY CAN BE MADE EXCEPTIONALLY STABLE. "ATLANTIC-CLASS" LIFEBOATS ARE RIGID INFLATABLES, WITH THE BUOYANCY TUBES FIXED TO A SHALLOW FIBREGLASS HULL.

☆ INVENTIONS ☆

NOVEL, ORIGINAL DEVICES & PROCESSES

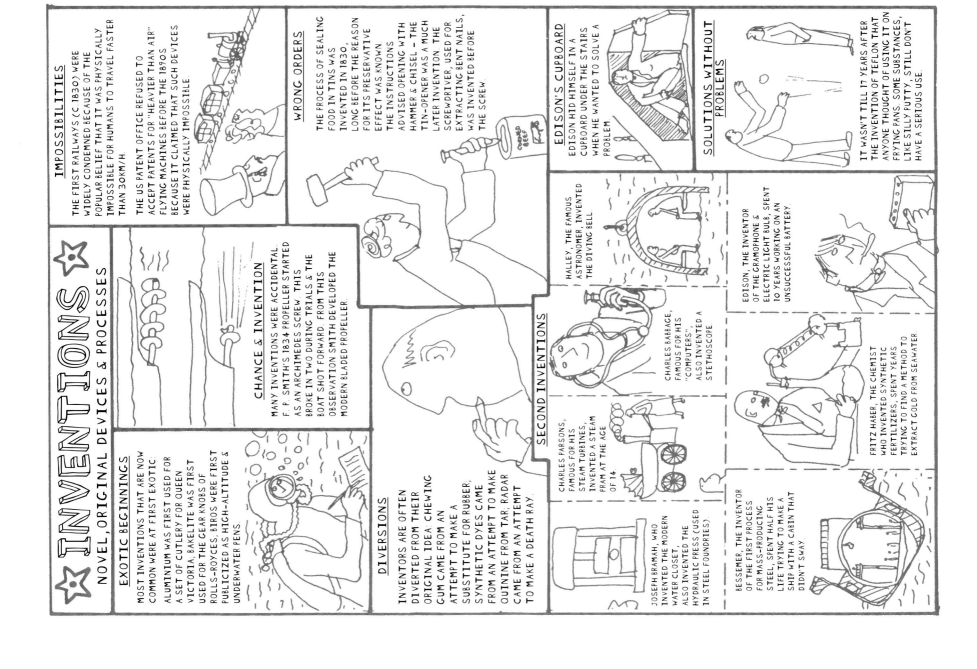

EXOTIC BEGINNINGS

MOST INVENTIONS THAT ARE NOW COMMON WERE AT FIRST EXOTIC.

ALUMINIUM WAS FIRST USED FOR A SET OF CUTLERY FOR QUEEN VICTORIA. BAKELITE WAS FIRST USED FOR THE GEAR KNOBS OF ROLLS-ROYCES. BIROS WERE FIRST PUBLICIZED AS HIGH-ALTITUDE & UNDERWATER PENS.

CHANCE & INVENTION

MANY INVENTIONS WERE ACCIDENTAL. F. P. SMITH'S 1834 PROPELLER STARTED AS AN ARCHIMEDES SCREW. THIS BROKE IN TWO DURING TRIALS & THE BOAT SHOT FORWARD. FROM THIS OBSERVATION SMITH DEVELOPED THE MODERN BLADED PROPELLER.

DIVERSIONS

INVENTORS ARE OFTEN DIVERTED FROM THEIR ORIGINAL IDEA. CHEWING GUM CAME FROM AN ATTEMPT TO MAKE A SUBSTITUTE FOR RUBBER, SYNTHETIC DYES CAME FROM AN ATTEMPT TO MAKE QUININE FROM TAR, RADAR CAME FROM AN ATTEMPT TO MAKE A DEATH RAY.

IMPOSSIBILITIES

THE FIRST RAILWAYS (C. 1830) WERE WIDELY CONDEMNED BECAUSE OF THE POPULAR BELIEF THAT IT WAS PHYSICALLY IMPOSSIBLE FOR HUMANS TO TRAVEL FASTER THAN 30KM/H.

THE US PATENT OFFICE REFUSED TO ACCEPT PATENTS FOR "HEAVIER THAN AIR" FLYING MACHINES BEFORE THE 1890S BECAUSE IT CLAIMED THAT SUCH DEVICES WERE PHYSICALLY IMPOSSIBLE.

WRONG ORDERS

THE PROCESS OF SEALING FOOD IN TINS WAS INVENTED IN 1830, LONG BEFORE THE REASON FOR ITS PRESERVATIVE EFFECT WAS KNOWN. THE INSTRUCTIONS ADVISED OPENING WITH HAMMER & CHISEL — THE TIN-OPENER WAS A MUCH LATER INVENTION. THE SCREWDRIVER, USED FOR EXTRACTING BENT NAILS, WAS INVENTED BEFORE THE SCREW.

SECOND INVENTIONS

CHARLES PARSONS, FAMOUS FOR HIS STEAM TURBINES, INVENTED A STEAM PRAM AT THE AGE OF 14.

JOSEPH BRAMAH, WHO INVENTED THE MODERN WATER CLOSET, ALSO INVENTED THE HYDRAULIC PRESS (USED IN STEEL FOUNDRIES).

HALLEY, THE FAMOUS ASTRONOMER, INVENTED THE DIVING BELL.

CHARLES BABBAGE, FAMOUS FOR HIS "COMPUTERS" ALSO INVENTED A STETHOSCOPE.

BESSEMER, THE INVENTOR OF THE FIRST PROCESS FOR MASS-PRODUCING STEEL, SPENT HALF HIS LIFE TRYING TO MAKE A SHIP WITH A CABIN THAT DIDN'T SWAY.

EDISON, THE INVENTOR OF THE GRAMOPHONE & ELECTRIC LIGHT BULB, SPENT 10 YEARS WORKING ON AN UNSUCCESSFUL BATTERY.

FRITZ HABER, THE CHEMIST WHO INVENTED SYNTHETIC FERTILIZERS, SPENT YEARS TRYING TO FIND A METHOD TO EXTRACT GOLD FROM SEAWATER.

EDISON'S CUPBOARD

EDISON HID HIMSELF IN A CUPBOARD UNDER THE STAIRS WHEN HE WANTED TO SOLVE A PROBLEM.

SOLUTIONS WITHOUT PROBLEMS

IT WASN'T TILL 17 YEARS AFTER THE INVENTION OF TEFLON THAT ANYONE THOUGHT OF USING IT ON FRYING PANS. SOME SUBSTANCES, LIKE SILLY PUTTY, STILL DON'T HAVE A SERIOUS USE.

✪ JELLYFISH ✪

RADIALLY SYMMETRICAL PRIMITIVE ANIMALS

CLASSIFICATION

JELLYFISH ARE COELENTERATES – THE SAME CLASS OF THE ANIMAL KINGDOM AS CORALS & SEA ANEMONES. THEY ALL HAVE RADIALLY SYMMETRICAL BODIES WHICH ARE PRINCIPALLY RADIALLY SYMMETRICAL STOMACHS, & MOST ARE FRINGED WITH POISONOUS TENTACLES FOR PARALYSING PREY.

LENGTH

THE LARGEST JELLYFISH EVER RECORDED HAD A 2M-DIAMETER BELL & 37M-LONG TENTACLES. THIS GIVES A THEORETICAL LENGTH OF 75M, MAKING IT THE LONGEST ANIMAL EVER FOUND ALIVE. IT WAS FOUND IN THE NORTH-WEST ATLANTIC IN 1865.

PORTUGUESE MEN-OF-WAR

THESE ARE CLASSED AS SIPHONOPHORES AFTER THEIR MECHANISM FOR TRAPPING A POCKET OF AIR IN THEIR BODIES TO ACT AS A FLOAT. THEIR TENTACLES ARE POISONOUS BUT NOT USUALLY FATAL TO MAN. THE POISON PRODUCES A BURNING PAIN AND RESULTS IN A LARGE WEAL THAT LASTS FOR ABOUT A WEEK.

BOX JELLYFISH

THE DEADLIEST JELLYFISH ARE THE "BOX JELLIES" OF THE INDO-PACIFIC OCEAN, SO CALLED BECAUSE OF THEIR CUBOID BODIES WITH FLATTENED SIDES. THESE CARRY A NEUROTOXIC VENOM SIMILAR IN STRENGTH TO THAT OF THE ASIATIC COBRA. IT KILLS IN LESS THAN 10 MINUTES & NO KNOWN ANTIDOTE ACTS FAST ENOUGH TO HELP. IN THE LAST 25 YEARS BOX JELLIES ARE KNOWN TO HAVE KILLED AT LEAST 60 PEOPLE IN AUSTRALIA & 40 ELSEWHERE.

STING

THE MECHANISM OF THE JELLYFISH'S STING IS UNIQUE IN THE ANIMAL KINGDOM. CELLS FULL OF TOXIN CONTAIN NEEDLE-LIKE HOLLOW THREADS. WHEN CELLS CONTACT PREY THEY LITERALLY EXPLODE, SHOOTING OUT THE THREADS, TURNING THEM INSIDE OUT & EMBEDDING THEIR TIPS IN THE PREY. THE EXPLODED CELLS ARE REPLACED BY OTHERS MANUFACTURED IN THE CENTRE OF THE JELLYFISH WHICH MIGRATE TO THE TIPS OF THE TENTACLES AS REQUIRED.

JELLYFISH ROBBED BY OCTOPUSES

THE OCTOPUS TREMOCTOPUS VIOLACEUS REMOVES TENTACLES FROM MAN-OF-WAR JELLYFISH & DRAPES THEM ALONG ITS FRONT FOUR ARMS TO USE AS A DEFENSIVE WEAPON.

REPRODUCTION

JELLYFISH MAY BE PRODUCED FROM GROWTHS OR LARVA BUDS ON AN ADULT WHICH DETACH THEMSELVES & GROW INTO ADULTS. YOUNG WILL ALSO GROW FROM EGGS DISCHARGED INTO THE SEA BY ADULT FEMALES & LATER FERTILIZED BY MALES. BUDDED JELLYFISH ARE CALLED POLYPS, SEXUALLY REPRODUCED JELLYFISH ARE CALLED MEDUSAE.

HOW TO MAKE A DOUBLE BASS

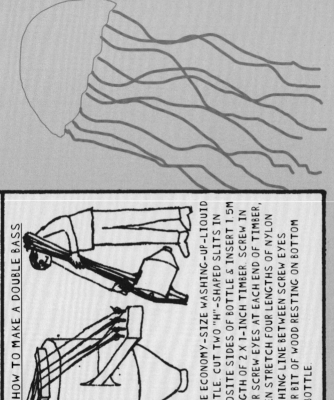

TAKE ECONOMY-SIZE WASHING-UP-LIQUID BOTTLE. CUT TWO "H"-SHAPED SLITS IN OPPOSITE SIDES OF BOTTLE & INSERT 1.5M LENGTH OF 2 X 1-INCH TIMBER. SCREW IN FOUR SCREW EYES AT EACH END OF TIMBER, THEN STRETCH FOUR LENGTHS OF NYLON FISHING LINE BETWEEN SCREW EYES OVER BIT OF WOOD RESTING ON BOTTOM OF BOTTLE.

JET ENGINES

DEVICES PRODUCING THRUST BY ACCELERATING MASSES OF AIR

FRANK WHITTLE'S IDEA

SIR FRANK WHITTLE INVENTED THE FIRST PRACTICAL JET ENGINE. HIS INSPIRATION WAS TO POWER THE COMPRESSOR BY A TURBINE (SEE BELOW)

FRANK WHITTLE'S FATHER

WHITTLE'S FATHER RAN A SMALL ENGINEERING WORKSHOP IN LEAMINGTON SPA & SPENT HIS SPARE TIME TRYING TO BUILD A PERPETUAL-MOTION MACHINE

TURBOPROPS

IN A TURBOPROP ENGINE, A BIG TURBINE ENABLES ALL THE ENERGY OF THE HOT GASES TO BE CONVERTED INTO ROTATION & USED TO POWER A PROPELLER.

HIGH SPEEDS

ENGINES ARE INEFFICIENT AT HIGH SPEEDS BECAUSE THE AIR AT THE TIPS OF PROPELLER BLADES BECOMES TURBULENT AT HIGH SPEEDS. THIS GENERATES HEAT BUT NO FORWARD THRUST.

LOW SPEEDS

JET ENGINES ARE INEFFICIENT AT LOW SPEEDS BECAUSE THEY NEED A LOT OF AIR RUSHING INTO THEM TO ACHIEVE THE RIGHT HEAT.

FRANK WHITTLE'S PROPHECY (1930)

"PISTON ENGINES HAVE HUNDREDS OF MOVING PARTS JERKING TO & FRO & THEY CANNOT BE MADE MORE POWERFUL WITHOUT BECOMING TOO COMPLEX. THE ENGINE OF THE FUTURE MUST PRODUCE 2,000HP WITH ONE MOVING PART — A SPINNING TURBINE & COMPRESSOR"

HOW IT WORKS

AIR SUCKED IN BY FAN & COMPRESSOR

FUEL IGNITED WITH AIR

HOT GASES PUSH TURBINE ROUND

HOT GASES ESCAPE AT HIGH SPEED

EXHAUST

TURBINE

BURNERS

COMPRESSOR

COOLING

THE COMPRESSOR ALWAYS PULLS IN ABOUT 5 TIMES AS MUCH AIR AS IS NEEDED TO BURN THE FUEL. THE EXCESS AIR MIXES WITH THE EXHAUST GASES & COOLS THE ENGINE.

PREDICTING BREAKDOWNS

JET ENGINES HAVE LOTS OF SENSORS WHICH RECORD VIBRATIONS & TEMPERATURES TO CHECK WHETHER ANYTHING IS ABOUT TO GO WRONG. SOME AIRLINES EXAMINE ALL THE USED OIL FILTERS & KEEP A RECORD OF ALL THE METALLIC PARTICLES THAT HAVE WORN OFF EACH ENGINE

HOW TO TEST WHETHER A NUMBER DIVIDES BY 13

SPLIT NUMBER INTO GROUPS OF 3 DIGITS, & ARRANGE WITH ALTERNATE PLUS & MINUS SIGNS. IF THE TOTAL OF THIS "SUM" IS 0 OR A MULTIPLE OF 13 THEN THE ORIGINAL NUMBER CAN BE DIVIDED BY 13:

67, 630, 563

$67 - 630 + 563 = 0$

so 67, 630, 563 is divisible by 13

11, 350, 286

$11 - 350 + 286 = 53$

so 11, 350, 286 isn't divisible by 13

JET BRAKES

THE ROAR & VIBRATION OF JET ENGINES FELT AFTER LANDING IS CAUSED BY THE THRUST-REVERSERS. THESE ARE BAFFLES WHICH DEFLECT THE EXHAUST GASES FORWARD TO SLOW DOWN THE AIRCRAFT.

DOORS OPEN

DOORS CLOSED

ANTI-NOISE

JET ENGINES MAY EVENTUALLY BE SILENCED BY ANTI-NOISE NOISE, PICKED UP BY A MICROPHONE, IS REPLAYED THROUGH SPEAKERS WITH A SLIGHT DELAY. THIS CAN CANCEL OUT THE VIBRATIONS THAT CAUSE THE NOISE. ANTI-NOISE IS ALREADY USED IN THE PILOTS' EAR PHONES ON SOME MILITARY PLANES.

RADIOACTIVE JETS

JETS PICK UP RADIO-ACTIVITY IN THE UPPER ATMOSPHERE, SO WORKSHOPS NEED DECONTAMINATION EQUIPMENT

FAN ENGINES

THE LARGE FAN ON THE FRONT OF MODERN JET ENGINES REDUCES THE SIZE OF THE COMPRESSOR NEEDED & MIXES MORE AIR WITH THE EXHAUST. THE TWO MAIN SOURCES OF NOISE IN JET ENGINES ARE AIR TURBULENCE IN THE COMPRESSOR & ROARING HOT EXHAUST GASES. THE FAN REDUCES BOTH THESE NOISES.

JUNGLES
AREAS OF DENSE TROPICAL VEGETATION

JUNGLE PRODUCTS: STRYCHNINE, QUININE, GAMBOGE (COLOURING PIGMENT), BALATA (GOLF-BALL OUTER COVER), PINE RESIN,

TURPENTINE, MAHOGANY, BALSA, TEAK, ALLSPICE, CARDAMOM, CINNAMON, NUTMEG,

PATCHOULI OIL (PERFUMES), YAM (DIOSGENIN MEDICINES), QUASSIA (INSECTICIDES)

CLOUD FORESTS

TROPICAL JUNGLES ABOVE 1,000M ARE FOGGY MOST OF THE TIME. WATER DRIPS CONSTANTLY & THE TREES ARE DRAPED IN MOSSES & LICHEN.

MANGROVE JUNGLES

SALTWATER SWAMP JUNGLES ARE DOMINATED BY ONLY ONE TREE FAMILY (RHIZOPHORACEAE). THESE HAVE BREATHING ROOTS WHICH EXTRACT OXYGEN FROM THE AIR RATHER THAN THE WATERLOGGED SOIL.

SANDY JUNGLES

HEATH JUNGLE OCCURS ON SANDY SOIL. IT IS UNSTABLE & READILY REVERTS TO SCRUBLAND IF A FEW TREES ARE FELLED.

CLIMATE

JUNGLES ARE HOT AND WET ALL YEAR ROUND, WITH TWELVE HOURS OF SUN EVERY DAY AND ABOUT 2,000MM OF RAINFALL A YEAR

POLLEN HISTORY

POLLEN IS NORMALLY BROKEN DOWN BY BACTERIA BUT, IN CERTAIN AIRLESS CONDITIONS (LIKE BOGS), IT REMAINS INTACT. SUCCESSIVE LAYERS OF SEDIMENTS IN BOGS CAN BE ANALYSED TO REVEAL THE JUNGLE VEGETATION OF THE PAST.

TROPICAL SOIL

SOILS IN TEMPERATE ZONES ARE GENERALLY RICHER THAN THOSE IN THE TROPICS BECAUSE THEY ARE RELATIVELY RECENT (DEVELOPED OR REWORKED IN THE LAST ICE AGE). TROPICAL SOILS DERIVE MOST OF THEIR NUTRIENTS FROM THEIR SURFACE LAYER OF ROTTING VEGETATION.

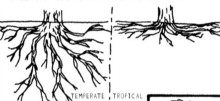

TEMPERATE   TROPICAL

LEAVES

LEAVES ON JUNGLE TREES ARE LESS VARIED THAN THOSE ON TEMPERATE TREES. JUNGLE LEAVES MUST ALL BE SMOOTH (TO HINDER LICHEN GROWTH) & POINTED (TO ENSURE GOOD DRAINAGE)

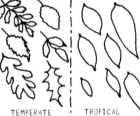

TEMPERATE   TROPICAL

FELLING PROBLEMS

BUTTRESS ROOTS OFTEN COMPEL FORESTERS TO ERECT PLATFORMS SO THEY CAN CUT THROUGH THE TRUNK ABOVE

OFTEN THE CANOPY OF LEAVES IS SO ENTWINED WITH NEIGHBOURING BRANCHES THAT A TREE WILL NOT FALL WHEN THE TRUNK IS CUT. ALL THE SURROUNDING TREES MUST BE CUT AS WELL.

STRANGLERS

PLANTS CALLED STRANGLER FIGS ATTACH THEMSELVES TO THE ROOTS OF A TREE & GROW, USING THE TREE'S FOOD & WATER. THEY EVENTUALLY SMOTHER & KILL THE TREE

CLIMBERS

WOODY CLIMBERS, LIKE RATTAN, CAN GROW UP TO 150M. THE SUCTION CARRYING WATER TO THE LEAVES AT THE TOP IS SO STRONG THAT, IF THE STEM IS SLIT, HISSING CAN BE HEARD AS AIR RUSHES IN

HOW TO MAKE A SPINNING-CARD PUZZLE

BEND A POSTCARD INTO AN "S" SHAPE BY RUBBING EACH EDGE OVER A TABLE.

THE PROBLEM IS TO GUESS WHICH WAY IT WILL SPIN WHEN DROPPED

IDEA FROM K. GEARY, ASHTEAD, SURREY, UK

CLOVES, PEPPER, VANILLA, RATTAN (CANE FURNITURE), BAMBOO, KAPOK (STUFFING FOR PILLOWS ETC.), ROSEWOOD OIL (PERFUMES), DAMMARS (RESINS USED IN PAINTS), CHICLE (CHEWING GUM), SAPELE (HARDWOOD), VANILLA

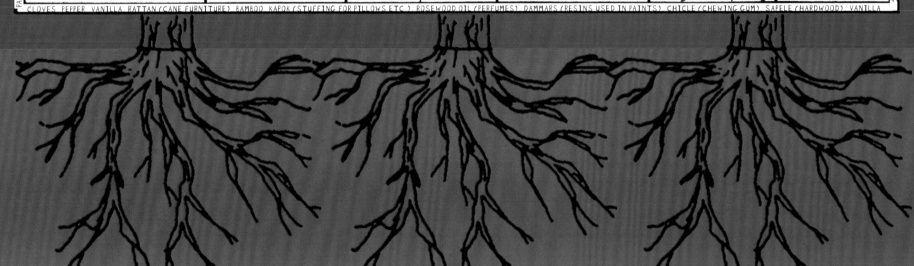

⭐ KANGAROOS ⭐

POUCHED MAMMALS WITH ENLARGED HIND LIMBS

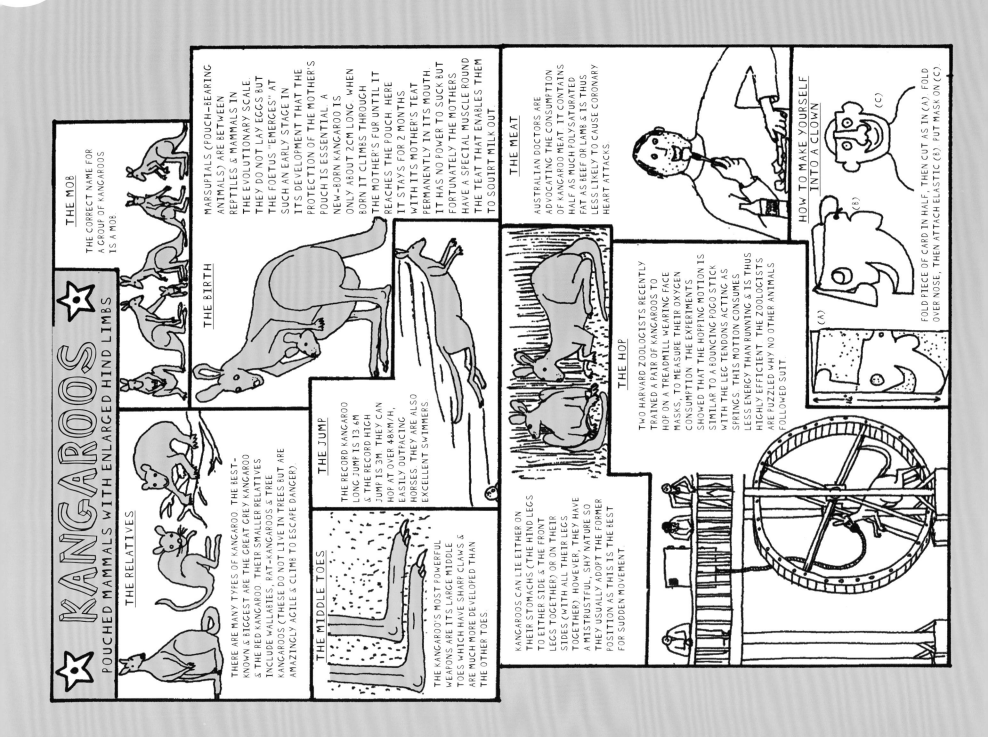

THE MOB

THE CORRECT NAME FOR A GROUP OF KANGAROOS IS A MOB.

THE RELATIVES

THERE ARE MANY TYPES OF KANGAROO. THE BEST-KNOWN & BIGGEST ARE THE GREAT GREY KANGAROO & THE RED KANGAROO. THEIR SMALLER RELATIVES INCLUDE WALLABIES, RAT-KANGAROOS & TREE KANGAROOS (THESE DO NOT LIVE IN TREES BUT ARE AMAZINGLY AGILE & CLIMB TO ESCAPE DANGER).

THE BIRTH

MARSUPIALS (POUCH-BEARING ANIMALS) ARE BETWEEN REPTILES & MAMMALS IN THE EVOLUTIONARY SCALE. THEY DO NOT LAY EGGS BUT THE FOETUS "EMERGES" AT SUCH AN EARLY STAGE IN ITS DEVELOPMENT THAT THE PROTECTION OF THE MOTHER'S POUCH IS ESSENTIAL. A NEW-BORN KANGAROO IS ONLY ABOUT 2CM LONG. WHEN BORN IT CLIMBS THROUGH THE MOTHER'S FUR UNTIL IT REACHES THE POUCH. HERE IT STAYS FOR 2 MONTHS WITH ITS MOTHER'S TEAT PERMANENTLY IN ITS MOUTH. IT HAS NO POWER TO SUCK BUT FORTUNATELY THE MOTHERS HAVE A SPECIAL MUSCLE ROUND THE TEAT THAT ENABLES THEM TO SQUIRT MILK OUT.

THE JUMP

THE RECORD KANGAROO LONG JUMP IS 13.6M & THE RECORD HIGH JUMP IS 3M. THEY CAN HOP AT OVER 48KM/H, EASILY OUTPACING HORSES. THEY ARE ALSO EXCELLENT SWIMMERS.

THE MIDDLE TOES

THE KANGAROO'S MOST POWERFUL WEAPONS ARE ITS LARGE MIDDLE TOES WHICH HAVE SHARP CLAWS & ARE MUCH MORE DEVELOPED THAN THE OTHER TOES.

THE HOP

TWO HARVARD ZOOLOGISTS RECENTLY TRAINED A PAIR OF KANGAROOS TO HOP ON A TREADMILL WEARING FACE MASKS, TO MEASURE THEIR OXYGEN CONSUMPTION. THE EXPERIMENTS SHOWED THAT THE HOPPING MOTION IS SIMILAR TO A BOUNCING POGO STICK WITH THE LEG TENDONS ACTING AS SPRINGS. THIS MOTION CONSUMES LESS ENERGY THAN RUNNING & IS THUS HIGHLY EFFICIENT. THE ZOOLOGISTS ARE PUZZLED WHY NO OTHER ANIMALS FOLLOWED SUIT.

KANGAROOS CAN LIE EITHER ON THEIR STOMACHS (THE HIND LEGS TO EITHER SIDE & THE FRONT LEGS TOGETHER) OR ON THEIR SIDES (WITH ALL THEIR LEGS TOGETHER) HOWEVER, THEY HAVE A MISTRUSTFUL, SHY NATURE SO THEY USUALLY ADOPT THE FORMER POSITION AS THIS IS THE BEST FOR SUDDEN MOVEMENT.

THE MEAT

AUSTRALIAN DOCTORS ARE ADVOCATING THE CONSUMPTION OF KANGAROO MEAT. IT CONTAINS HALF AS MUCH POLYSATURATED FAT AS BEEF OR LAMB & IS THUS LESS LIKELY TO CAUSE CORONARY HEART ATTACKS.

HOW TO MAKE YOURSELF INTO A CLOWN

FOLD PIECE OF CARD IN HALF, THEN CUT AS IN (A). FOLD OVER NOSE, THEN ATTACH ELASTIC (B). PUT MASK ON (C).

LEAVES

ORGANS OF PHOTOSYNTHESIS OF HIGHER PLANTS

THE FUNCTION OF LEAVES IS THE PRODUCTION OF ENERGY FROM LIGHT & CARBON DIOXIDE IN THE AIR (PHOTOSYNTHESIS)

STRUCTURE

CARBON DIOXIDE ENTERS LEAVES THROUGH SMALL HOLES (STOMA) IN THE SURFACE

THE GREEN COLOUR OF LEAVES IS CAUSED BY THE GREEN PIGMENT CALLED CHLOROPHYLL, WHICH IS INSIDE SMALL STRUCTURES CALLED CHLOROPLASTS. THE CHLOROPHYLL TRAPS THE SUN'S LIGHT ENERGY

THE LEAF SKELETON IS THE NETWORK OF VASCULAR STRANDS WHICH SUPPORTS THE LEAF & KEEPS IT SUPPLIED WITH WATER & NUTRIENTS

LEAVES & FLOWERS

THE STIMULUS THAT CAUSES PLANTS TO FLOWER AT A PARTICULAR TIME OF YEAR COMES FROM THE LEAVES. SOME PLANTS CAN BE MADE TO FLOWER AT ANY TIME BY BEING GRAFTING WITH LEAVES ARTIFICIALLY EXPOSED TO THE REQUIRED PERIOD OF "DAYLIGHT"

LEAF RHYTHMS

IN MANY PLANTS THE LEAVES MOVE SLIGHTLY IN DAILY RHYTHMS. THIS CONTINUES EVEN IF THE PLANTS ARE KEPT IN DARKNESS.

LEAF FALL

LEAVES FALL WHEN A SECTION OF THE STEM FORMS A WEAK SCARRED ZONE. THIS IS CAUSED BY THE PLANT RELEASING SMALL AMOUNTS OF ETHYLENE (THE SAME PETROCHEMICAL FROM WHICH POLYTHENE IS MADE). THE LEAVES OF DEAD TREES DO NOT FALL

EVAPORATION

THE LARGE AREA OF MOIST CELL SURFACE NECESSARY FOR PHOTOSYNTHESIS LEADS TO AN ENORMOUS WATER LOSS THROUGH EVAPORATION. A BEECH-TREE LEAF CAN LOSE UP TO 5 TIMES ITS OWN WEIGHT OF WATER PER DAY.

LEAF PROTEIN

EDIBLE PROTEIN CAN BE EXTRACTED FROM LEAVES BY PRESSING OUT THEIR JUICE, HEATING IT AND THEN FILTERING IT TO OBTAIN THE PROTEIN. LEAVES HAVE POTENTIAL AS A CHEAP, ABUNDANT SOURCE OF PROTEIN BUT CONTAIN A LOT OF FIBRE AND SOME NASTY CHEMICALS, SUCH AS CYANIDE & TANNINS

COMPASS LEAVES

THE LEAVES OF THE US PRAIRIE COMPASS PLANT ARE ALWAYS ALIGNED NORTH-SOUTH. THIS AVOIDS THEIR CATCHING THE SUN AT ITS FULL MIDDAY STRENGTH (THUS REDUCING EVAPORATION)

RAIN FROM LEAVES

LEAVES INDIRECTLY CAUSE RAIN. ANALYSIS OF THE DUST PARTICLES AROUND WHICH ICE & RAIN DROPLETS FORM HAS REVEALED THAT MANY COME FROM DEAD, DRY LEAVES, BLOWN INTO THE UPPER ATMOSPHERE

HOW TO BLEACH FLOWERS

SUSPEND FLOWERS UPSIDE-DOWN IN JAR CONTAINING A LITTLE HOUSEHOLD AMMONIA. RED FLOWERS WILL TURN GREEN YELLOW & WHITE FLOWERS WILL NOT CHANGE

LEFT-HANDEDNESS

AN UNCOMMON PREDISPOSITION

LANGUAGE

MOST LANGUAGES ARE BIASED AGAINST LEFT-HANDERS

ENGLISH   RIGHT   LEFT
(CORRECT) (LEFT OUT)

FRENCH   DROIT   GAUCHE
(ADROIT)

LATIN   DEXTER   SINISTER
(DEXTROUS)

GREEK IS AN EXCEPTION ARISTEROS (LEFT-HANDED) ALSO MEANS BETTER

INTERNATIONAL

THE ESKIMOS, MAORIS, AFRICANS & CHINESE ARE ALL PREDOMINANTLY RIGHT-HANDED. SO WERE THE ANCIENT EGYPTIANS, GREEKS & ROMANS.

ELEPHANTS

AFRICAN ELEPHANTS ARE LEFT- OR RIGHT-TUSKED ONE TUSK IS USED FOR DIGGING & IS SLIGHTLY LARGER THAN THE OTHER

MONKEYS

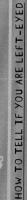

A RECENT STUDY OF JAPANESE MACAQUE MONKEYS REVEALED

40% LEFT-PAWED

20% RIGHT-PAWED

40% AMBIDEXTROUS

FEET

MANY RIGHT-HANDED FOOTBALLERS PREFER TO USE THEIR LEFT FOOT

HOW TO TELL IF YOU ARE LEFT-EYED

FOCUS EYES ON DISTANT OBJECT. RAISE FINGER IN FRONT OF OBJECT SO YOU SEE IT "OUT OF FOCUS". WINK ONE EYE, THEN THE OTHER. FINGER WILL APPEAR TO JUMP WHEN YOU WINK DOMINANT EYE BUT NOT THE OTHER

MOST RIGHT-HANDERS ARE RIGHT-EYED. THERE IS SOME EVIDENCE THAT THEY ALSO CHEW MORE WITH THE RIGHT SIDE OF THE JAW.

SIAMESE TWINS

SIAMESE TWINS ARE MIRROR IMAGES OF EACH OTHER. ONE WILL BE LEFT-HANDED & THE OTHER RIGHT-HANDED

THE US ARMY REJECTS A HIGHER PERCENTAGE OF LEFT-HANDERS THAN RIGHT-HANDERS

LEFT-HANDED US SCHOOLCHILDREN HAVE, ON AVERAGE, SLIGHTLY HIGHER IQS

IN MENTAL INSTITUTIONS, MORE PEOPLE THAN AVERAGE ARE LEFT-HANDED

HUNKIN IS LEFT-HANDED

THEORY 1

WHY MAN DEVELOPED A RIGHT-HAND BIAS

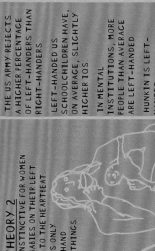

WHEN ONE-HAND-SIDED TOOLS, SUCH AS SCYTHES & SICKLES, FIRST APPEARED, THEY WERE PRECIOUS OBJECTS OWNED BY THE COMMUNITY, NOT BY INDIVIDUALS. IT WAS OBVIOUSLY DESIRABLE THAT EVERYBODY SHOULD BE ABLE TO USE THE SAME TOOLS, SO A ONE-HAND-SIDED BIAS DEVELOPED

THEORY 2

IT MAY BE INSTINCTIVE FOR WOMEN TO CRADLE BABIES ON THEIR LEFT SIDE, NEXT TO THE HEARTBEAT. THIS LEAVES ONLY THE RIGHT HAND FREE TO DO THINGS.

SPORT

IN MANY SPORTS, SUCH AS CRICKET, TENNIS & FENCING, IT IS AN ADVANTAGE TO BE LEFT-HANDED. LEFT-HANDED PLAYERS GET USED TO RIGHT-HANDED OPPONENTS, BUT RIGHT-HANDED PLAYERS ARE OFTEN CONFUSED BY A LEFT-HANDED OPPONENT

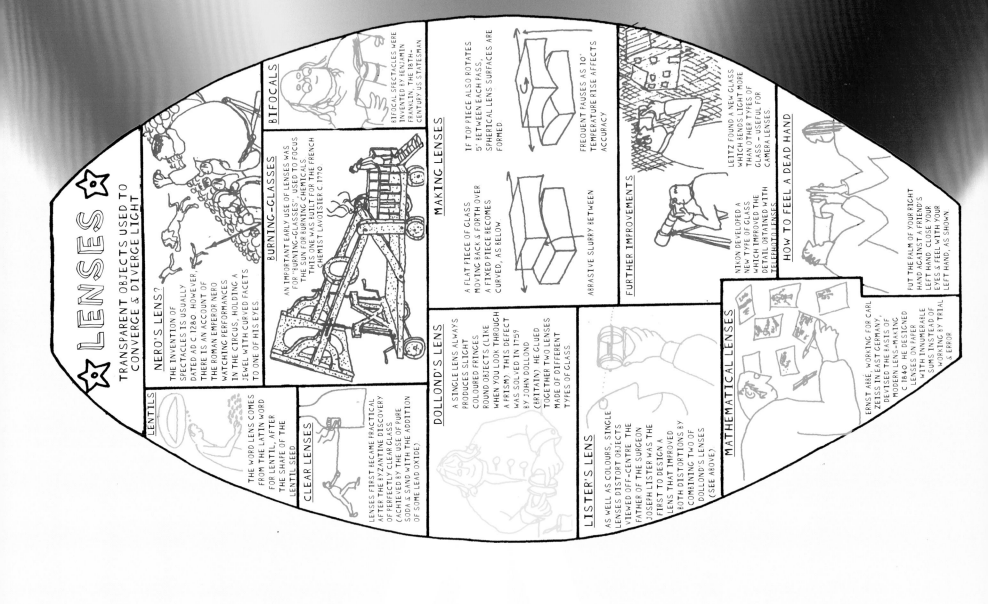

☆ LENSES ☆

TRANSPARENT OBJECTS USED TO CONVERGE & DIVERGE LIGHT

NERO'S LENS?

THE INVENTION OF SPECTACLES IS USUALLY DATED AD C 1280. HOWEVER, THERE IS AN ACCOUNT OF THE ROMAN EMPEROR NERO WATCHING PERFORMANCES IN THE CIRCUS, HOLDING A JEWEL WITH CURVED FACETS TO ONE OF HIS EYES

LENTILS

THE WORD LENS COMES FROM THE LATIN WORD FOR LENTIL, AFTER THE SHAPE OF THE LENTIL SEED

CLEAR LENSES

LENSES FIRST BECAME PRACTICAL AFTER THE BYZANTINE DISCOVERY OF PERFECTLY CLEAR GLASS (ACHIEVED BY THE USE OF PURE SODA & SAND WITH THE ADDITION OF SOME LEAD OXIDE)

BURNING-GLASSES

AN IMPORTANT EARLY USE OF LENSES WAS FOR "BURNING-GLASSES", USED TO FOCUS THE SUN FOR BURNING CHEMICALS. THIS ONE WAS BUILT FOR THE FRENCH CHEMIST LAVOISIER C 1770

BIFOCALS

BIFOCAL SPECTACLES WERE INVENTED BY BENJAMIN FRANKLIN, THE 18TH-CENTURY US STATESMAN

DOLLOND'S LENS

A SINGLE LENS ALWAYS PRODUCES SLIGHT COLOURED FRINGES ROUND OBJECTS (LIKE WHEN YOU LOOK THROUGH A PRISM) THIS DEFECT WAS SOLVED IN 1759 BY JOHN DOLLOND (BRITAIN) HE GLUED TOGETHER TWO LENSES MADE OF DIFFERENT TYPES OF GLASS

LISTER'S LENS

AS WELL AS COLOURS, SINGLE LENSES DISTORT OBJECTS VIEWED OFF-CENTRE THE FATHER OF THE SURGEON JOSEPH LISTER WAS THE FIRST TO DESIGN A LENS THAT IMPROVED BOTH DISTORTIONS BY COMBINING TWO OF DOLLOND'S LENSES (SEE ABOVE)

MAKING LENSES

A FLAT PIECE OF GLASS MOVING BACK & FORTH OVER A FIXED PIECE BECOMES CURVED, AS BELOW

ABRASIVE SLURRY BETWEEN

IF TOP PIECE ALSO ROTATES 5° BETWEEN EACH PASS, SPHERICAL LENS SURFACES ARE FORMED

FREQUENT PAUSES AS 10° TEMPERATURE RISE AFFECTS ACCURACY

FURTHER IMPROVEMENTS

LEITZ FOUND A NEW GLASS WHICH BENDS LIGHT MORE THAN OTHER TYPES OF GLASS — USEFUL FOR CAMERA LENSES

NIKON DEVELOPED A NEW TYPE OF GLASS WHICH IMPROVED THE DETAIL OBTAINED WITH TELEPHOTO LENSES

MATHEMATICAL LENSES

ERNST ABBÉ, WORKING FOR CARL ZEISS IN EAST GERMANY, DEVISED THE BASIS OF MODERN LENS-MAKING C 1840 HE DESIGNED LENSES ON PAPER WITH INNUMERABLE SUMS INSTEAD OF WORKING BY TRIAL & ERROR

HOW TO FEEL A DEAD HAND

PUT THE PALM OF YOUR RIGHT HAND AGAINST A FRIEND'S LEFT HAND, CLOSE YOUR EYES & FEEL WITH YOUR LEFT HAND, AS SHOWN

LIBRARIES
COLLECTIONS OF BOOKS

POTTERY LIBRARIES

A LARGE MESOPOTAMIAN LIBRARY OF CLAY TABLETS (C.650 BC) WAS FOUND AT NINEVEH IN THE 19TH CENTURY. THE 30,943 TABLETS WERE KEPT IN LABELLED POTTERY JARS ARRANGED ON SHELVES. CATALOGUE TABLETS HAVE ALSO BEEN FOUND.

AUTHENTICITY

BEFORE THE INVENTION OF PRINTING, BOOKS WERE COPIED BY HAND & MISTAKES WERE COMMON. AN IMPORTANT FUNCTION OF GREEK LIBRARIES WAS TO RETAIN THE ORIGINAL MANUSCRIPTS SO THAT PEOPLE COULD CHECK THEIR COPIES.

SECURITY

IMPORTANT LEGAL TEXTS WERE BAKED ON TABLETS & WRAPPED IN CLAY ENVELOPES ON WHICH THE TEXT WAS REPEATED. ANY TAMPERING WITH THE TEXT COULD THUS BE CHECKED.

EXPANDING SHELVES

BRITAIN'S BIGGEST LIBRARY (THE BRITISH LIBRARY) TAKES MORE THAN 3 MILLION NEW ITEMS EACH YEAR. THESE CONSUME 12KM OF EXTRA SHELVING A YEAR.

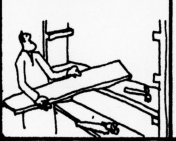

CHEST LIBRARIES

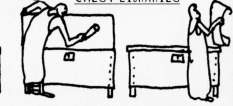

ANCIENT ROME IS SAID TO HAVE BOASTED 29 PUBLIC LIBRARIES (MOSTLY IN TEMPLES) BY AD 350. THE BOOKS WERE WRITTEN ON ROLLS OF PARCHMENT & KEPT IN WOODEN CHESTS.

LOCAL LIBRARIES

THE LAW ALLOWING COUNCILS TO RAISE RATES TO HELP FOUND LIBRARIES WAS PASSED IN 1850. FREE PUBLIC ACCESS TO BOOKS WAS NOT GENERALLY INTRODUCED UNTIL THE 20TH CENTURY, HOWEVER, PIONEERED BY LONDON'S CLERKENWELL LIBRARY IN 1894.

GLASGOW

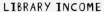

BRITAIN'S BIGGEST PUBLIC LIBRARY IS GLASGOW'S MITCHELL LIBRARY.

OVERDUE RECORD

THE LONGEST OVERDUE BOOK KNOWN WAS CHECKED OUT OF CINCINNATI MEDICAL LIBRARY IN 1823 & RETURNED IN 1968. THE FINE OF $1,102 WAS NOT CHARGED.

LIBRARY INCOME

BRITISH PUBLIC LIBRARIES SPEND LESS THAN 15% OF THEIR INCOME ON BOOKS. WAGES CONSUME ABOUT 55% & THE REST GOES ON OVERHEADS & OTHER SERVICES.

NEW BOOKS

ROBOT LIBRARIANS

KANAZAWA UNIVERSITY, JAPAN, USED TO HAVE A VIDEO LIBRARY RUN BY ROBOTS (CALLED INTELIBOTS). THESE BATTERY-POWERED, WHEELED DEVICES LOCATED SELECTED TAPES FROM RACKS RESEMBLING MINIATURE MULTI-STOREY CAR-PARKS & TOOK THEM TO THE NEAREST VIDEO PLAYER.

HOW TO MAKE A CAT SPARK

STROKE A CAT WITH A BIT OF NYLON IN THE DARK & YOU SHOULD SEE SPARKS. LIKE ALL EXPERIMENTS WITH STATIC ELECTRICITY, IT WORKS BETTER IN COLD, DRY WEATHER.

LICE

WINGLESS BLOODSUCKING INSECTS

BITING OR SUCKING?
BITING LICE (MALLOPHAGA) FEED ON FEATHERS & BITS OF SKIN & HAIR. THEY INFEST MANY ANIMALS BUT NOT HUMANS. FROM BITING LICE, SUCKING LICE (ANOPLURA) HAVE DEVELOPED, FEEDING ON BLOOD & INFESTING MAMMALS, INCLUDING HUMANS.

RACIAL LICE
AMERICAN, CHINESE, AFRICAN & EUROPEAN HEAD LICE ARE STRUCTURALLY DISTINCT. THE EUROPEAN VARIETY CANNOT GRIP ONTO AN OVAL CROSS-SECTION OF A BLACK PERSON'S HAIR. THE AFRICAN VARIETY HAS A CLAW EQUIPPED FOR THIS.

SUPER LICE
LICE HAVE ALREADY BECOME IMMUNE TO DDT & OTHER INSECTICIDES. THEY CAN STILL BE KILLED BY MALATHION BUT THEY ARE EXPECTED TO DEVELOP IMMUNITY TO IT EVENTUALLY.

LOUSY CHILDREN
ONE INSPECTION SUGGESTED THAT 26% OF BRITISH SCHOOLCHILDREN HAD HEAD LICE.

COLOUR MATCH
HEAD LICE ADJUST THEIR COLOUR AT BIRTH TO MATCH THE SCALP OF THEIR HOST.

STRENGTH
THE FORCE NEEDED TO CRUSH A LOUSE IS ABOUT 500,000 TIMES ITS OWN WEIGHT.

FEVER
IF A PERSON DEVELOPS A FEVER, THEIR LICE WILL MOVE RAPIDLY AWAY IN SEARCH OF ANOTHER HOST. THIS BENEFITS THEM AS SWEAT CAN CONTAIN MICRO-ORGANISMS FATAL TO THEIR SURVIVAL.

TYPHUS
LICE ARE THE MAIN CARRIERS OF TYPHUS. THE TYPHOID ORGANISMS MULTIPLY IN THE GUT OF THE LOUSE, WHICH SWELLS & BURSTS. THE DISEASE IS CONTRACTED IF THE REMAINS OF THE LOUSE ARE INHALED OR SCRATCHED INTO THE SKIN.

POP

BODY LICE
BODY LICE ARE NOW FAIRLY UNCOMMON. THEY USED TO NEST & LAY EGGS IN CLOTHES BUT FREQUENT WASHING & IRONING HAVE KILLED THEM OFF.

ELECTORAL LICE
TRADITIONALLY, THE MAYOR OF THE SWEDISH TOWN HURDENBURG WAS ELECTED BY A LOUSE. THE ELDERS SAT ROUND A TABLE ON WHICH THE LOUSE WAS PLACED, TOUCHING IT WITH THEIR LONG BEARDS. THE BEARD SELECTED BY THE LOUSE DETERMINED THE FUTURE MAYOR.

YOUNG WOMEN IN SIBERIA USED TO FLIRT WITH THEIR SUITORS BY THROWING LICE AT THEM.

BENEFICIAL LICE?
THE NATURALIST LINNAEUS THOUGHT LICE PROTECTED CHILDREN FROM DISEASE.

IN POLAND IT WAS TRADITIONALLY THOUGHT THAT A LOUSY SCALP WAS HEALTHY.

HOW TO LOOK FOR LICE
THE EASIEST THINGS TO FIND ARE THE EGGS (NITS) - SMALL WHITE BALLS GLUED TO THE HAIR ROOT. THE GLUE SECRETED BY THE LOUSE IS SO STRONG THAT THE NITS USUALLY REMAIN ATTACHED, GROWING WITH THE HAIR UNTIL IT IS CUT.

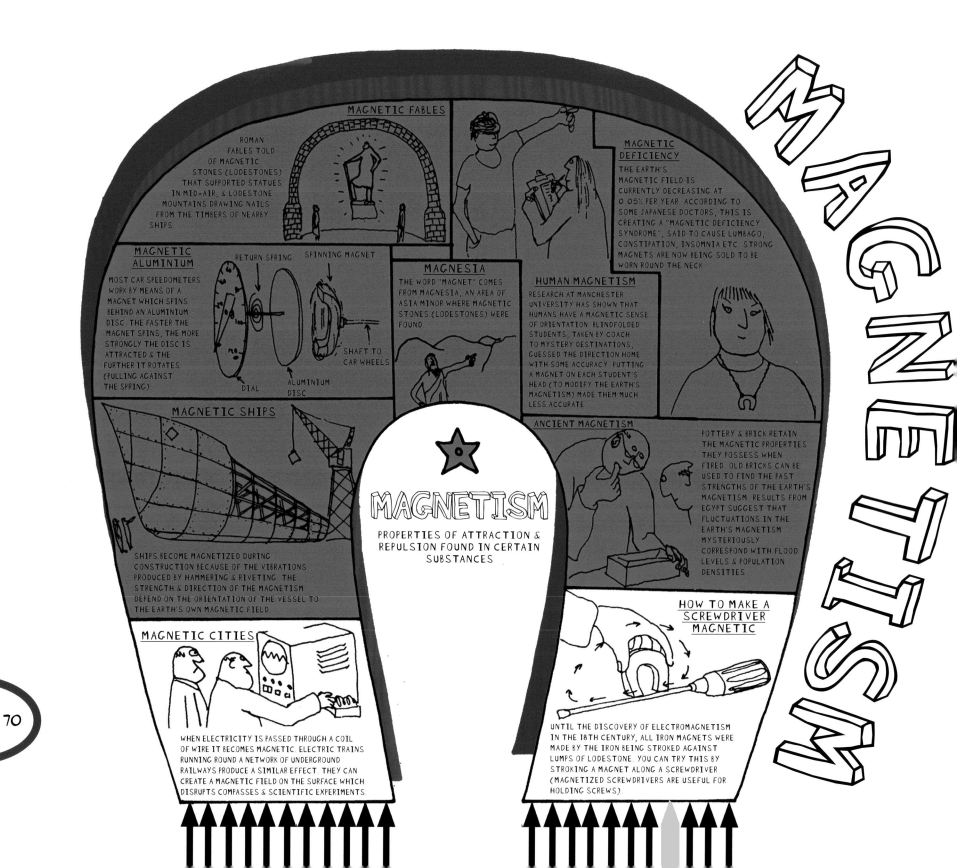

MAGNETISM

MAGNETIC FABLES

ROMAN FABLES TOLD OF MAGNETIC STONES (LODESTONES) THAT SUPPORTED STATUES IN MID-AIR, & LODESTONE MOUNTAINS DRAWING NAILS FROM THE TIMBERS OF NEARBY SHIPS.

MAGNETIC DEFICIENCY

THE EARTH'S MAGNETIC FIELD IS CURRENTLY DECREASING AT 0.05% PER YEAR. ACCORDING TO SOME JAPANESE DOCTORS, THIS IS CREATING A "MAGNETIC DEFICIENCY SYNDROME", SAID TO CAUSE LUMBAGO, CONSTIPATION, INSOMNIA ETC. STRONG MAGNETS ARE NOW BEING SOLD TO BE WORN ROUND THE NECK.

MAGNETIC ALUMINIUM

MOST CAR SPEEDOMETERS WORK BY MEANS OF A MAGNET WHICH SPINS BEHIND AN ALUMINIUM DISC. THE FASTER THE MAGNET SPINS, THE MORE STRONGLY THE DISC IS ATTRACTED & THE FURTHER IT ROTATES (PULLING AGAINST THE SPRING.)

RETURN SPRING

SPINNING MAGNET

SHAFT TO CAR WHEELS

DIAL

ALUMINIUM DISC

MAGNESIA

THE WORD "MAGNET" COMES FROM MAGNESIA, AN AREA OF ASIA MINOR WHERE MAGNETIC STONES (LODESTONES) WERE FOUND

HUMAN MAGNETISM

RESEARCH AT MANCHESTER UNIVERSITY HAS SHOWN THAT HUMANS HAVE A MAGNETIC SENSE OF ORIENTATION. BLINDFOLDED STUDENTS, TAKEN BY COACH TO MYSTERY DESTINATIONS, GUESSED THE DIRECTION HOME WITH SOME ACCURACY. PUTTING A MAGNET ON EACH STUDENT'S HEAD (TO MODIFY THE EARTH'S MAGNETISM) MADE THEM MUCH LESS ACCURATE

MAGNETIC SHIPS

SHIPS BECOME MAGNETIZED DURING CONSTRUCTION BECAUSE OF THE VIBRATIONS PRODUCED BY HAMMERING & RIVETING. THE STRENGTH & DIRECTION OF THE MAGNETISM DEPEND ON THE ORIENTATION OF THE VESSEL TO THE EARTH'S OWN MAGNETIC FIELD.

MAGNETISM

PROPERTIES OF ATTRACTION & REPULSION FOUND IN CERTAIN SUBSTANCES

ANCIENT MAGNETISM

POTTERY & BRICK RETAIN THE MAGNETIC PROPERTIES THEY POSSESS WHEN FIRED. OLD BRICKS CAN BE USED TO FIND THE PAST STRENGTHS OF THE EARTH'S MAGNETISM. RESULTS FROM EGYPT SUGGEST THAT FLUCTUATIONS IN THE EARTH'S MAGNETISM MYSTERIOUSLY CORRESPOND WITH FLOOD LEVELS & POPULATION DENSITIES

HOW TO MAKE A SCREWDRIVER MAGNETIC

UNTIL THE DISCOVERY OF ELECTROMAGNETISM IN THE 18TH CENTURY, ALL IRON MAGNETS WERE MADE BY THE IRON BEING STROKED AGAINST LUMPS OF LODESTONE. YOU CAN TRY THIS BY STROKING A MAGNET ALONG A SCREWDRIVER (MAGNETIZED SCREWDRIVERS ARE USEFUL FOR HOLDING SCREWS).

MAGNETIC CITIES

WHEN ELECTRICITY IS PASSED THROUGH A COIL OF WIRE IT BECOMES MAGNETIC. ELECTRIC TRAINS RUNNING ROUND A NETWORK OF UNDERGROUND RAILWAYS PRODUCE A SIMILAR EFFECT. THEY CAN CREATE A MAGNETIC FIELD ON THE SURFACE WHICH DISRUPTS COMPASSES & SCIENTIFIC EXPERIMENTS.

MALARIA

TROPICAL DISEASE CAUSING FEVER & SOMETIMES DEATH

THE LIFE CYCLE OF THE MALARIA PARASITE

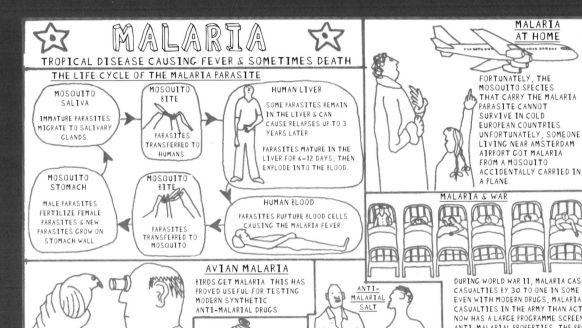

MOSQUITO SALIVA — IMMATURE PARASITES MIGRATE TO SALIVARY GLANDS.

MOSQUITO BITE — PARASITES TRANSFERRED TO HUMANS.

HUMAN LIVER — SOME PARASITES REMAIN IN THE LIVER & CAN CAUSE RELAPSES UP TO 3 YEARS LATER. PARASITES MATURE IN THE LIVER FOR 6-12 DAYS, THEN EXPLODE INTO THE BLOOD.

MOSQUITO STOMACH — MALE PARASITES FERTILIZE FEMALE PARASITES & NEW PARASITES GROW ON STOMACH WALL.

MOSQUITO BITE — PARASITES TRANSFERRED TO MOSQUITO.

HUMAN BLOOD — PARASITES RUPTURE BLOOD CELLS CAUSING THE MALARIA FEVER.

MALARIA AT HOME

FORTUNATELY, THE MOSQUITO SPECIES THAT CARRY THE MALARIA PARASITE CANNOT SURVIVE IN COLD EUROPEAN COUNTRIES. UNFORTUNATELY, SOMEONE LIVING NEAR AMSTERDAM AIRPORT GOT MALARIA FROM A MOSQUITO ACCIDENTALLY CARRIED IN A PLANE.

DDT ERADICATION

DDT IS SPRAYED ON WALLS & DRIES IN SMALL CRYSTALS.

MOSQUITOES REST ON WALLS AFTER FEEDING TO DIGEST THEIR BLOOD MEAL.

DDT STICKS TO HAIRS ON THE MOSQUITOES' FEET & THEY EVENTUALLY DIE.

CRYSTALS ON WALL REMAIN EFFECTIVE FOR 6-12 MONTHS.

DDT RESISTANCE

IN THE 1960S IT WAS THOUGHT THAT MALARIA COULD BE COMPLETELY ERADICATED BY THE EXTENSIVE USE OF DDT. ALTHOUGH PROGRAMMES WERE SUCCESSFUL IN PARTS OF AMERICA & SOUTHERN EUROPE, MANY PARTS OF ASIA HAVE SUFFERED INCREASES IN THE MOSQUITO POPULATION. THE MAIN REASON FOR THIS IS THE GROWING RESISTANCE OF MOSQUITOES TO DDT.

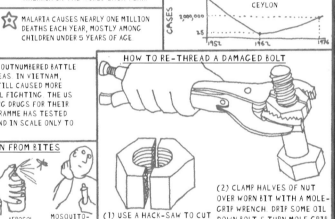

INDIA

CEYLON

☆ IT IS ESTIMATED THAT THERE ARE 350-500 MILLION CASES OF MALARIA IN THE WORLD EACH YEAR.

☆ MALARIA CAUSES NEARLY ONE MILLION DEATHS EACH YEAR, MOSTLY AMONG CHILDREN UNDER 5 YEARS OF AGE.

MALARIA & WAR

DURING WORLD WAR II, MALARIA CASES OUTNUMBERED BATTLE CASUALTIES BY 30 TO ONE IN SOME AREAS. IN VIETNAM, EVEN WITH MODERN DRUGS, MALARIA STILL CAUSED MORE CASUALTIES IN THE ARMY THAN ACTUAL FIGHTING. THE US NOW HAS A LARGE PROGRAMME SCREENING DRUGS FOR THEIR ANTI-MALARIAL PROPERTIES. THE PROGRAMME HAS TESTED WELL OVER 240,000 DRUGS & IS SECOND IN SCALE ONLY TO THE SEARCH FOR ANTI-CANCER DRUGS.

AVIAN MALARIA

BIRDS GET MALARIA. THIS HAS PROVED USEFUL FOR TESTING MODERN SYNTHETIC ANTI-MALARIAL DRUGS.

ANTI-MALARIAL SALT

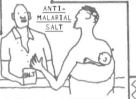

MALARIA WAS SUCCESSFULLY ERADICATED FROM IRAN & GUYANA WHEN ANTI-MALARIAL DRUGS WERE MIXED WITH THE PUBLIC SUPPLY OF COOKING SALT. THESE KILLED ALL THE PARASITES IN THE HUMANS' BLOOD SO NO MOSQUITO COULD BE REINFECTED.

MALARIA & QUININE

NO CURE FOR MALARIA EXISTED UNTIL THE 1600S, WHEN THE BARK OF THE CINCHONA TREE WAS INTRODUCED FROM PERU. QUININE, THE ACTIVE INGREDIENT, IS STILL USED AGAINST CERTAIN TYPES OF MALARIA.

PROTECTION FROM BITES

BURNING PYRETHRUM

MOSQUITO GAUZE ON WINDOWS

MOSQUITO NETS ON BEDS

AEROSOL INSECTICIDES

MOSQUITO-REPELLENT CREAMS

HOW TO RE-THREAD A DAMAGED BOLT

(1) USE A HACK-SAW TO CUT A SUITABLE NUT IN HALF.

(2) CLAMP HALVES OF NUT OVER WORN BIT WITH A MOLE-GRIP WRENCH. DRIP SOME OIL DOWN BOLT & TURN MOLE GRIP TO RECUT THREAD.

MALARIA

☆ MEMORY ☆
THE ABILITY TO REMEMBER EXPERIENCE

REMEMBERING

THE ANCIENT "ART OF MEMORY" WAS INVENTED, ACCORDING TO CICERO, BY SIMONIDES IN 477 BC. THIS ART CONSISTED OF ORGANIZING SYSTEMATICALLY THE MATERIAL TO BE REMEMBERED & LINKING IT WITH VISUAL IMAGES IN THE BRAIN. PEOPLE OFTEN MEMORIZED THEM BY IMAGINING WALKING THROUGH A HOUSE, WITH ROOMS & FURNITURE LINKED TO A KEY PHRASE OF THE SPEECH.

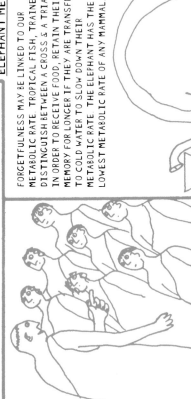

ELEPHANT MEMORY

FORGETFULNESS MAY BE LINKED TO OUR METABOLIC RATE. TROPICAL FISH, TRAINED TO DISTINGUISH BETWEEN A CROSS & A TRIANGLE IN ORDER TO RECEIVE FOOD, RETAIN THEIR MEMORY FOR LONGER IF THEY ARE TRANSFERRED TO COLD WATER TO SLOW DOWN THEIR METABOLIC RATE. THE ELEPHANT HAS THE LOWEST METABOLIC RATE OF ANY MAMMAL.

MORNING MEMORY

TIME OF DAY HAS A STRONG INFLUENCE ON MEMORY. EXPERIMENTS TESTING PEOPLE ON THINGS THAT THEY HAVE JUST LEARNED SHOW THAT SHORT-TERM MEMORY GETS WORSE AS THE DAY PROGRESSES (PRESUMABLY WITH INCREASED TIREDNESS).

HOW TO TEST YOUR VISUAL MEMORY

MOST PEOPLE CAN FORM SHARP "PICTURES" IN THEIR MINDS OF FAMILIAR FACES, OBJECTS & PLACES. HOWEVER, THE DETAILS OF THESE PICTURES ARE EXTREMELY ELUSIVE. FOR EXAMPLE

VISUALIZE A SOLID CUBE BALANCED ON ONE CORNER. IT IS CUT HORIZONTALLY INTO TWO EQUAL HALVES. WHEN THE TOP HALF IS LIFTED OFF, WHAT IS THE SHAPE OF THE CUT SURFACE? (ANSWER TOP LEFT. THE VISUALIZATION OF THE CUBE IS NOT USUALLY VERY HELPFUL.)

FORGETTING

OUR BRAINS HAVE A FINITE TOTAL CAPACITY. FORGETTING ALLOWS US TO ADAPT, MAKING ROOM FOR NEW MEMORIES.

IF WE COULD REMEMBER OUR WHOLE LIVES IN AS MUCH DETAIL AS WE CAN REMEMBER THE LAST HOUR WE WOULD BECOME VERY CONFUSED. IT IS THE PROCESS OF THE "FADING" OF THE IMMEDIATE PAST THAT ORIENTATES US IN TIME.

EVENING MEMORY

TESTS ALSO SHOW THAT LONG-TERM MEMORY IMPROVES AS THE DAY PROGRESSES.

EUREKA!

MEMORY DRUG

STUDENTS TESTED ON THEIR ABILITY TO REMEMBER LISTS OF WORDS IMPROVED THEIR SCORES AFTER TAKING A DRUG CALLED PIRACETAM. THE RESEARCHERS, AT CARDIFF UNIVERSITY, DO NOT KNOW HOW ANY CHEMICAL COULD CAUSE THIS.

EVIDENCE

MANY CRIMINAL CONVICTIONS DEPEND ON THE MEMORY OF WITNESSES. AN EXTENSIVE TRIAL ASKING STUDENTS TO REMEMBER 60 DETAILS OF A PHOTO SHOWS THE ALARMING INACCURACY OF "WITNESS EVIDENCE".

DAYS SINCE SEEING PHOTO	0	5	15	45
AVERAGE QUESTIONS ANSWERED	59	57	57	57
AVERAGE WRONG ANSWERS	8	10	12	13
AVERAGE QUESTIONS SWORN TO	43	39	38	35
AVERAGE WRONG SWORN ANSWERS	3	4	6	7

THREE TIERS

THERE ARE NOW BELIEVED TO BE THREE SORTS OF MEMORY IN OUR BRAIN. SHORT-TERM MEMORY IS STORED AS ELECTRICAL CHARGE, MEDIUM-TERM MEMORY IS STORED AS SODIUM SALTS (CHEMICAL CHANGES), & LONG-TERM MEMORY IS FIXED BY PROTEIN CHANGES.

PROTEIN
CHEMICAL
ELECTRICAL
MEMORY
10 30 60 MINUTES

MOSQUES

VARIETIES

THERE ARE 3 TYPES OF MOSQUE. THE IGDAH IS USED FOR THE TWO ANNUAL FESTIVALS (THE BREAKING OF THE FAST & THE SACRIFICE OF ABRAHAM). IT IS LARGE ENOUGH TO ACCOMMODATE THE WHOLE POPULATION OF A CITY. IT IS USUALLY SIMPLY A LARGE OPEN SPACE WITH A WALL & A MINARET ON ONE SIDE.

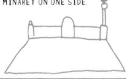

THE MASJID IS USED FOR DAILY PRAYER BY SMALL GROUPS OR INDIVIDUALS. THE ONLY ESSENTIAL ELEMENTS ARE A CLEAN FLOOR & A WALL FACING MECCA.

THE JUMA IS USED FOR THE WEEKLY CONGREGATIONAL SERVICE EVERY FRIDAY. IT IS USUALLY AN ENCLOSED COURTYARD WITH A FOUNTAIN FOR WASHING, A MINARET FOR CALLING THE FAITHFUL & A PULPIT (MINBAR) FOR THE WEEKLY SERMON.

SERMONS

IT IS UNLIKELY THAT ARCHITECTURE WAS EVER CONSIDERED TO BE A "PROFESSION" IN THE ISLAMIC WORLD. ARCHITECTS' NAMES RARELY APPEAR ON INSCRIPTIONS OR DOCUMENTS. MOST OF THE DETAILED DESIGN & DECORATION WAS PROBABLY LEFT TO THE MASTER BUILDERS. THERE IS SOME EVIDENCE THAT THE OUTLINE PLANS WERE DEVISED BY MEMBERS OF THE RULING CLASS WITH A MATHEMATICAL INCLINATION & REGARDED SIMPLY AS A HOBBY.

ISLAMIC ARCHITECTS

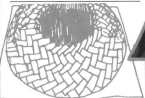

THE PREACHER (OR IMAM) SOMETIMES GIVES HIS SERMONS FROM A LOWER STEP OF THE PULPIT. THE EMPTY CANOPIED SPACE IS LEFT VACANT FOR THE ABSENT PROPHET (MUHAMMAD).

DOMES WITHOUT SUPPORTS

WOOD WAS NOT ALWAYS AVAILABLE IN THE ISLAMIC WORLD, SO AN INGENIOUS METHOD WAS DEVELOPED FOR CONSTRUCTING DOMES & VAULTS WITHOUT THE USE OF A TEMPORARY SUPPORTING WOODEN FRAMEWORK. THE BRICKS WERE LAID AT AN ANGLE, SO THEY WOULD PRECARIOUSLY SUPPORT ONE ANOTHER UNTIL A COMPLETE COURSE HAD BEEN LAID.

CHANTING

THE JEWS USED A RAM'S-HORN TRUMPET TO CALL THE FAITHFUL TO WORSHIP. THE CHRISTIANS USED BELLS & WOODEN CLAPPERS. MUHAMMAD IS SAID TO HAVE FOUND BOTH CALLS CACOPHONOUS & UNPLEASANT. THE IDEA OF A CHANTED PRAYER SUMMONING THE FAITHFUL CAME TO HIM FROM ALLAH IN A VISION.

DECORATION

EARLY ISLAMIC DECORATION IS SIMILAR IN STYLE TO THAT OF THE LATE-CLASSICAL WORLD. GRADUALLY, THE NATURAL FOLIAGE IN THE CLASSICAL STYLE BECAME INCREASINGLY ABSTRACT. FROM THE 1400S, WITH AN INCREASING VARIETY OF MINERAL PIGMENTS AVAILABLE, BRIGHTLY COLOURED TILES & MOSAICS BEGAN TO REPLACE CARVED RELIEF DECORATION.

REINFORCED COLUMNS

UNTIL THE 1400S, THE ISLAMIC BUILDERS DID NOT GENERALLY QUARRY THEIR OWN STONE, PREFERRING TO REUSE MATERIALS FROM EARLIER BUILDINGS. THE USE OF SUCH STONES, USUALLY OF ILL-ASSORTED SIZES, LED TO THE ELABORATE PRACTICE OF REINFORCING HOLLOW COLUMNS BY POURING MOLTEN LEAD DOWN THE MIDDLE OR BY INSERTING IRON BANDS.

HOW TO MAKE A SET OF CHIMES

TIE A SELECTION OF LARGE NAILS OF VARIOUS SIZES TO A METAL COAT HANGER WITH COTTON THREAD AS ABOVE. PLAY BY HITTING NAILS WITH AN EXTRA NAIL.

MOSQUES

73

MUMMIES
EMBALMED OR OTHERWISE-PRESERVED DEAD BODIES

MUMMIYA

THE WORD "MUMMY" COMES FROM THE ARABIC WORD "MUMMIYA", WHICH MEANS RAW PITCH. PITCH OR RESIN WAS USED IN EMBALMING FOR GLUING THE LAYERS OF BANDAGES TOGETHER & THE RESULTING OBJECT CAME TO BE CALLED A MUMMIYA.

BANDAGING
ONE MUMMY UNWRAPPED RECENTLY WAS COVERED IN A TOTAL OF 3 MILES OF 7CM-WIDE LINEN BANDAGE.

PRESERVATION
BODIES BURIED IN SMALL ENCLOSED EARTH TOMBS WILL SURVIVE INTACT IN EGYPT WITHOUT ANY EMBALMING TREATMENT, OWING TO THE UNIQUE DRYNESS & STERILITY OF THE SOIL COMBINED WITH THE CONSTANT HEAT. IT WAS ONLY WHEN THE TOMBS BECAME LARGER, TO ACCOMMODATE POSSESSIONS, THAT BODIES WERE FOUND TO BE ROTTING. MUMMIFICATION WAS ADOPTED TO PREVENT THIS.

THE PROCESS
1) REMOVE LUNGS, LIVER, INTESTINES & STOMACH FROM BODY, & PLACE IN JARS.
2) COVER BODY INSIDE & OUT WITH NATRON (A TYPE OF SALT) FOR 40 DAYS. THEN WASH & COVER WITH OILS.
3) PAD OUT BODY WHERE REQUIRED TO RESTORE LIFELIKE APPEARANCE.
4) SEW ON FINGERNAILS (OTHERWISE THEY FALL OFF) & INSERT ARTIFICIAL EYES.
5) PAINT IN RED-OCHRE & ROUGE PAINT ALL OVER.
6) WRAP IN BANDAGES SOAKED IN RESIN OR PITCH.

REMOVING THE ENTRAILS
A SCRIBE MARKED A LINE ON THE LEFT SIDE OF THE BODY, BENEATH THE RIBS, ALONG WHICH THE PARASCHISTES, OR RIPPER OF THE DISTRICT (AN OFFICER OF LOW CLASS), MADE A DEEP INCISION WITH A CRUDE STONE KNIFE. HE WAS THEN PELTED WITH STONES & CURSED. HE IS ALWAYS SHOWN SMALLER THAN THE OTHER FIGURES IN EGYPTIAN PICTURES OF EMBALMING BECAUSE THE RELATIVE SIZES OF THE FIGURES ALWAYS DENOTE THEIR RELATIVE STATUS.

HOW TO MIND-READ

HAND A COIN TO A FRIEND & BLINDFOLD YOURSELF. ASK HIM TO PUT THE COIN IN ONE HAND & HOLD THIS HAND ABOVE HIS HEAD FOR 30 SECONDS, CONCENTRATING HARD ON THE COIN. NOW ASK HIM TO HOLD OUT BOTH HANDS. REMOVE THE BLINDFOLD & YOU CAN TELL WHICH HAND CONTAINS THE COIN. BLOOD TENDS TO DRAIN SLIGHTLY FROM THE UPHELD HAND, MAKING IT A DISTINCTLY PALER COLOUR THAN THE OTHER HAND.

FINDING A MUMMY'S DESCENDANTS
A DR STASTNY, OF TEXAS UNIVERSITY, DEVELOPED A METHOD OF ANALYSING FRAGMENTS OF MUMMIES, WITH THE OBJECT OF RELATING MUMMIFIED INDIVIDUALS TO PRESENT-DAY PEOPLE. DIFFERENT TRIBES, ESPECIALLY IN ISOLATED PLACES, HAVE CLEAR ANTIGEN PROFILES. HE WORKED ON PERUVIAN MUMMIES, ATTEMPTING TO DETERMINE WHETHER THE EGYPTIANS EVER CROSSED TO AMERICA.

MUMMIES RISING FROM THE DEAD
THE REASON WHY THE EGYPTIANS MUMMIFIED THEIR DEAD WAS PROBABLY BECAUSE THEY BELIEVED THAT AT SOME FUTURE DATE THE DEAD WOULD COME TO LIFE AGAIN, IF ONLY THEY COULD BE PREVENTED FROM ROTTING AWAY. TO ENSURE COMFORT ON THEIR RETURN THEIR POSSESSIONS & SOMETIMES EVEN MUMMIFIED JOINTS OF MEAT WERE SEALED INSIDE THEIR TOMBS.

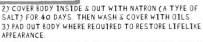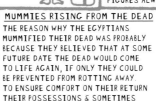

MUSIC

THE ART OF EXPRESSION IN SOUND

SILENT MUSIC

THE INDIANS TRADITIONALLY BELIEVE THAT THERE ARE TWO TYPES OF SOUND. THE FIRST IS "UNSTRUCK SOUND", THE MUSIC OF THE GODS, INAUDIBLE TO MEN, & CREATED BY VIBRATION OF THE ETHER. THE SECOND IS "STRUCK SOUND", MAN-MADE MUSIC, CREATED BY VIBRATION OF THE AIR. A TUNE IS SAID TO RESULT FROM A UNION BETWEEN PHYSICAL BREATH & THE FIRE OF INTELLECT.

THE INDIAN SCALE

THE INDIANS USE A 7-NOTE SCALE WITH THE SAME INTERVALS AS THE EUROPEAN MAJOR SCALE. THE NOTES ARE CALLED SA (THE KEY NOTE), RE, GA, MA, PA, DHA & NI. EACH NOTE REPRESENTS A PARTICULAR MOOD: SA & MA = TRANQUILLITY, RE = ANGER, GA & DHA = SOLEMNITY. PA = JOY & NI = SORROW. THE NOTES ARE ALSO LIKENED TO ANIMAL NOISES, E.G. RE = A COW'S MOO, NI = AN ELEPHANT'S TRUMPET, ETC.

THE CHINESE FOUNDATION

CHINESE MUSIC IS BASED ON A FOUNDATION NOTE WHICH WAS HELD TO BE ONE OF THE ETERNAL PRINCIPLES OF THE UNIVERSE. GREAT CARE HAD TO BE TAKEN TO DETERMINE THE EXACT PITCH OF THIS NOTE TO ENSURE THE WELL-BEING OF THE STATE. IN THE FIRST CENTURY BC AN IMPERIAL OFFICE OF MUSIC WAS SET UP TO STANDARDIZE THE NOTE. IT WAS DECREED TO BE THE PITCH OBTAINED FROM BLOWING THROUGH A PIPE WITH A HEIGHT EQUAL TO 90 GRAINS OF MILLET OF AVERAGE SIZE LAID END TO END.

THE ORIGIN OF THE FLAT

IN THE 6TH CENTURY AD ST GREGORY SELECTED A SCALE OF 8 NOTES FOR USE IN CHURCH MUSIC. THESE WERE ADHERED TO FOR SOME 10 CENTURIES WITH ONE EXCEPTION. THE NOTE B WAS SOMETIMES FELT TO PRODUCE A "FALSE RELATION OF SOUND" CALLED THE TRITONUS, SO THEY SOMETIMES USED B FLAT. THIS IS THE ORIGIN OF OUR SYMBOL FOR A FLAT NOTE, SINCE THIS CHANGE WAS INDICATED BY WRITING A SMALL B INSTEAD OF A CAPITAL B.

CHINESE INSTRUMENTS

THE CHINESE CLASSIFY THEIR INSTRUMENTS ACCORDING TO 8 CLASSES OF MATERIAL FROM WHICH THE NOISE STEMS.

METAL	STONE	SILK	BAMBOO	WOOD	SKIN	GOURD	CLAY
BELLS	CHIMES	STRINGS	FLUTES	PERCUSSIVE EFFECTS	DRUMS	WINDBOX FOR REED INSTRUMENT	PIPES

FOSSILIZATION OF MUSIC

THE ISLAMIC WORLD NEVER DEVELOPED A SYSTEM OF MUSIC-WRITING. PERFORMERS IMPROVISED, WITHIN DEFINED LIMITS, BUT TO PLAY THE SAME PIECE TWICE IN THE SAME WAY WAS UNTHINKABLE. ANY SYSTEM OF MUSIC-WRITING WAS REGARDED AS DANGEROUS & LIABLE TO FOSSILIZE THE INTERPRETATION.

HOW TO FIND THE HEIGHT OF A CHURCH SPIRE

FIND A STICK TALLER THAN YOURSELF & MARK IT LEVEL WITH THE TOP OF YOUR HEAD. ASK SOMEONE TO MOVE SLOWLY FORWARD HOLDING STICK TILL, WITH YOUR EYE AT GROUND LEVEL, THE MARK ON THE STICK IS IN LINE WITH THE TOP OF THE SPIRE (SEE LEFT). COUNT THE PACES FROM YOUR EYE TO THE STICK & TO THE BASE OF THE SPIRE. YOU CAN NOW FIND THE HEIGHT OF THE SPIRE FROM YOUR OWN HEIGHT USING THIS SUM:

(YOUR HEIGHT) ✗ (PACES TO SPIRE) ÷ (PACES TO STICK)

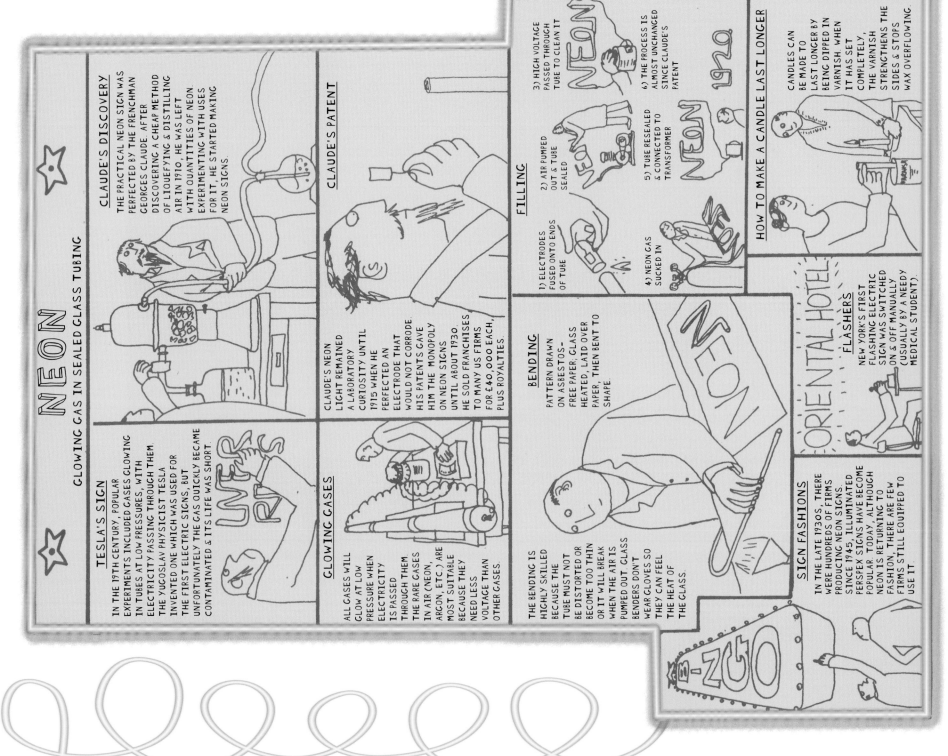

NEON

GLOWING GAS IN SEALED GLASS TUBING

CLAUDE'S DISCOVERY

THE PRACTICAL NEON SIGN WAS PERFECTED BY THE FRENCHMAN GEORGES CLAUDE. AFTER DISCOVERING A CHEAP METHOD OF LIQUEFYING & DISTILLING AIR IN 1910, HE WAS LEFT WITH QUANTITIES OF NEON EXPERIMENTING WITH USES FOR IT, HE STARTED MAKING NEON SIGNS.

CLAUDE'S PATENT

CLAUDE'S NEON LIGHT REMAINED A LABORATORY CURIOSITY UNTIL 1915 WHEN HE PERFECTED AN ELECTRODE THAT WOULD NOT CORRODE. HIS PATENTS GAVE HIM THE MONOPOLY ON NEON SIGNS UNTIL ABOUT 1930. HE SOLD FRANCHISES TO MANY US FIRMS FOR £40,000 EACH, PLUS ROYALTIES.

TESLA'S SIGN

IN THE 19TH CENTURY, POPULAR EXPERIMENTS INCLUDED GASES GLOWING IN TUBES AT LOW PRESSURES, WITH ELECTRICITY PASSING THROUGH THEM. THE YUGOSLAV PHYSICIST TESLA INVENTED ONE WHICH WAS USED FOR THE FIRST ELECTRIC SIGNS, BUT UNFORTUNATELY THE GAS QUICKLY BECAME CONTAMINATED & ITS LIFE WAS SHORT

GLOWING GASES

ALL GASES WILL GLOW AT LOW PRESSURE WHEN ELECTRICITY IS PASSED THROUGH THEM. THE RARE GASES IN AIR (NEON, ARGON, ETC.) ARE MOST SUITABLE BECAUSE THEY NEED LESS VOLTAGE THAN OTHER GASES.

FILLING

1) ELECTRODES FUSED ONTO ENDS OF TUBE

2) AIR PUMPED OUT & TUBE SEALED

3) HIGH VOLTAGE PASSED THROUGH TUBE TO CLEAN IT

4) NEON GAS SUCKED IN

5) TUBE RESEALED & CONNECTED TO TRANSFORMER

6) THE PROCESS IS ALMOST UNCHANGED SINCE CLAUDE'S PATENT

NEON 1920

HOW TO MAKE A CANDLE LAST LONGER

CANDLES CAN BE MADE TO LAST LONGER BY BEING DIPPED IN VARNISH. WHEN IT HAS SET COMPLETELY, THE VARNISH STRENGTHENS THE SIDES & STOPS WAX OVERFLOWING.

BENDING

PATTERN DRAWN ON ASBESTOS-FREE PAPER; GLASS HEATED, LAID OVER PAPER, THEN BENT TO SHAPE.

THE BENDING IS HIGHLY SKILLED BECAUSE THE TUBE MUST NOT BE DISTORTED OR BECOME TOO THIN OR IT WILL BREAK WHEN THE AIR IS PUMPED OUT. GLASS BENDERS DON'T WEAR GLOVES SO THEY CAN FEEL THE HEAT OF THE GLASS.

FLASHERS

NEW YORK'S FIRST FLASHING ELECTRIC SIGN WAS SWITCHED ON & OFF MANUALLY (USUALLY BY A NEEDY MEDICAL STUDENT).

ORIENTAL HOTEL

SIGN FASHIONS

IN THE LATE 1930s, THERE WERE HUNDREDS OF FIRMS PRODUCING NEON SIGNS. SINCE 1945, ILLUMINATED PERSPEX SIGNS HAVE BECOME POPULAR. TODAY, ALTHOUGH NEON IS RETURNING TO FASHION, THERE ARE FEW FIRMS STILL EQUIPPED TO USE IT.

NERVES

FIBRES CONNECTING THE BRAIN TO ALL PARTS OF THE BODY

NERVES AS PIPES

RENAISSANCE PHILOSOPHERS & MAGICIANS THOUGHT THAT IMPULSES OF THE MIND (OR SOUL) WERE TRANSLATED INTO MOVEMENTS BY ETHER – A FIFTH MEDIATING ELEMENT LINKING MIND & BODY. THE BRAIN & NERVES WERE THOUGHT TO BE LIKE A CISTERN & PIPES DISTRIBUTING THE ETHER.

NERVES AS WIRES

NERVES SEND SIGNALS BETWEEN THE BRAIN & THE MUSCLES & SENSES, USUALLY VIA THE SPINAL CORD, WHICH ACTS AS A SORT OF JUNCTION BOX.

ELECTRIC NERVES

UNTIL THE 18TH CENTURY, LIGHTNING & STATIC ELECTRICITY WERE THE ONLY KNOWN ELECTRICAL PHENOMENA. THE DISCOVERY, BY THE ITALIAN SCIENTIST GALVANI (C. 1780), THAT FROGS' LEGS COULD BE MADE TO MOVE BY THE APPLICATION OF ELECTRICITY TO THE NERVES CAME AS A COMPLETE SURPRISE.

STRONG SIGNAL

WEAK SIGNAL

NERVE PULSES

NERVES CONTROL MUSCLES BY VARYING THE FREQUENCY OF THE IMPULSES THEY SEND, NOT BY VARYING THE POWER OF THE INDIVIDUAL IMPULSE. IMPULSES FROM THE SENSE ORGANS WORK IN THE SAME WAY.

AT JUNCTIONS, NERVES RELEASE CHEMICALS CALLED NEUROTRANSMITTERS WHICH STIMULATE NEIGHBOURING CELLS. ABOUT 15 DIFFERENT TYPES ARE KNOWN. ONE IS MUCH LIKE CURARE (THE PARALYSING POISON). ANOTHER IS SIMILAR TO MORPHINE (THE ADDICTIVE PAIN-KILLING DRUG).

NEUROTRANSMITTERS

GIANT NERVES

GIANT SQUIDS ARE USEFUL IN NERVE RESEARCH BECAUSE THEY HAVE THE LARGEST NERVE FIBRES OF ANY KNOWN ANIMAL – UP TO 2CM IN DIAMETER (1,000 TIMES THICKER THAN HUMAN NERVES).

MYSTERY GROWTH

IN THE FOETUS, NERVES GROW OUTWARDS FROM THE SPINAL COLUMN. HOW THEY NAVIGATE TO THEIR CORRECT LIMB IS THE SUBJECT OF MUCH RESEARCH BUT REMAINS A MYSTERY.

SIXTH SENSE

THE NERVES WITHIN MUSCLES ARE SOMETIMES REGARDED AS A SIXTH SENSE. THESE NERVES SENSE THE POSITION OF EACH MUSCLE, WHICH IS HOW WE MANAGE TO MOVE WITH GREAT ACCURACY, EVEN IN THE DARK. IT IS THESE NERVES, TOO, THAT TRIGGER REFLEXES LIKE THE JERK OF THE LEG IN RESPONSE TO A BLOW ON THE KNEE.

ELECTRIC GROWTH

ELECTRIC FIELDS DRAMATICALLY AFFECT THE SPEED AT WHICH NERVES GROW. FOR EXAMPLE, THEY WILL CAUSE A FROG TO REGROW AN AMPUTATED LIMB TWICE AS FAST.

HOW TO LEVITATE

GET 4 FRIENDS TO PRESS DOWN ON YOUR HEAD. AFTER 10 SEC, CLOSE YOUR EYES & ASK FRIENDS TO PRETEND TO LIFT YOU WITH THEIR FINGERS AS SHOWN.

THIS CONFUSES THE NERVES WITHIN THE MUSCLES (SEE "SIXTH SENSE", ABOVE) & YOU WILL FEEL AS IF YOU HAVE BEEN LIFTED HIGH INTO THE AIR.

NICKEL

A WHITE MAGNETIC DUCTILE METAL

EMBEDDED NICKEL

NICKEL IS ONE OF THE MOST ABUNDANT ELEMENTS ON EARTH. HOWEVER, OF THE ESTIMATED 160 BILLION TONNES ONLY 0.001% IS CONTAINED IN THE EARTH'S CRUST. THE REST IS LOCKED UP IN THE EARTH'S CENTRAL CORE, WHICH IS BELIEVED TO CONSIST OF A MIXTURE OF IRON & NICKEL.

FALSE COPPER

NICKEL GOT ITS NAME FROM THE GERMAN "KUPFERNIKKEL" (MEANING FALSE COPPER) AFTER IT HAD BEEN FOUND IN VARIOUS GERMAN COPPER MINES.

CHINESE NICKEL

VARIOUS EARLY CIVILIZATIONS MANUFACTURED BRONZE FROM ORES WITH UP TO 10% NICKEL. THE CHINESE MADE A METAL FROM AN ORE WITH A HIGH NICKEL CONTENT. THEY CALLED IT PAI-THUNG (WHITE COPPER). THIS WAS PROBABLY THE FIRST CUPRONICKEL ALLOY. IT WAS THE ARRIVAL OF BOWLS MADE OF PAI-THUNG IN THE WEST THAT STIMULATED RESEARCH INTO THE UNUSED GERMAN KUPFERNIKKEL ORE. THE FIRST USE OF NICKEL ALLOY IN THE WEST WAS FOR CUTLERY, IN ABOUT 1830.

SICKLY NICKEL MINERS

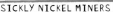

IN THE EARLY GERMAN MINES THE EXTRACTION OF NICKEL ORE WAS A DANGEROUS BUSINESS AS IT ALSO CONTAINED SOME ARSENIC. MINERS WERE ADVISED TO WEAR LONG LEATHER BOOTS, GLOVES & VEILS TO MINIMIZE CONTACT. SMELTING THE ORE WAS ALSO DANGEROUS (FUMES OF ARSENIC WERE GIVEN OFF). THE FOREMAN TRADITIONALLY ATE BUTTER WHILE WORKING, AS PREVENTIVE MEDICINE.

BATTLESHIP ARMOUR

NICKEL WAS PRODUCED IN RELATIVELY SMALL QUANTITIES UNTIL THE 1890S WHEN IT WAS FOUND THAT ADDING A SMALL PERCENTAGE TO STEEL PRODUCED A PLATE WITH GREATLY SUPERIOR SHELL-RESISTANT PROPERTIES. VAST NICKEL-RICH DEPOSITS IN CANADA WERE OPENED UP, REFINED & INCORPORATED IN THE ARMOUR PLATE USED FOR ALL THE WORLD WAR I BATTLESHIPS.

NICHROME

NICHROME IS A NICKEL & CHROME ALLOY WHICH HAS A PARTICULARLY HIGH RESISTANCE TO ELECTRICITY. IT IS USED FOR THE ELEMENTS OF ELECTRIC FIRES, IRONS & TOASTERS.

CHROMIUM NICKEL STAINLESS STEEL

CHROMIUM NICKEL STAINLESS STEEL IS ONE OF THE MOST CORROSION-RESISTANT ALLOYS KNOWN. IT IS USED, AMONG OTHER THINGS, FOR CONCENTRATED NITRIC ACID STORAGE TANKS.

INVAR

INVAR IS A USEFUL NICKEL IRON ALLOY WHICH DOES NOT EXPAND WHEN HEATED. IT IS USED FOR ACCURATE RULERS & LENS MOUNTINGS. (WITH A SLIGHTLY LOWER NICKEL CONTENT, THE THERMAL EXPANSION EQUALS THAT OF GLASS.)

MONEL

MONEL IS A NICKEL COPPER ALLOY WHICH REVOLUTIONIZED THE MANUFACTURE OF PERMANENT MAGNETS IN THE 1930S, ABSORBING & RETAINING FAR MORE MAGNETISM THAN ANY PREVIOUS MATERIAL.

COINAGE

CUPRO-NICKEL COINS ARE WIDELY USED. THEY WERE PARTICULARLY WARMLY WELCOMED BY THE FIJIANS. THESE ISLANDERS HAD AN AVERSION TO THE TASTE OF THEIR PREVIOUS BRONZE COINAGE (IN THE ABSENCE OF POCKET OR PURSE THEY TRADITIONALLY CARRIED MONEY IN THEIR MOUTHS).

HOW TO FLOAT A BOATER

PUT THE BOATER UPSIDE DOWN ON SMOOTH SURFACE. SPIN IT ROUND WITH FOREFINGER. WHEN GOING FAST ENOUGH, RAISE FINGER & THE BOATER WILL FLOAT.

☆ NYLON ☆

COPOLYMER OF DICARBOXYLIC ACIDS & DIAMINES

DISCOVERY

NYLON WAS INVENTED IN AMERICA IN 1930 BY W. CAROTHERS, A CHEMIST. HE SUCCEEDED IN PRODUCING THE FIRST MAN-MADE CHEMICAL TO CONTAIN LONG-CHAIN MOLECULES (SIMILAR TO THOSE IN NATURAL FIBRES).

ONE MONTH LATER HIS ASSISTANT DISCOVERED THAT FROM THIS CHEMICAL (A GLUEY MASS) IT WAS POSSIBLE TO PULL OUT A FIBRE.

UNFORTUNATELY, THIS FIRST FIBRE WAS EASILY MELTED OR DISSOLVED & THE COMMERCIAL VARIETY (NYLON) WAS NOT PERFECTED FOR ANOTHER 7 YEARS.

CAROTHERS NEVER LIVED TO SEE THE SUCCESS OF HIS DISCOVERY. HE SUFFERED FROM DEPRESSION & COMMITTED SUICIDE IN 1937.

NYLON BRISTLE

THE FIRST NYLON PRODUCT WAS TOOTHBRUSH BRISTLE (1938).

PRODUCTION

ABOUT 10% OF ALL FABRICS TODAY ARE MADE OF NYLON. WORLD PRODUCTION IS ABOUT 2.5 MILLION TONNES A YEAR.

"NATURAL LOOK" NYLON

MOST NYLON FABRICS ARE MADE OF NYLON FILAMENTS WHICH HAVE BEEN CHOPPED INTO SHORT UNEQUAL LENGTHS & THEN SPUN TO MAKE A YARN (LIKE NATURAL FIBRES).

FILAMENTS

CHOPPED FILAMENTS

SPUN CHOPPED FILAMENTS

SOLID NYLON

NYLON IS NOT ONLY USED FOR FILAMENTS. IT CAN ALSO BE CAST INTO SOLID OBJECTS INCLUDING SHOE HEELS, FOOD BOXES & ELECTRIC-DRILL CASINGS. IT IS ALSO USED FOR GEARS THAT ARE INACCESSIBLE & CANNOT BE LUBRICATED.

HOW TO DO A SIMPLE CARD TRICK

TURN BOTTOM CARD OF PACK BACK TO FRONT. ASK FRIEND TO PICK CARD. SECRETLY TURN PACK OVER. NOW ASK FRIEND TO MEMORIZE THE CARD & REPLACE IT. SHUFFLE PACK. THE "BOTTOM" CARD & CHOSEN CARD WILL BE THE ONLY ONES BACK TO FRONT.

TOUGH NYLON

NYLON FIBRES ARE VERY TOUGH. EVEN BULLET-PROOF VESTS CAN BE MADE OF NYLON.

STRETCHING NYLON

THE LONG-CHAIN MOLECULES IN NYLON ARE NORMALLY ARRANGED AT RANDOM. HOWEVER, IF A NYLON ROD IS STRETCHED TO A THIN FILAMENT, THE LONG MOLECULES LINE UP & LOCK INTO EACH OTHER. THIS IS WHAT GIVES NYLON FILAMENTS THEIR STRENGTH.

RAW NYLON MOLECULES

STRETCHED NYLON MOLECULES

SHINY NYLON

NYLON FILAMENTS (& HENCE NYLON CLOTHES) ARE NATURALLY SHINY. HOWEVER, A WHITE POWDER (TITANIUM DIOXIDE) IS OFTEN ADDED TO THE CHEMICAL MIX TO MAKE MATT FILAMENTS.

COLD NYLON

NYLON GARMENTS TEND TO FEEL COLD WHEN FIRST PUT ON. THIS IS BECAUSE NYLON IS AN INSULATOR (& THUS WARMS UP SLOWLY) & BECAUSE ITS SMOOTH SURFACE INCREASES THE AREA OF SKIN CONTACT.

NYLON CRIMP

NYLON FILAMENTS CAN BE "CRIMPED". ONE METHOD (USED FOR ACRILAN & ORLON) IS TO SPIN A MIXTURE OF HIGHLY STRETCHED & UNSTRETCHED FILAMENTS. WHEN THIS IS HEATED, THE HIGHLY STRETCHED FILAMENTS RELAX & SHRINK, CAUSING THE YARN TO "CRIMP".

NATURAL CRIMP

MOST NATURAL FIBRES ARE WAVY OR "CRIMPED". THIS CREATES FABRICS THAT HAVE A LARGE AMOUNT OF AIR TRAPPED IN THEM, GIVING GOOD INSULATION & MOISTURE ABSORPTION.

NYLON STOCKINGS WERE LAUNCHED SIMULTANEOUSLY THROUGHOUT THE USA ON 15 MAY 1940. 12M GIANT STOCKINGED LEGS WERE BUILT FOR THE OCCASION. IN THE FIRST YEAR 64 MILLION PAIRS OF NYLONS WERE SOLD.

OBESITY

ABNORMAL FATNESS

PHYSIOLOGY v. PSYCHOLOGY

THERE IS AN UNRESOLVED DEBATE AMONG SCIENTISTS ABOUT WHETHER OBESE PEOPLE OVEREAT BECAUSE OF A BIOLOGICAL FAULT IN THEIR MAKE-UP, OR THROUGH A PSYCHOLOGICAL NEED FOR COMFORT

APPETITE & FULL STOMACHS

SOME DOCTORS BELIEVE THAT MODERN CONVENIENCE FOODS (HIGH IN SUGAR, PROTEIN & FATS) ARE THE ROOT CAUSE OF OBESITY. THEY ARE SUCH CONCENTRATED SOURCES OF ENERGY THAT THE BODY'S ENERGY REQUIREMENTS ARE MET BEFORE THE STOMACH FEELS FULL. HOWEVER, DIETS THAT INCLUDE UNABSORBABLE ROUGHAGE (WHICH MAKES THE STOMACH FEEL FULL) ARE NOT VERY SUCCESSFUL IN PROMOTING WEIGHT LOSS. IT APPEARS THAT THE ABSORPTION OF FOOD IS ESSENTIAL IN SATISFYING HUNGER.

APPETITE & ENERGY

IN ONE US STUDY, VOLUNTEERS WERE FED INTRAVENOUSLY WITH 2,000 CALORIES EVERY NIGHT. THIS HAD NO EFFECT ON THEIR DAYTIME APPETITE, SUGGESTING THAT CALORIE INTAKE IS AN UNRELIABLE REGULATOR OF APPETITE

OBESITY & NUTRITION

FOETUSES EXPOSED TO INSUFFICIENT NUTRITION DURING THE FIRST 6 MONTHS OF PREGNANCY ARE MORE LIKELY TO GROW UP TO BE FATTER THAN NORMAL. THOSE EXPOSED DURING THE LAST 3 MONTHS ARE MORE LIKELY TO BE THINNER THAN NORMAL. POOR NUTRITION IN EARLY PREGNANCY AFFECTS THE HYPOTHALAMUS WHICH CONTROLS GROWTH. POOR NUTRITION IN LATE PREGNANCY REDUCES THE NUMBER OF FAT CELLS CREATED

OBESITY & METABOLISM

ONE CURRENT THEORY ON OBESITY IS THAT FAT PEOPLE ARE METABOLICALLY TOO EFFICIENT, SO THEY DO NOT BURN UP SO MUCH ENERGY. THIS RAISES THE POSSIBILITY OF DISCOVERING A DRUG TO INCREASE ENERGY CONSUMPTION AND SO CURE OBESITY.

DIETING & BINGES

IN A STUDY AT WEST VIRGINIA UNIVERSITY, SUBJECTS WERE GIVEN A 500-CALORIE MILK DRINK, BUT SOME WERE TOLD THAT IT WAS A SPECIAL LOW-CALORIE DRINK. THE SUBJECTS WERE THEN ASKED TO SAMPLE 3 ICE-CREAMS, UNDER THE ILLUSION THAT THE OBJECT OF THE EXPERIMENT WAS TO TEST THE FLAVOURS. THE REAL EXPERIMENT WAS TO MEASURE HOW MUCH ICE-CREAM THEY ATE. THE RESULT WAS THAT SUBJECTS WHO WERE ON A DIET & WHO ALSO HAD BEEN TOLD THAT THE DRINK WAS HIGH-CALORIE ATE MORE OF THE ICE-CREAM. THEY SEEMED TO BE TAKING THE ATTITUDE "IT'S TOO LATE NOW, SO I MIGHT AS WELL ENJOY MYSELF PROPERLY". THE RESEARCHERS SUGGEST THAT AN AWARENESS OF THIS REACTION MIGHT HELP MANY OBESE PEOPLE TO DIET.

THE MOST OBESE

THE WORLD'S HEAVIEST MAN WAS PROBABLY MANUEL URIBE OF MEXICO, WHO WEIGHED 560KG AT HIS PEAK.

OLYMPICS

THE PANKRATION

THE MOST DANGEROUS EVENT WAS THE PANKRATION, ORIGINALLY A SERIES OF DUELS TO THE DEATH. THE NECESSITY OF KILLING EVERY OPPONENT IN THIS EVENT LATER CEASED, BUT THE FIGHTS REMAINED VICIOUS, SINCE GOUGING, LIMB BREAKING & STRANGLING WERE ALL PERMITTED. THE GOLD MEDAL OFTEN HAD TO BE AWARDED POSTHUMOUSLY.

MARRIED WOMEN

ONLY MEN OF PURE GREEK DESCENT WERE ALLOWED TO COMPETE. MARRIED WOMEN WERE NOT EVEN PERMITTED TO WATCH. ANY UNFORTUNATE ENOUGH TO BE DISCOVERED WERE RITUALLY THROWN OVER A CLIFF.

THE STADE

THE WORD "STADIUM" COMES FROM THE GREEK "STADE". THIS WAS THE LENGTH OF THE RUNNING TRACK AT OLYMPIA (192.27M). IT WAS SAID TO HAVE BEEN MEASURED BY HERCULES AS BEING THE DISTANCE HE COULD WALK WHILE HOLDING HIS BREATH.

THE PAGAN RITES

THE GREEK OLYMPICS WERE HELD FROM BC 776 UNTIL 393 AD, WHEN THEY WERE STOPPED BY THE ROMAN EMPEROR, THEODOSIUS. YEARS AFTER BANNING ALL PAGAN RELIGIONS HE DECIDED THAT THE GAMES WERE A PAGAN FESTIVAL, WITH SOME JUSTIFICATION. THE GAMES STARTED WITH THE JUDGES, THE HELLANODIKAI, DIPPING THEIR HANDS IN BLOOD, WHILE TAKING A SOLEMN OATH AGAINST CHEATING. THE GAMES ENDED WITH A DECIDEDLY PAGAN THANKSGIVING.

ACHILLES

THETIS DROPPED HER SON ACHILLES IN THE WATER OF THE RIVER STYX. THIS MADE HIM INVULNERABLE. UNFORTUNATELY, SHE DID NOT WANT TO GET WET. THE PART OF HIS HEEL BY WHICH SHE WAS HOLDING HIM REMAINED DRY & THEREFORE VULNERABLE – HENCE THE PROVERBIAL ACHILLES HEEL.

ATHELIOS

THE WORD "ATHLETE" COMES FROM THE GREEK KING ATHELIOS. HE DEPOSED ANOTHER KING (CLYMENOS) WHO HAD ERECTED AN ALTAR AT OLYMPIA & WAS PROMOTING GAMES THERE. ATHELIOS LIKED THE GAMES SO MUCH THAT HE OFFERED HIS KINGDOM TO WHICHEVER OF HIS SONS RAN FASTEST IN THE GAMES.

NERO'S GAMES

IN AD 67 THE EMPEROR NERO BRIBED THE JUDGES TO POSTPONE THE GAMES SINCE HE HOPED HE WOULD HAVE A BETTER CHANCE OF WINNING IF HE HAD AN EXTRA YEAR'S TRAINING. DESPITE BEING THROWN FROM HIS 10-HORSE CHARIOT & BEING UNABLE TO REMOUNT, HE WAS AWARDED THE PRIZE. HE ALSO WON CONTESTS FOR SINGING & ACTING.

☆ ORANGES ☆

ROUND GOLD-COLOURED FRUIT OF CERTAIN CITRUS TREES

FERTILIZING ORANGES

CITRUS TREES ARE MONOECIOUS – BOTH SEXES ARE IN THE SAME BLOSSOM. IN SOME VARIETIES THE POLLEN & OVULES ARE ALWAYS IMPERFECT SO SELF-FERTILIZATION RARELY OCCURS. THESE TREES CONTINUE TO DEVELOP FRUIT BUT IT WILL BE VIRTUALLY SEEDLESS. VARIETIES THAT LIKE THEIR OWN POLLEN WILL BEAR FRUIT FULL OF INCESTUOUS SEEDS.

SPRAYING ORANGES

ORANGES ARE PRONE TO NUMEROUS PESTS & DISEASES & REQUIRE FREQUENT SPRAYING. THIS HAS BEEN SO EFFECTIVE IN FLORIDA THAT LIGHTNING NOW KILLS AS MANY TREES AS ANY DISEASE.

HYBRID ORANGES

MOST CITRUS TREES CONSIST OF 2 PARTS. THE UPPER FRAMEWORK IS ONE KIND OF CITRUS & THE ROOTS & TRUNK ARE ANOTHER. THE PARTS MEET IN A VISIBLE LINE ROUND THE TRUNK. ALL THE LEMON TREES IN CALIFORNIA ARE GROWN ON ORANGE-TREE ROOTSTOCK. EXTENSIVE CROSSING RESULTS IN MULTI-FRUIT TREES, WITH UP TO 6 DIFFERENT FRUITS – LEMONS, LIMES, GRAPEFRUIT, TANGERINES, ORANGES & KUMQUATS.

PICKING ORANGES

EXPERIMENTAL ORANGE-PICKING MACHINES INCLUDE COMBS, SHAKERS & BLOWERS WHICH DELIVER GUSTS OF WIND, SWINGING THE ORANGES LIKE PENDULUMS TILL THEY FALL. ROBOTS MAY PICK ORANGES IN THE FUTURE – ONE ROBOT TO FIND THE ORANGES AND ANOTHER TO PICK THEM. AN EXPERIENCED PERSON CAN PICK A TREE IN ABOUT AN HOUR – THAT'S AROUND 20,000 ORANGES A DAY.

FROSTY ORANGES

-3°C IS THE CRITICAL MINIMUM TEMPERATURE FOR THE HEALTH OF ORANGE TREES & THEIR FRUIT. OIL, COAL, WOOD & OLD TYRES ARE BURNED BETWEEN THE TREES ON FROSTY NIGHTS. SOME GROVES HAVE GIANT FANS TO MIX THE COLD LOW AIR WITH THE WARMER AIR ABOVE. ANOTHER METHOD OF HEATING IS TO TURN ON THE WATER-SPRINKLERS. AS LONG AS FREEZING WATER IS IN CONTACT WITH THE FRUIT THE TEMPERATURE CANNOT FALL BELOW 0°C. THE DANGER IS THAT THE ACCUMULATING WEIGHT OF ICE ON THE BRANCHES WILL BREAK THEM UNLESS THERE IS A RAPID THAW.

WAXED ORANGES

ORANGES HAVE TO BE WASHED AFTER PICKING TO REMOVE THE RESIDUE OF THE SPRAYS. THIS REMOVES THEIR NATURAL SURFACE WAX, WITHOUT WHICH THEY QUICKLY SHRIVEL UP, SO MOST ORANGES ARE POLISHED WITH WAX POLISH AFTER WASHING.

GASSING ORANGES

NAVEL ORANGES

THE NAVEL ORANGE DERIVES ITS NAME FROM THE NAVEL-LIKE OPENING IN THE TOP OF EACH ORANGE, CONTAINING A SMALL "FOETAL" ORANGE WITH 5 OR 6 PITHY SEGMENTS.

MANY RIPE ORANGES REMAIN GREEN ON THE OUTSIDE. THIS USED TO REDUCE THEIR MARKET VALUE, SO MOST ORANGES ARE NOW "GASSED" IN CHAMBERS WITH AN ATMOSPHERE OF ETHYLENE. THIS IS NOT QUITE AS UNNATURAL AS IT SOUNDS, MANY FRUITS, INCLUDING BANANAS, GIVE OFF ETHYLENE, & GREEN ORANGES LEFT IN A ROOM FULL OF BANANAS WOULD TURN ORANGE.

HOW TO MAKE A PING-PONG BALL FLOAT IN THE MIDDLE OF A GLASS OF WATER

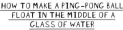

IF YOUR FRIENDS TRY THIS FIRST THEY WILL FIND THAT THE BALL WILL ALWAYS BE ATTRACTED TO THE SIDE OF THE GLASS BY SURFACE-TENSION FORCES. HOWEVER, IF YOU FILL THE GLASS TO THE BRIM, THE SURFACE TENSION WILL REPEL THE BALL FROM THE SIDES, MAKING IT SIT IN THE MIDDLE.

☆ ORCHIDS ☆

A FAMILY OF MONOCOTYLEDONS WITH SPECIALIZED FLOWERS

ORCHIDS EVERYWHERE

ORCHIDACEAE ARE ONE OF THE LARGEST PLANT FAMILIES, COMPRISING ABOUT 22,000 SPECIES – NEARLY ONE SEVENTH OF ALL FLOWER-BEARING PLANTS. THEY ARE FOUND EVERYWHERE IN THE WORLD EXCEPT IN THE ARCTIC, & SOME FLOURISH AT ALTITUDES OF UP TO 3 MILES. ONE AUSTRALIAN SPECIES, RHIZANTHELLA GARDNERI, GROWS & FLOWERS COMPLETELY UNDERGROUND.

ENTICING AN INSECT

MOST ORCHIDS ARE FERTILIZED BY INSECTS WHICH TRANSFER POLLEN FROM ONE FLOWER TO ANOTHER. MANY SPECIES ATTRACT BEES & WASPS WITH A DELICIOUS-TASTING NECTAR. OTHER SPECIES MIMIC THE SHAPE & COLOUR OF CERTAIN MOTHS WHICH ATTEMPT TO MATE WITH THE FLOWERS. THE GENUS OPHRYS EVEN EMITS THE MATING SMELL OF THE FEMALE WASP IT MIMICS.

DARWIN & ORCHIDS

DARWIN CLAIMED THAT THERE MUST BE AN INSECT WITH A 30CM-LONG TONGUE AFTER HE HAD EXAMINED THE ORCHID ANGRAECUM SESQUIPEDALE, WHOSE NECTAR IS PARTICULARLY INACCESSIBLE. HIS SURMISE WAS PROVED CORRECT 40 YEARS LATER WHEN THE LONG-TONGUED XANTHOPAN MORGANI PRAEDICTA WAS FIRST SEEN. DARWIN ALSO CALCULATED THAT IF EVERY SEED FROM ONE EUROPEAN SPOTTED ORCHID GERMINATED SUCCESSFULLY, IT WOULD COVER THE ENTIRE LAND SURFACE OF THE EARTH IN 3 GENERATIONS. FORTUNATELY THE SEEDS DEVELOP ONLY IF THEY LAND ON CERTAIN FUNGI.

ORCHID-HUNTING

IN THE LATE-19TH CENTURY NEW SPECIES OF ORCHID WERE SOUGHT WITH GREAT ZEAL. THE RIVALRY BETWEEN THE NURSERY COMPANIES WAS INTENSE & THEIR EXPLORERS WERE OFTEN INSTRUCTED TO DESTROY ANY EXAMPLE OF A NEW SPECIES TO HINDER THEIR OPPONENTS. ONLY WITH THE METHOD OF PRODUCING NEW SPECIES BY HYBRIDIZING DID THE DEMAND SLACKEN.

THE USELESS ORCHIDS

OF THE 22,000 ORCHID SPECIES THE ONLY ONE THAT HAS ANY COMMERCIAL USE IS VANILLA. THE VANILLA POD CONTAINS THE ORCHID'S SEEDS, & IS DRIED & STEEPED IN CASHEW-NUT OIL. THE PLANT CLINGS TO TREES, HAS NO ROOTS IN THE GROUND & DERIVES ITS SUSTENANCE FROM THE AIR.

UNHEALTHY AIR

WHEN TROPICAL ORCHIDS WERE FIRST BROUGHT TO BRITAIN THEY COULD NOT BE INDUCED TO SURVIVE FOR LONG. THIS WAS CHIEFLY DUE TO THE PRACTICE OF HEATING GREEN-HOUSES BY A BRICKED FIRE BELOW. THIS TENDED TO DRY OUT THE PLANTS SO VAST QUANTITIES OF WATER WERE USED, USUALLY CREATING AN EXCESSIVELY DAMP ATMOSPHERE SAID TO BE LIKE A MIXTURE OF A TURKISH BATH & A LONDON FOG. IT WAS ONLY WHEN CAST IRON, HOT-WATER-FILLED PIPES WERE ADOPTED FOR HEATING IN THE 1850S THAT THE HUMIDITY COULD BE CONTROLLED.

ORCHID AWARDS

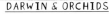

THE ROYAL HORTICULTURAL SOCIETY TAKES ORCHIDS SERIOUSLY. AN ORCHID COMMITTEE EXAMINES NEW HYBRIDS &, BY A COMPLEX VOTING SYSTEM, AWARDS THEM PRELIMINARY COMMENDATIONS, AWARDS OF MERIT OR FIRST-CLASS CERTIFICATES. A PAINTING IS MADE OF EACH PLANT THAT RECEIVES AN AWARD & THIS IS CAREFULLY FILED IN THE ORCHID ROOM.

HOW TO MAKE NEWSPAPER LOGS

TIE UP A ROLL OF NEWSPAPER 30CM LONG & 10CM IN DIAMETER VERY TIGHTLY WITH TWO LOOPS OF STRING. SOAK ROLL IN HOT WATER & DETERGENT FOR 2 HOURS TO CEMENT PAPER TOGETHER. LEAVE TO DRY OUT THOROUGHLY & ROLL WILL BURN LIKE A LOG.

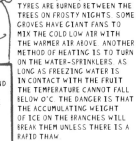

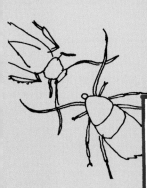

PARASITES
ANIMALS & PLANTS THAT LIVE & FEED ON ANOTHER

SIMPLICITY

THE STRUCTURE & DIGESTIVE SYSTEM OF PARASITES TEND TO BE VERY SIMPLE. THERE IS NO NEED FOR COMPLEXITY AS THE HOST PROVIDES SHELTER, WARMTH & ABUNDANT FOOD & WATER.

LIFE CYCLE OF FISH TAPEWORM:

INTESTINES   FAECES   FRESH WATER   PLANKTON   FISH   MAN

PROFUSION

PRACTICALLY ALL ANIMALS HAVE BEEN FOUND TO HARBOUR AT LEAST ONE SPECIALLY ADAPTED PARASITE. THIS IMPLIES THAT THERE ARE MORE PARASITE SPECIES THAN ANIMALS.

COMPLEXITY

THE PARASITE'S LIFE IS EASY UNTIL ITS HOST DIES. FINDING A NEW HOST IS ALWAYS CHANCY & HAS LED TO ELABORATE PARASITE LIFE CYCLES & PROLIFIC REPRODUCTION TO INCREASE ITS CHANCES.

HARMLESS

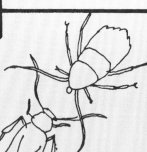

THE FOLLICLE MITE

MOST PARASITES ARE HARMLESS. IT IS NOT IN THEIR INTERESTS TO HARM THE HOST (THEY CANNOT LIVE ON A DEAD HOST). HARMFUL PARASITES ARE SAID TO BE "BADLY ADJUSTED".

MUTUAL BENEFIT

SOME ANIMALS, LIKE THE COCKROACH, DEPEND ON PARASITES FOR THEIR SURVIVAL. THE SPECIES TRICHONYMPHA, WHICH INHABITS THE COCKROACH STOMACH, IS ESSENTIAL FOR BREAKING DOWN THE WOOD IN ITS DIET.

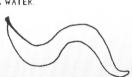

PARASITIC MALES

IN SOME SPECIES OF DEEP-SEA ANGLER FISH, THE MALE IS A PARASITE ON THE FEMALE, FIXED PERMANENTLY TO HER SKIN.

DOMINANCE

RECENT EXPERIMENTS AT OHIO UNIVERSITY SUGGEST THAT DOMINANCE OF CERTAIN INDIVIDUALS AMONG SOCIAL ANIMALS MAY BE INFLUENCED BY PARASITES. DOMINANT LABORATORY MICE WERE FOUND TO HARBOUR FEWER PARASITES THAN THE REST.

HYPERPARASITES

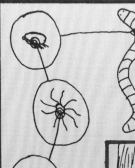

33 PARASITE SPECIES HAVE BEEN FOUND ON THE US CATERPILLAR HEMEROCAMPA LEUCOSTIGMA. ON THESE PARASITES, 13 SECONDARY PARASITES HAVE BEEN FOUND &, ON THESE, 2 TO 5 SPECIES OF TERTIARY PARASITES.

HOW TO MAKE CLEAR ICE CUBES

MISTLETOE

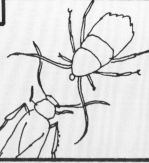

MISTLETOE IS A PARASITE ON TREES AND IS PARTICULARLY DESTRUCTIVE IN THE SIVAJI REGION OF INDIA. SCIENTISTS HAVE NOW FOUND A SECOND MISTLETOE SPECIES WHICH IS PARASITIC ON THE HARMFUL VARIETY. THIS HAS NOW BEEN INTRODUCED IN INDIA & IS REDUCING THE DAMAGE.

ROTATING-HEADED PARASITE

THE TERMITE PARASITE DEVESCOVINID CAN TWIST ITS HEAD ON ITS BODY FOR ANY NUMBER OF COMPLETE REVOLUTIONS. IT USES ITS HEAD ROTATION (UP TO 40 REVS A MINUTE) AS A FORM OF PROPULSION.

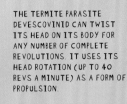

AIR DISSOLVED IN WATER CAUSES CLOUDINESS IN ICE CUBES. HEATING REMOVES THIS AIR, SO CUBES MADE FROM VERY HOT WATER WILL BE CLEAR. PUT ICE TRAY IN POLYTHENE BAG TO AVOID CONDENSATION.

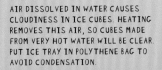

✦ PENICILLIN ✦
GROUP OF MOULDS THAT STOP THE GROWTH OF BACTERIA

FLEMING'S DISCOVERY

PENICILLIN WAS DISCOVERED BY SIR ALEXANDER FLEMING IN 1928. WHILE EXAMINING SOME DISHES OF BACTERIA, HE NOTICED THAT ONE HAD DEVELOPED A MOULD WHICH APPEARED TO BE DISSOLVING HIS BACTERIA. THIS MOULD HE CALLED PENICILLIN.

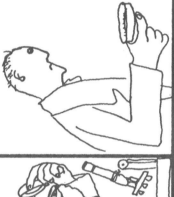

FLEMING'S OVERSIGHT

FLEMING DID NOT REALIZE THE IMPORTANCE OF HIS DISCOVERY BECAUSE HIS MOULD BROTH WAS UNMANAGEABLE. HE COULD NOT ISOLATE THE ACTIVE INGREDIENT – IT DISAPPEARED IF HE TRIED TO CONCENTRATE IT. IT TOOK 8 DAYS TO GROW & THEN DIED WITHIN 10 DAYS, SO CLINICAL TRIALS ON PATIENTS WERE NOT EASY.

ANCIENT PENICILLIN

PENICILLIN MAY NOT BE ONLY A RECENT DISCOVERY. THE USE OF MOULDS & MOULDY SUBSTANCES FOR CURING INFECTIONS & WOUNDS IS RECORDED IN ANCIENT DOCUMENTS FROM CHINA, GREECE & ROME, & IN WEST-EUROPEAN FOLKLORE.

PENICILLIN BRUSHES

PENICILLIN WAS FIRST PRODUCED FROM A MOULD OF THE PENICILLIUM FAMILY. THESE MOULDS LOOK LIKE MICROSCOPIC BRUSHES (IN LATIN, PENICILLUS = BRUSH) & RELEASE SPORES FROM THE ENDS OF THEIR "BRISTLES".

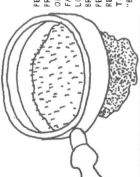

MELON PENICILLIN

THERE ARE SEVERAL THOUSAND PENICILLIUM MOULDS. WHEN COMMERCIAL PRODUCTION OF PENICILLIN STARTED IN AMERICA IN 1941, MOULDS FROM ALL OVER THE WORLD WERE COLLECTED & TESTED. FINALLY, A MOULD FOUND ON A CANTALOUPE MELON AT A LOCAL MARKET WAS SELECTED.

PENICILLIN ACTION

PENICILLIN KILLS BACTERIA BY BURSTING THE CELL WALLS. FORTUNATELY, THE WALLS OF ANIMAL CELLS ARE COMPLETELY DIFFERENT SO THEY ARE UNAFFECTED BY PENICILLIN.

POP

DANGEROUS DRUG

PENICILLIN WOULD PROBABLY NOT BE ALLOWED TO COME ONTO THE MARKET IF IT WERE "DISCOVERED" TODAY. THE US FEDERAL DRUGS AUTHORITY & THE BRITISH MEDICINES COMMISSION WOULD ADVISE AGAINST IT ON ACCOUNT OF THE FREQUENCY OF ALLERGIC SIDE-EFFECTS.

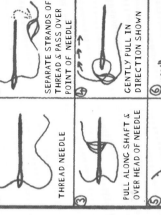

PENICILLIN FOOD

UNTIL RECENTLY, PENICILLIN WAS ADDED TO MANY ANIMAL FOODS TO PROMOTE GROWTH & PREVENT DISEASE. THIS PRACTICE LED TO AN ALARMING INCREASE IN PENICILLIN-RESISTANT BACTERIA & HAS BEEN BANNED. MANY SCIENTISTS ARE CONCERNED AT THE VAST QUANTITIES STILL PRESCRIBED BY VETS.

PENICILLIN RESISTANCE

BACTERIA CAN DEVELOP A RESISTANCE TO PENICILLIN. STRAINS OF SALMONELLA, FLU & GONORRHOEA THAT DO NOT RESPOND TO PENICILLIN HAVE APPEARED. DOCTORS ARE NOW ADVISED TO PRESCRIBE PENICILLIN (AND ALL ANTIBIOTICS) SPARINGLY TO REDUCE THE SPREAD OF RESISTANT BACTERIA.

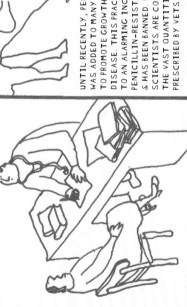

HOW TO THREAD A NEEDLE 12 TIMES

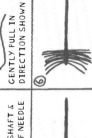

1. THREAD NEEDLE
2. SEPARATE STRANDS OF THREAD & PASS OVER POINT OF NEEDLE
3. PULL ALONG SHAFT & OVER HEAD OF NEEDLE
4. GENTLY PULL IN DIRECTION SHOWN
5. KEEP PULLING
6. CUT ENDS

PENS

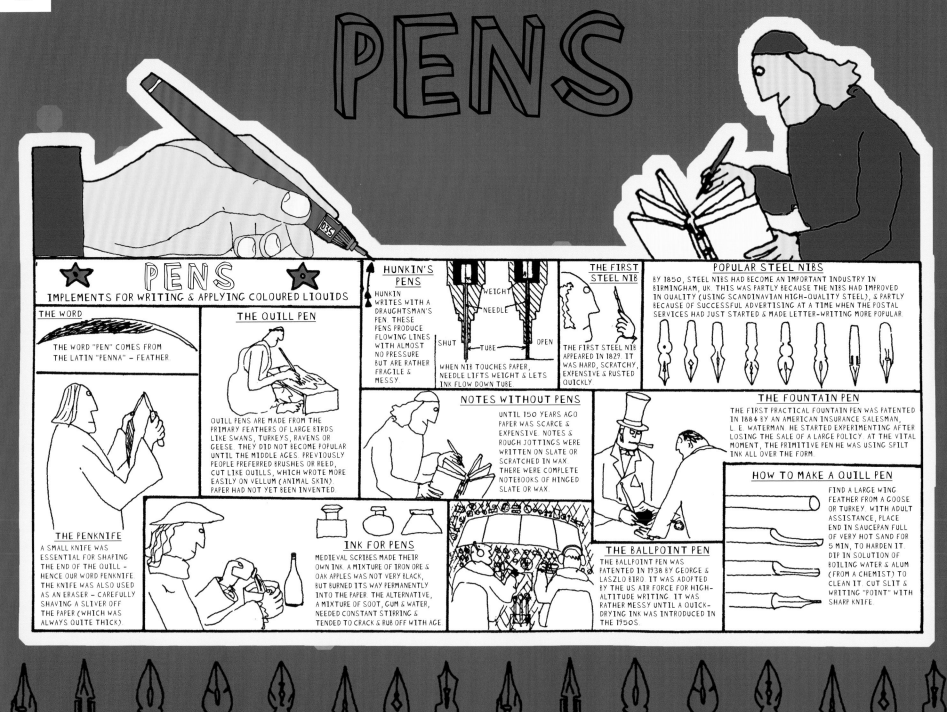

PENS
IMPLEMENTS FOR WRITING & APPLYING COLOURED LIQUIDS

THE WORD
THE WORD "PEN" COMES FROM THE LATIN "PENNA" – FEATHER.

THE QUILL PEN
QUILL PENS ARE MADE FROM THE PRIMARY FEATHERS OF LARGE BIRDS LIKE SWANS, TURKEYS, RAVENS OR GEESE. THEY DID NOT BECOME POPULAR UNTIL THE MIDDLE AGES. PREVIOUSLY PEOPLE PREFERRED BRUSHES OR REED, CUT LIKE QUILLS, WHICH WROTE MORE EASILY ON VELLUM (ANIMAL SKIN). PAPER HAD NOT YET BEEN INVENTED.

THE PENKNIFE
A SMALL KNIFE WAS ESSENTIAL FOR SHAPING THE END OF THE QUILL – HENCE OUR WORD PENKNIFE. THE KNIFE WAS ALSO USED AS AN ERASER – CAREFULLY SHAVING A SLIVER OFF THE PAPER (WHICH WAS ALWAYS QUITE THICK).

INK FOR PENS
MEDIEVAL SCRIBES MADE THEIR OWN INK. A MIXTURE OF IRON ORE & OAK APPLES WAS NOT VERY BLACK, BUT BURNED ITS WAY PERMANENTLY INTO THE PAPER. THE ALTERNATIVE, A MIXTURE OF SOOT, GUM & WATER, NEEDED CONSTANT STIRRING & TENDED TO CRACK & RUB OFF WITH AGE.

HUNKIN'S PENS
HUNKIN WRITES WITH A DRAUGHTSMAN'S PEN. THESE PENS PRODUCE FLOWING LINES WITH ALMOST NO PRESSURE BUT ARE RATHER FRAGILE & MESSY.

WEIGHT

NEEDLE

SHUT — TUBE — OPEN

WHEN NIB TOUCHES PAPER, NEEDLE LIFTS WEIGHT & LETS INK FLOW DOWN TUBE

NOTES WITHOUT PENS
UNTIL 150 YEARS AGO PAPER WAS SCARCE & EXPENSIVE. NOTES & ROUGH JOTTINGS WERE WRITTEN ON SLATE OR SCRATCHED IN WAX. THERE WERE COMPLETE NOTEBOOKS OF HINGED SLATE OR WAX.

THE FIRST STEEL NIB
THE FIRST STEEL NIB APPEARED IN 1829. IT WAS HARD, SCRATCHY, EXPENSIVE & RUSTED QUICKLY.

POPULAR STEEL NIBS
BY 1850, STEEL NIBS HAD BECOME AN IMPORTANT INDUSTRY IN BIRMINGHAM, UK. THIS WAS PARTLY BECAUSE THE NIBS HAD IMPROVED IN QUALITY (USING SCANDINAVIAN HIGH-QUALITY STEEL), & PARTLY BECAUSE OF SUCCESSFUL ADVERTISING AT A TIME WHEN THE POSTAL SERVICES HAD JUST STARTED & MADE LETTER-WRITING MORE POPULAR.

THE FOUNTAIN PEN
THE FIRST PRACTICAL FOUNTAIN PEN WAS PATENTED IN 1884 BY AN AMERICAN INSURANCE SALESMAN, L. E. WATERMAN. HE STARTED EXPERIMENTING AFTER LOSING THE SALE OF A LARGE POLICY. AT THE VITAL MOMENT, THE PRIMITIVE PEN HE WAS USING SPILT INK ALL OVER THE FORM.

THE BALLPOINT PEN
THE BALLPOINT PEN WAS PATENTED IN 1938 BY GEORGE & LASZLO BIRO. IT WAS ADOPTED BY THE US AIR FORCE FOR HIGH-ALTITUDE WRITING. IT WAS RATHER MESSY UNTIL A QUICK-DRYING INK WAS INTRODUCED IN THE 1950S.

HOW TO MAKE A QUILL PEN
FIND A LARGE WING FEATHER FROM A GOOSE OR TURKEY. WITH ADULT ASSISTANCE, PLACE END IN SAUCEPAN FULL OF VERY HOT SAND FOR 5 MIN, TO HARDEN IT. DIP IN SOLUTION OF BOILING WATER & ALUM (FROM A CHEMIST) TO CLEAN IT. CUT SLIT & WRITING "POINT" WITH SHARP KNIFE.

☆ PERPETUAL MOTION ☆

HYPOTHETICAL MECHANISMS

PERPETUAL WATER POWER

DESIGNS FOR PERPETUAL-MOTION MACHINES BASED ON WATER WHEELS WERE POPULAR IN THE RENAISSANCE. PRIMITIVE PEG GEARS ALWAYS CREATED A LOT OF NOISE & FRICTION. IT WOULD HAVE SEEMED OBVIOUS THAT IF THIS COULD BE REDUCED – BY THE ADDITION OF SOME EXTRA WHEELS PERHAPS – THE DEVICE COULD RUN FOR EVER.

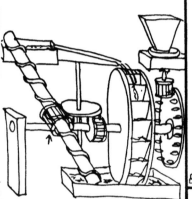

PERPETUAL BATTERIES

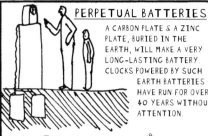

A CARBON PLATE & A ZINC PLATE, BURIED IN THE EARTH, WILL MAKE A VERY LONG-LASTING BATTERY. CLOCKS POWERED BY SUCH EARTH BATTERIES HAVE RUN FOR OVER 40 YEARS WITHOUT ATTENTION.

DISCS TIGHTLY CLAMPED TOGETHER

PAPER SILVER ZINC PAPER SILVER ZINC ETC

DRY BATTERIES MADE OF STACKS OF DISCS OF PAPER, ZINC & SILVER HAVE BEEN USED TO POWER PERPETUAL CHIMES (ONE OF WHICH IS STILL WORKING AFTER 140 YEARS).

SCIENTIFIC PERPETUAL MOTION

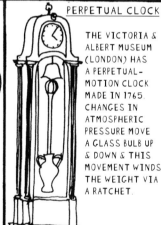

PERPETUAL MOTION IS IMPOSSIBLE ONLY WHEN IT DEFIES GRAVITY & OTHER SCIENTIFIC LAWS. VARIOUS FORMS ARE SCIENTIFICALLY ACCEPTABLE.

ANY OBJECT MOVING IN SPACE WILL CONTINUE FOR EVER (UNLESS ATTRACTED BY ANOTHER OBJECT).

THE MOLECULES IN EVERY LIQUID ARE IN A STATE OF CONTINUAL AGITATION (CALLED BROWNIAN MOTION).

AT VERY LOW TEMPERATURES SOME SUBSTANCES BECOME SUPERCONDUCTORS. THESE CAN ALLOW AN ELECTRIC CURRENT TO FLOW FOR EVER.

PERPETUAL FRAUD

IN 1873, AN AMERICAN CALLED KEELY CONSTRUCTED A PERPETUAL-MOTION MACHINE WHICH APPEARED TO WORK. HE CONVINCED MANY SCIENTISTS & AN HEIRESS & SECURED A COMFORTABLE INCOME FOR ITS DEVELOPMENT FROM HER UNTIL HIS DEATH IN 1898. IT WAS THEN DISCOVERED THAT HIS SECRET WAS AN ELABORATE SYSTEM OF COMPRESSED-AIR JETS & HIDDEN SWITCHES IN HIS LABORATORY.

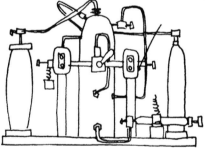

PERPETUAL BICYCLE

VARIOUS DESIGNS FOR BICYCLES USING THE FORCE OF THE BODY BUMPING UP & DOWN ON THE SADDLE HAVE BEEN PROPOSED. WHILE THIS MIGHT NOT ACHIEVE PERPETUAL MOTION, IT COULD REDUCE THE EFFORT OF CYCLING IF A PRACTICAL DESIGN COULD BE FOUND.

PERPETUAL CLOCK

THE VICTORIA & ALBERT MUSEUM (LONDON) HAS A PERPETUAL-MOTION CLOCK MADE IN 1765. CHANGES IN ATMOSPHERIC PRESSURE MOVE A GLASS BULB UP & DOWN & THIS MOVEMENT WINDS THE WEIGHT VIA A RATCHET.

PERPETUAL MAGNETISM

MAGNET
HOLE
STEEL BALL

MAGNET PULLS STEEL BALL UP SLOPE, THEN STEEL BALL FALLS THROUGH HOLE

THIS DESIGN WAS THOUGHT UP BY A JESUIT PRIEST IN 1570. THE MYSTERIOUS FORCE OF MAGNETISM MUST HAVE SEEMED SO MAGICAL THAT IT MIGHT EASILY BE HARNESSED FOR PERPETUAL MOTION.

PERPETUAL CAPILLARY

THIS INGENIOUS DEVICE WAS INVENTED IN 1827, BASED ON THE OBSERVATION THAT WATER RISES UP INTO A SPONGE. ANOTHER HEROIC FAILURE.

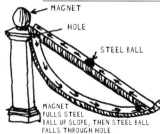

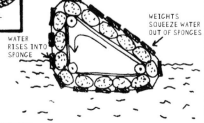

WATER RISES INTO SPONGE

WEIGHTS SQUEEZE WATER OUT OF SPONGES

PERPETUAL WHEELS

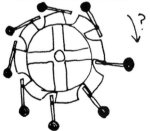

WHEELS WITH MOVING WEIGHTS HAVE BEEN THE BASIS OF MANY FAILED ATTEMPTS AT PERPETUAL MOTION. ALTHOUGH THEY OFTEN APPEAR PROMISING, THE MOVEMENTS OF THE WEIGHTS ON ONE SIDE ALWAYS CANCEL THE MOVEMENTS OF THE WEIGHTS ON THE OTHER.

PERPETUAL WIND

THIS WAS PROBABLY THE FIRST ATTEMPT TO DESIGN A PERPETUAL-MOTION MACHINE WORKED BY AIR (BY AN ITALIAN DOCTOR, ZIMARA C.1,500).

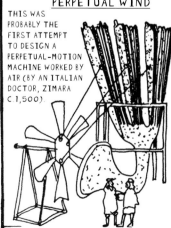

P V C

SYNTHETIC THERMOPLASTIC POLYMER OF VINYL CHLORIDE

HISTORY

POLY-VINYL CHLORIDE WAS FIRST MADE AS A WHITE POWDER BY THE FRENCH SCIENTIST REGNAULT IN 1835

IT WAS THEN FORGOTTEN ABOUT UNTIL 1912, WHEN A RUSSIAN CHEMIST CREATED A RUBBERY PLASTIC FORM OF THE CHEMICAL

COMMERCIAL PRODUCTION STARTED IN GERMANY BETWEEN THE WARS TO MEET THE SHORTAGE OF RUBBER

VINYLITE

THE FIRST PVC PLASTIC TO BE MADE IN AMERICA WAS VINYLITE (1928). IT WAS SOMETIMES MIXED WITH BRONZE DUST, ALUMINIUM DUST OR EVEN FISH SCALES TO GIVE A SPARKLING EFFECT. OLD, MARBLE-PATTERNED RUBBERY BATHROOM TILES ARE MADE OF VINYLITE

INFERIORITY

EARLY PVC WAS PARTLY RESPONSIBLE FOR PLASTICS GETTING A BAD REPUTATION AS A "CHEAP INFERIOR" MATERIAL. IT WAS NOT ACCURATELY MIXED & BATCHES OFTEN SMELLED DISGUSTING & BECAME INCREASINGLY BRITTLE WITH AGE

MAKING ROAD CONES

① FORMER HOT PVC LIQUID
② FORMER IS DIPPED IN PVC
③ COATING IS ALLOWED TO COOL
④ CONE IS REMOVED

COATING ELECTRIC CABLE

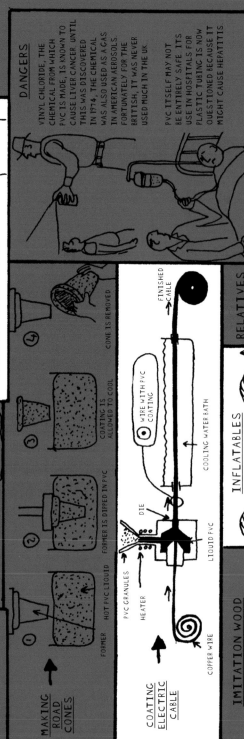

PVC GRANULES
HEATER
COPPER WIRE
LIQUID PVC
DIE
COOLING WATER BATH
WIRE WITH PVC COATING
FINISHED CABLE

IMITATION WOOD

RIGID PVC FOAM, ALTHOUGH EXPENSIVE TO MAKE, IS STRONGER THAN FOAMS MADE FROM OTHER PLASTICS. IT CAN BE SAWN, NAILED, STAPLED & GLUED JUST LIKE WOOD. IN AMERICA IT IS WIDELY USED FOR IMITATION-WOOD MOULDINGS & EVEN WHOLE COFFINS

DANGERS

VINYL CHLORIDE, THE CHEMICAL FROM WHICH PVC IS MADE, IS KNOWN TO CAUSE LIVER CANCER. UNTIL THIS WAS DISCOVERED IN 1974, THE CHEMICAL WAS ALSO USED AS A GAS IN AMERICAN AEROSOLS. FORTUNATELY FOR THE BRITISH, IT WAS NEVER USED MUCH IN THE UK.

PVC ITSELF MAY NOT BE ENTIRELY SAFE. ITS USE IN HOSPITALS FOR PLASTIC TUBING IS NOW QUESTIONED BECAUSE IT MIGHT CAUSE HEPATITIS.

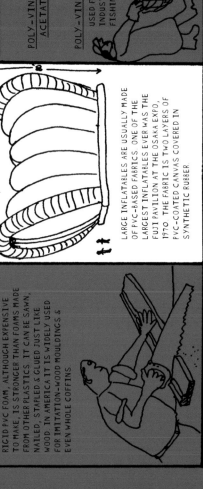

INFLATABLES

LARGE INFLATABLES ARE USUALLY MADE OF PVC-BASED FABRICS. ONE OF THE LARGEST INFLATABLES EVER WAS THE FUJI PAVILION AT THE OSAKA EXPO, 1970. THE FABRIC IS TWO LAYERS OF PVC-COATED CANVAS COVERED IN SYNTHETIC RUBBER.

RELATIVES

POLY-VINYL-ACETATE
USED AS GLUE, FOR WATERPROOFING PAINTS, & IN SOME CHEWING GUMS

POLY-VINYLIDENE CHLORIDE
USED FOR MAKING YARN FOR INDUSTRIAL CLOTHING & FISHING NETS

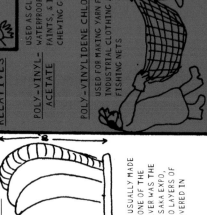

HOW TO MAKE RICE KRISPIES JUMP

RUB A PLASTIC SPOON ON SOME FUR & THEN HOLD IT OVER SOME DRY RICE KRISPIES.

☆ QUARTZ ☆

ABUNDANCE

QUARTZ IS THE CRYSTALLINE FORM OF SILICON DIOXIDE (SILICA). FLINTS, SANDSTONE AND SEA SAND ARE ALMOST PURE QUARTZ. IT IS THE COMMONEST MINERAL IN THE WORLD AFTER FELDSPAR.

HARDNESS

QUARTZ IS HARDER THAN STEEL, GLASS & MOST OTHER MINERALS. THIS IS WHY STONE-AGE MAN USED FLINT AXES & KNIVES, & WHY QUARTZ GRAINS ARE USED AS SANDPAPER.

ICE

THE ANCIENT GREEKS REFERRED TO CLEAR QUARTZ CRYSTALS (ROCK CRYSTAL) AS "PERMANENT ICE".

JEWELS

MANY SEMIPRECIOUS STONES ARE BASICALLY COLOURED QUARTZ. THESE INCLUDE AGATE, AMETHYST, CARNELIAN, JASPER & ONYX.

GLASS

MOST GLASS IS A MIXTURE OF SAND (QUARTZ) AND OTHER CHEMICALS. PURE QUARTZ GLASS IS MORE DIFFICULT TO MAKE, BUT EXPANDS ONLY A TENTH AS MUCH AS ORDINARY GLASS WHEN HEATED & CAN BE PLUNGED INTO WATER WHEN RED-HOT WITHOUT BREAKING. THIS IS WHY IT IS USED FOR HIGH-TEMPERATURE (QUARTZ HALOGEN) LIGHT BULBS SUCH AS CAR HEADLIGHTS.

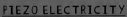

PIEZO ELECTRICITY

WHEN A QUARTZ CRYSTAL IS COMPRESSED IT PRODUCES A VERY SMALL ELECTRIC CURRENT. CONVERSELY, IF A CURRENT IS APPLIED TO THE CRYSTAL, IT EXPANDS SLIGHTLY. THIS EFFECT IS CALLED PIEZO ELECTRICITY.

WATCHES

EVERY QUARTZ CRYSTAL HAS A NATURAL RESONATING FREQUENCY. IN A QUARTZ WATCH AN ELECTRICAL CIRCUIT STIMULATES THE CRYSTAL & MAKES IT VIBRATE (THE PIEZO ELECTRIC EFFECT). THE OUTPUT FROM THE CRYSTAL IS THEN FED BACK TO THE CIRCUIT, REGULATING ITS SPEED.

BENDERS

WHEN A CURRENT IS PASSED THROUGH A LAYER OF QUARTZ CRYSTALS GLUED TO A THIN METAL STRIP, THE PIEZO ELECTRIC EFFECT WILL CAUSE THE METAL TO BEND. THIS DEVICE IS USED FOR COMPUTER COOLING FANS & DOT MATRIX PRINTERS, & EVEN LOUDSPEAKERS.

GENERATORS

PIEZO QUARTZ GENERATORS HAVE BEEN DEVELOPED IN AMERICA. WHEN PLACED IN CAR SILENCERS THEY CONVERT NOISE (VIBRATION) INTO ELECTRICITY. THEY COULD EVENTUALLY REPLACE ALTERNATORS, & SO REDUCE FUEL CONSUMPTION.

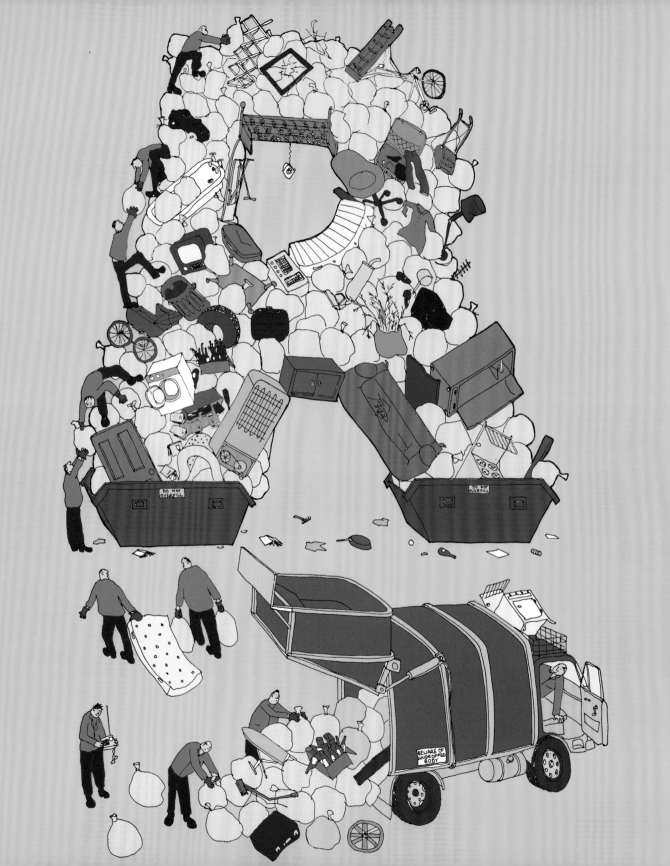

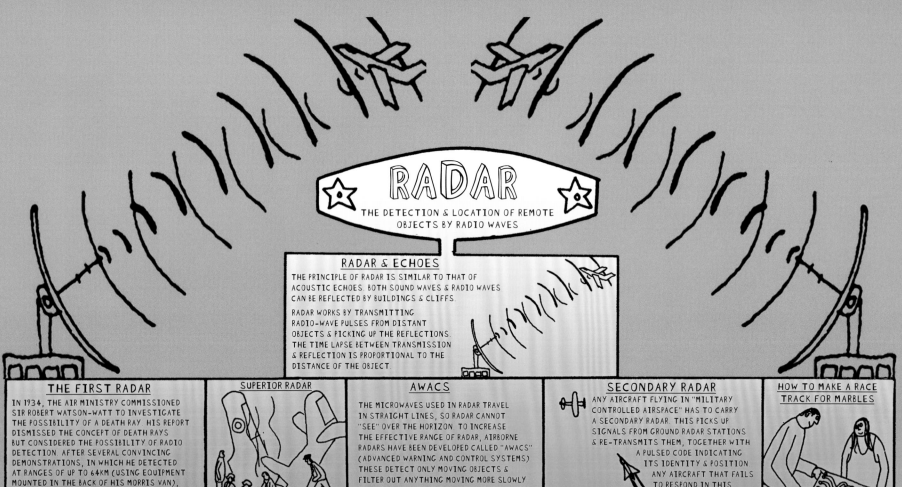

RADAR

THE DETECTION & LOCATION OF REMOTE OBJECTS BY RADIO WAVES

RADAR & ECHOES

THE PRINCIPLE OF RADAR IS SIMILAR TO THAT OF ACOUSTIC ECHOES. BOTH SOUND WAVES & RADIO WAVES CAN BE REFLECTED BY BUILDINGS & CLIFFS.

RADAR WORKS BY TRANSMITTING RADIO-WAVE PULSES FROM DISTANT OBJECTS & PICKING UP THE REFLECTIONS. THE TIME LAPSE BETWEEN TRANSMISSION & REFLECTION IS PROPORTIONAL TO THE DISTANCE OF THE OBJECT.

THE FIRST RADAR

IN 1934, THE AIR MINISTRY COMMISSIONED SIR ROBERT WATSON-WATT TO INVESTIGATE THE POSSIBILITY OF A DEATH RAY. HIS REPORT DISMISSED THE CONCEPT OF DEATH RAYS BUT CONSIDERED THE POSSIBILITY OF RADIO DETECTION. AFTER SEVERAL CONVINCING DEMONSTRATIONS, IN WHICH HE DETECTED AT RANGES OF UP TO 64KM (USING EQUIPMENT MOUNTED IN THE BACK OF HIS MORRIS VAN), THE AIR MINISTRY'S FIRST PRACTICAL RADAR STATIONS WERE SET UP TO PROTECT THE THAMES ESTUARY.

SUPERIOR RADAR

IN WORLD WAR II, THE ALLIES' RADAR WAS SUPERIOR TO THE NAZIS' BECAUSE OF THE DISCOVERY OF THE CAVITY MAGNETRON, A DEVICE THAT TRANSMITS MICROWAVE FREQUENCIES. THIS WAS MUCH SMALLER & MORE POWERFUL THAN PREVIOUS TRANSMITTERS, & IT REMAINED UNKNOWN TO THE NAZIS UNTIL THEY FOUND ONE IN A CRASHED PLANE IN 1943.

AWACS

THE MICROWAVES USED IN RADAR TRAVEL IN STRAIGHT LINES, SO RADAR CANNOT "SEE" OVER THE HORIZON. TO INCREASE THE EFFECTIVE RANGE OF RADAR, AIRBORNE RADARS HAVE BEEN DEVELOPED CALLED "AWACS" (ADVANCED WARNING AND CONTROL SYSTEMS). THESE DETECT ONLY MOVING OBJECTS & FILTER OUT ANYTHING MOVING MORE SLOWLY THAN 145KM/H SO THE RADAR IS NOT SWAMPED WITH ROAD TRAFFIC.

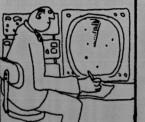

SECONDARY RADAR

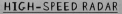

ANY AIRCRAFT FLYING IN "MILITARY CONTROLLED AIRSPACE" HAS TO CARRY A SECONDARY RADAR. THIS PICKS UP SIGNALS FROM GROUND RADAR STATIONS & RE-TRANSMITS THEM, TOGETHER WITH A PULSED CODE INDICATING ITS IDENTITY & POSITION. ANY AIRCRAFT THAT FAILS TO RESPOND IN THIS MANNER IS INTERCEPTED BY A FIGHTER PLANE & INSPECTED VISUALLY.

HIGH-SPEED RADAR

THE LATEST RADARS ROTATE AT 750 RPM (10 TIMES FASTER THAN THE TRADITIONAL TYPES). THESE GIVE A PICTURE THAT DOESN'T FLICKER ON THE SCREEN & THAT IS ACCURATE ENOUGH TO DISTINGUISH AIRCRAFT TYPES. THEY CAN EVEN DETECT A DEAD HARE ON THE RUNWAY.

HOW TO MAKE A RACE TRACK FOR MARBLES

BUY A LUMP OF MODELLING CLAY & ROLL IT OUT TO A 1CM-THICK RECTANGLE. SCOOP OUT TRACKS FOR MARBLES WITH LOOP OF WIRE. SMOOTH TRACKS WITH WETTED FINGER. WHEN CLAY HAS SET, PLACE TRACK ON GENTLE SLOPE & ROCK FROM SIDE TO SIDE TO CONTROL MARBLES' DESCENT.

RADAR

☆ RAILWAYS ☆
MAN'S MYRMIDONS OF LOCOMOTION

THE RAILWAY CIRCUS

THE FIRST STEAM ENGINE TO RUN ON RAILS WAS DESIGNED & BUILT BY AN EX-MINING ENGINEER CALLED TREVITHICK IN 1804. HE MADE SOME IMPROVEMENTS & BROUGHT HIS SECOND MODEL, CALLED "CATCH ME WHO CAN", TO LONDON. HERE HE OPENED A RAILWAY CIRCUS, CHARGING THE PUBLIC ONE SHILLING TO ENTER THE ENCLOSURE & HAVE A RIDE IF THEY DARED. UNFORTUNATELY IT DID NOT ATTRACT ENOUGH PEOPLE & TREVITHICK WENT BANKRUPT.

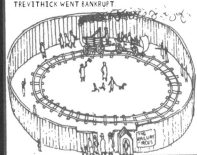

THE WORLD'S LARGEST WAITING ROOMS ARE IN PEKING CENTRAL STATION, WITH CAPACITY FOR 14,000 PEOPLE.

THE ORUKTER AMPHIBALOS

AMERICA'S FIRST LAND STEAM VEHICLE WAS SUPPOSED TO BE A DREDGER FOR PHILADELPHIA HARBOUR. IT WAS BUILT BY A BLACKSMITH, OLIVER EVANS, IN 1805 & NAMED GRANDLY THE ORUKTER AMPHIBALOS (MEANING LITERALLY THE SNORTING SWIMMER). HE ADDED THE WHEELS & DRIVING BELTS AS AN AFTERTHOUGHT TO TRANSPORT IT FROM HIS FORGE TO THE HARBOUR. SADLY THE WHEELS COLLAPSED UNDER ITS WEIGHT.

THE £1,250 TICKET

THE MOST EXPENSIVE SEASON TICKET EVER ISSUED BY BRITISH RAIL WAS A 1ST-CLASS WEEKLY RETURN FROM LONDON TO INVERNESS.

CLOCKWORK TRAINS

FULL-SCALE CLOCKWORK TRAINS ARE NOT AS IMPRACTICAL AS MIGHT BE IMAGINED. NOT QUITE AS FANCIFUL AS THE DRAWING BELOW, THEY STORE ENERGY IN HIGH-SPEED ROTATING FLYWHEELS WOUND BY ELECTRIC MOTORS. A SWISS "ELECTROGYRO OMNIBUS" OPERATED SUCCESSFULLY FROM 1953 TO 1969 DESPITE A MAXIMUM RANGE OF 0.8KM BETWEEN "REWINDS". A MORE PRACTICAL VERSION WAS TRIED ON NEW YORK'S UNDERGROUND. BOTH DRIVING WHEELS & FLYWHEELS WERE POWERED BY MOTORS THAT COULD ALSO ACT AS GENERATORS. THE DRIVING WHEELS COULD THEN BE PARTIALLY POWERED BY THE FLYWHEELS. WHEN THE TRAIN SLOWED DOWN, THE DRIVING WHEEL MOTORS SUPPLIED ELECTRICITY TO RECHARGE THE FLYWHEELS.

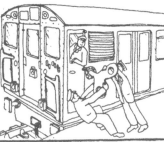

ONE OF THE LONGEST FREIGHT TRAINS EVER STRETCHED OVER 6KM WITH THREE 3,600-HP LOCOMOTIVES AT EACH END. RUN IN AMERICA IN 1967, IT WEIGHED 40,000 TONS.

THE WORLD'S MOST CROWDED TRAINS

THE JAPANESE RAIL SYSTEM IS PROBABLY THE WORLD'S MOST CROWDED. PROFESSIONAL PUSHERS ARE EMPLOYED AT TOKYO TO SQUEEZE IN PASSENGERS BEFORE THE DOORS CAN BE CLOSED. ARTICLES LOST IN 1970 INCLUDED:
- 419,929 UMBRELLAS
- 172,106 SHOES
- 250,630 PAIRS OF SPECTACLES
- PLUS VARIOUS SETS OF FALSE TEETH & ARTIFICIAL EYEBALLS.

HOW TO COLLECT OXYGEN FROM IVY

PUT SOME IVY IN A JAM JAR AND FILL THE JAR WITH WATER. IMMERSE JAR IN BOWL OF WATER, THEN TURN JAR UPSIDE-DOWN SO GAS COLLECTS IN IT.

TO PROVE GAS IS OXYGEN EMPTY JAM JAR OF WATER & PUT OVER LIGHTED CANDLE. IT WILL BURN MORE BRIGHTLY IN THE ENRICHED ATMOSPHERE.

☆ RAIN ☆
WATER ISSUING FROM CLOUDS IN DROPS

RAIN & SEA PLANTS

AN ESSENTIAL REQUIREMENT FOR THE PRODUCTION OF RAIN IS THE PRESENCE OF ATMOSPHERIC PARTICLES UPON WHICH ICE CRYSTALS CAN FORM (MOST RAIN STARTS AT HIGH ALTITUDE AS MINUTE ICE CRYSTALS). THE NATURE OF THESE NUCLEI IS UNCERTAIN BUT THE LATEST THEORY IS THAT DECAYING VEGETATION IS A PROLIFIC SOURCE. ONE MARINE PLANT (CACHONINA NIEI) APPEARS TO BE PARTICULARLY ACTIVE AS ITS PARTICLES ARE A SIMILAR SHAPE TO ICE CRYSTALS.

RAIN & THE MOON

PERIODS OF HIGH RAINFALL HAVE SOME CORRELATION WITH PHASES OF THE MOON. SOME METEOROLOGISTS THINK THAT THIS IS LINKED WITH THE DENSITY OF METEORIC DUST IN THE ATMOSPHERE, WHICH ALSO VARIES WITH THE MOON'S PHASES. THE DUST COULD PROVIDE NUCLEI TO PRECIPITATE RAIN FROM CLOUDS.

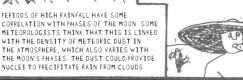

TOO LITTLE RAIN

THE DRIEST PART OF THE WORLD IS A DESERT IN CHILE WHICH HAS NOT HAD ANY RAIN FOR OVER 400 YEARS. SOME TROPICAL DESERTS HAVE AN ANNUAL RAINFALL AS HIGH AS BRITAIN'S, BUT THE WATER EVAPORATES SO FAST THAT IT HAS LITTLE EFFECT. A RESERVOIR 4M DEEP WOULD TAKE LESS THAN A YEAR TO EVAPORATE COMPLETELY IN PARTS OF THE SAHARA.

MAN-MADE RAIN

CLOUDS CAN BE MADE TO PRECIPITATE RAIN IF SILVER-IODIDE SMOKE IS BLOWN INTO THEM. ONE OF THE BIGGEST EXPERIMENTS, CARRIED OUT OVER CALIFORNIA FROM 1957 TO 1960, BROUGHT INCONCLUSIVE BENEFITS ALTHOUGH IT WAS HAMPERED BY POOR CO-OPERATION FROM OFFICIALS & A TENDENCY FOR SPORTSMEN TO USE THE RAIN GAUGES AS TARGETS. AN ATTEMPT TO DENUDE A HURRICANE OF ITS MOISTURE WHILE STILL AT SEA USING IODIDE SMOKE WAS DISASTROUS. THE HURRICANE TURNED INLAND WITH INCREASED VIOLENCE & DEVASTATED GEORGIA. OTHER INCONCLUSIVE RESULTS & THE HIGH COST OF SILVER IODIDE HAVE DISCOURAGED FURTHER RESEARCH.

TOO MUCH RAIN

CHERRAPUNJI, IN ASSAM, HAS THE WORLD'S HIGHEST ANNUAL RAINFALL. IT AVERAGES OVER 400 INCHES A YEAR & IN 1860 REACHED 1,041 INCHES. ABOUT 90% OF THIS FALLS BETWEEN APRIL & SEPTEMBER WHICH MEANS ABOUT 2 INCHES A DAY (LIKE GETTING LONDON'S AVERAGE ANNUAL RAINFALL EVERY TWO WEEKS).

ACCURATE FORECASTING

ADVANCES IN RADAR SYSTEMS HAVE ADDED TO MUCH GREATER ACCURACY IN BRITISH WEATHER FORECASTS. SYSTEMS OF RADARS LINKED BY COMPUTER NOW PROVIDE INSTANTANEOUS COUNTRYWIDE INFORMATION OF RAINFALL & CLOUD COVER. THESE COMPUTERS HAVE LARGE MEMORIES & CAN "LEARN" THE PROBABLE MOVEMENT OF CLOUDS.

ANTI-HAIL GUNS

A FRENCH FIRM PATENTED A DEVICE CONSISTING OF AN ACETYLENE GENERATOR THAT DETONATES A LOUD BANG EVERY 15 SEC. THE SUCCESSION OF RISING SHOCK WAVES IS SAID TO ALTER THE CLOUD STRUCTURE TO MAKE HAIL FALL AS RAIN, THUS PREVENTING CROP DAMAGE.

HOW TO MAKE THE SOUND OF APPLAUSE

PULL A 50CM LENGTH OF EMBROIDERY THREAD OVER AN UNLIT CANDLE TO COAT IT IN WAX. THREAD IT ONTO A NEEDLE AND PASS IT THROUGH THE SIDE OF WOODEN MATCHBOX. HOLD MATCHBOX TO EAR & SLOWLY PULL THREAD THROUGH HOLE. THE RESULTING NOISE IS UNCANNILY SIMILAR TO THE CLAPPING OF A THEATRE AUDIENCE.

RUBBER

VEGETABLE GUM COMMON IN TROPICAL TREES

RUBBER & THE AZTECS

THE AZTECS ATTACHED GREAT SIGNIFICANCE TO THIS STRANGE ELASTIC SUBSTANCE THAT BURNED WITH A DENSE BLACK SMOKE. THEY CALLED IT OLLI, A WORD THAT ALSO MEANT BLOOD, & IN THEIR PICTURE WRITING THE HEART WAS SYMBOLIZED AS A BALL OF RUBBER. THE PRIESTS COVERED THEMSELVES WITH FRESH LIQUID LATEX. THEY KEPT SOLIDIFIED LUMPS IN THE TEMPLES FOR HEALING & FOR BURNING TO PRODUCE RAIN.

RUBBER GLOVES

RUBBER GLOVES WERE THE BRAINWAVE OF A SURGEON CALLED HALSTEAD. HE INTRODUCED THEM FOR ONE OF HIS NURSES WHO HAD AN ALLERGY TO CARBOLIC ACID. THE USE OF RUBBER GLOVES FOR KEEPING INCISIONS STERILE WAS REALIZED ONLY LATER.

MR HANCOCK

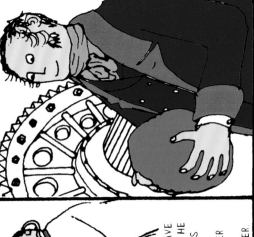

THOMAS HANCOCK (1820–56) WAS THE FATHER OF THE MODERN RUBBER INDUSTRY. THE LIQUID LATEX FROM THE TREES WAS VERY DIFFICULT TO UTILIZE AS IT SET TO A SOLID ELASTIC LUMP AFTER A FEW HOURS & IT WAS THEN IMPOSSIBLE TO REMOULD. HANCOCK STARTED MAKING ELASTIC BANDS THE SAME SIZE AS THE LUMPS HE RECEIVED. WHILE ATTEMPTING TO MAKE A MACHINE TO CUT THE LUMPS INTO BANDS HE MADE ONE THAT WAS TOO VIOLENT & TRANSFORMED THE SHREDS INTO A GLUTINOUS BUT REMOULDABLE MASS. HE CALLED HIS MACHINE A MASTICATOR & WENT ON TO UNITE WITH CHARLES MACINTOSH TO MAKE WATERPROOF FABRICS.

A RUBBER SKIN FOR DESERTS

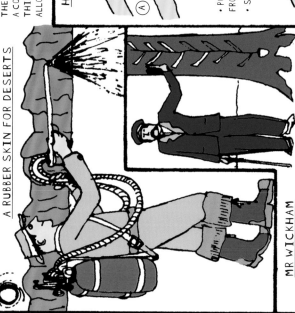

THE UNISOL SOIL STABILIZATION PROCESS INVOLVES A COATING OF RUBBER & OIL SPRAYED ON POOR SOIL. THIS TRAPS MOISTURE & COMBATS EROSION, ALLOWING PLANTS TO ESTABLISH THEMSELVES.

MR WICKHAM

SOUTH AMERICA HAD A MONOPOLY OF THE RUBBER TRADE UNTIL IT WAS DECIDED TO ATTEMPT TO ESTABLISH RUBBER TREES IN CEYLON (NOW SRI LANKA). AN EXPLORER CALLED WICKHAM WAS DISPATCHED TO COLLECT SEEDS IN 1878 &, DESPITE HAVING HIS BOAT & MONEY STOLEN, RETURNED IN RECORD TIME, CHARTERING ANOTHER VESSEL. KEW GARDENS THREW OUT MOST OF ITS TROPICAL PLANTS TO MAKE ROOM FOR HIS 70,000 SEEDS. 2,700 GREW INTO SAPLINGS & WERE RE-EXPORTED TO CEYLON.

HOW TO SEPARATE A & B WITHOUT UNTYING ANY KNOTS

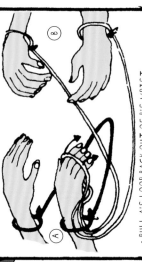

- PULL A'S LOOP THROUGH B'S RIGHT WRISTBAND FROM THE BACK.
- SLIP A'S LOOP OVER BACK OF B'S HAND.

- PULL A'S LOOP BACK OUT OF B'S WRIST
- A & B WILL NOW BE DISENTANGLED.

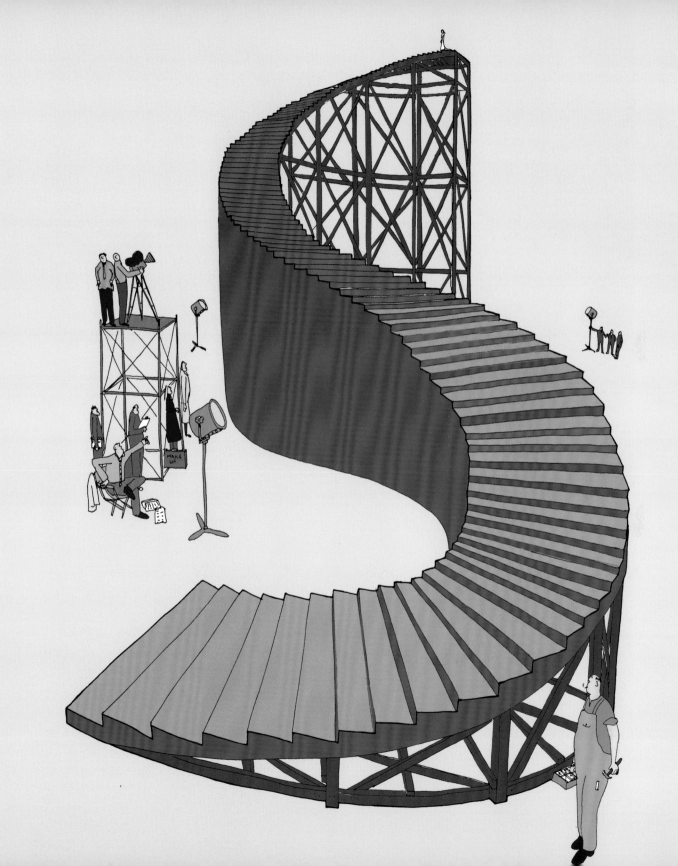

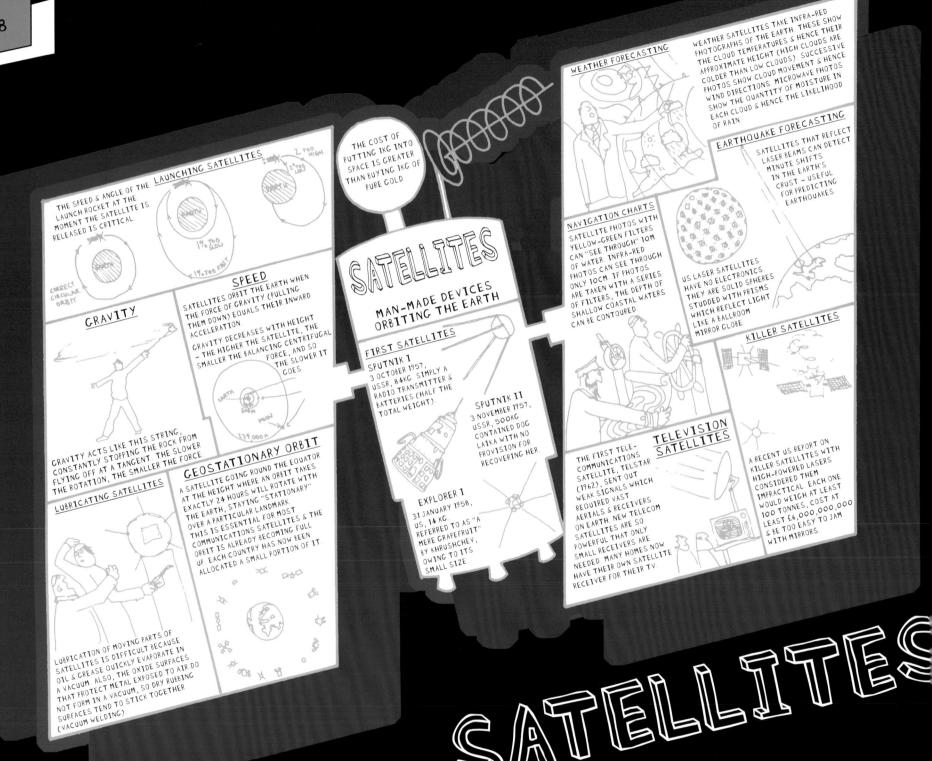

SATELLITES
MAN-MADE DEVICES ORBITING THE EARTH

THE COST OF PUTTING 1KG INTO SPACE IS GREATER THAN BUYING 1KG OF PURE GOLD

LAUNCHING SATELLITES

THE SPEED & ANGLE OF THE LAUNCH ROCKET AT THE MOMENT THE SATELLITE IS RELEASED IS CRITICAL

CORRECT CIRCULAR ORBIT

2 TOO HIGH
2 TOO LOW
1% TOO LOW
1% TOO FAST

GRAVITY

GRAVITY ACTS LIKE THIS STRING, CONSTANTLY STOPPING THE ROCK FROM FLYING OFF AT A TANGENT. THE SLOWER THE ROTATION, THE SMALLER THE FORCE

SPEED

SATELLITES ORBIT THE EARTH WHEN THE FORCE OF GRAVITY (PULLING THEM DOWN) EQUALS THEIR INWARD ACCELERATION

GRAVITY DECREASES WITH HEIGHT – THE HIGHER THE SATELLITE, THE SMALLER THE BALANCING CENTRIFUGAL FORCE, AND SO THE SLOWER IT GOES.

EARTH
500M
MOON
239,000 M

GEOSTATIONARY ORBIT

A SATELLITE GOING ROUND THE EQUATOR AT THE HEIGHT WHERE AN ORBIT TAKES EXACTLY 24 HOURS WILL ROTATE WITH THE EARTH, STAYING "STATIONARY" OVER A PARTICULAR LANDMARK. THIS IS ESSENTIAL FOR MOST COMMUNICATIONS SATELLITES & THE ORBIT IS ALREADY BECOMING FULL UP. EACH COUNTRY HAS NOW BEEN ALLOCATED A SMALL PORTION OF IT.

LUBRICATING SATELLITES

LUBRICATION OF MOVING PARTS OF SATELLITES IS DIFFICULT BECAUSE OIL & GREASE QUICKLY EVAPORATE IN A VACUUM. ALSO, THE OXIDE SURFACES THAT PROTECT METAL EXPOSED TO AIR DO NOT FORM IN A VACUUM, SO DRY RUBBING SURFACES TEND TO STICK TOGETHER (VACUUM WELDING).

FIRST SATELLITES

SPUTNIK I
3 OCTOBER 1957, USSR, 84KG SIMPLY A RADIO TRANSMITTER & BATTERIES (HALF THE TOTAL WEIGHT)

SPUTNIK II
3 NOVEMBER 1957, USSR, 500KG CONTAINED DOG LAIKA WITH NO PROVISION FOR RECOVERING HER

EXPLORER I
31 JANUARY 1958, US, 14 KG REFERRED TO AS "A MERE GRAPEFRUIT" BY KHRUSHCHEV, OWING TO ITS SMALL SIZE

WEATHER FORECASTING

WEATHER SATELLITES TAKE INFRA-RED PHOTOGRAPHS OF THE EARTH. THESE SHOW THE CLOUD TEMPERATURES & HENCE THEIR APPROXIMATE HEIGHT (HIGH CLOUDS ARE COLDER THAN LOW CLOUDS). SUCCESSIVE PHOTOS SHOW CLOUD MOVEMENT & HENCE WIND DIRECTIONS. MICROWAVE PHOTOS SHOW THE QUANTITY OF MOISTURE IN EACH CLOUD & HENCE THE LIKELIHOOD OF RAIN

NAVIGATION CHARTS

SATELLITE PHOTOS WITH YELLOW-GREEN FILTERS CAN "SEE THROUGH" 10M OF WATER. INFRA-RED PHOTOS CAN SEE THROUGH ONLY 10CM. IF PHOTOS ARE TAKEN WITH A SERIES OF FILTERS, THE DEPTH OF SHALLOW COASTAL WATERS CAN BE CONTOURED

EARTHQUAKE FORECASTING

SATELLITES THAT REFLECT LASER BEAMS CAN DETECT MINUTE SHIFTS IN THE EARTH'S CRUST – USEFUL FOR PREDICTING EARTHQUAKES

US LASER SATELLITES HAVE NO ELECTRONICS. THEY ARE SOLID SPHERES STUDDED WITH PRISMS WHICH REFLECT LIGHT LIKE A BALLROOM MIRROR GLOBE

TELEVISION SATELLITES

THE FIRST TELE-COMMUNICATIONS SATELLITE, TELSTAR (1962), SENT OUT WEAK SIGNALS WHICH REQUIRED VAST AERIALS & RECEIVERS ON EARTH. NEW TELECOM SATELLITES ARE SO POWERFUL THAT ONLY SMALL RECEIVERS ARE NEEDED. MANY HOMES NOW HAVE THEIR OWN SATELLITE RECEIVER FOR THEIR TV.

KILLER SATELLITES

A RECENT US REPORT ON KILLER SATELLITES WITH HIGH-POWERED LASERS CONSIDERED THEM IMPRACTICAL. EACH ONE WOULD WEIGH AT LEAST 100 TONNES, COST AT LEAST £6,000,000,000 & BE TOO EASY TO JAM WITH MIRRORS.

SATELLITES

MODEL T FORD CONVERTED FOR SNOW, 1913

SPIRAL AUGER SNOW VEHICLE, US, 1922

DRUM SNOW VEHICLE, US, 1942 – ENGINE INSIDE DRUM

☆ SNOW ☆
WATER FROZEN INTO SMALL 6-SIDED CRYSTALS

LABORATORY SNOW

MAKING SNOW IN A LABORATORY IS NOT SIMPLE. CHILLED WATER VAPOUR TENDS TO FREEZE ON THE SIDES OF ITS CONTAINER RATHER THAN FALL AS SNOW. IT WAS NOT UNTIL 1946 THAT SNOW WAS "SYNTHESIZED" BY THE WATER BEING COOLED SUDDENLY TO -70°C

DEEP SNOW

THE SNOWIEST RECORDED PLACE IN THE WORLD IS MOUNT RAINIER, WASHINGTON, US, WHERE AN AVERAGE OF 14.6M (575") FALLS PER YEAR.

COWS ON SNOW

CATTLE CAN FEED THROUGH UP TO 150MM (6IN) OF SNOW.

SHEEP ON SNOW

SHEEP CAN WALK THROUGH UP TO 300MM (12IN) OF SNOW.

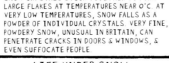

SHEEP IN SNOW

SHEEP CAN SURVIVE FOR SEVERAL WEEKS IN SNOW & EVEN GIVE BIRTH TO HEALTHY LAMBS.

DUSTY SNOW

SNOW CRYSTALS STICK TOGETHER TO FORM LARGE FLAKES AT TEMPERATURES NEAR 0°C. AT VERY LOW TEMPERATURES, SNOW FALLS AS A POWDER OF INDIVIDUAL CRYSTALS. VERY FINE, POWDERY SNOW, UNUSUAL IN BRITAIN, CAN PENETRATE CRACKS IN DOORS & WINDOWS, & EVEN SUFFOCATE PEOPLE.

LIFE UNDER SNOW

ALTHOUGH THE AIR ABOVE MAY BE FAR BELOW FREEZING POINT, SMALL ANIMALS CAN LIVE IN RELATIVELY WARM (NEAR 0°C) SHELTERED DENS UNDER SNOW. MANY DO NOT HIBERNATE. VOLES, LEMMINGS & SHREWS LEAD ACTIVE LIVES, EATING STORED FOOD & REPRODUCING FREELY.

WHITE-OUT

WHEN A BLIZZARD IS STRONG ENOUGH, CLOUD MERGES INTO SNOW WITHOUT ANY VISIBLE HORIZON OR SHADOWS – A CONDITION KNOWN AS WHITE-OUT. ALL SENSE OF DIRECTION, & EVEN BALANCE, MAY BE LOST

USEFUL SNOW

IN DEVON, CORN HAS GERMINATED & GROWN UP TO 75MM UNDER SNOW. IN MUCH OF THE US, SNOW COVER IS ESSENTIAL TO PROTECT CROPS PLANTED IN THE AUTUMN FROM COLD AIR TEMPERATURES. OCCASIONAL YEARS WITHOUT SNOW DO GREAT CROP DAMAGE.

ENCOURAGING SNOW

MANY REGIONS DEPEND ON THE SNOW MELTING IN THE SPRING FOR IRRIGATION. VARIOUS METHODS HAVE BEEN TRIED TO TRAP AS MUCH SNOW AS POSSIBLE. LEAVING STUBBLE & STRIPS OF UNCUT WHEAT, PLOUGHING RIDGES IN THE FIRST SNOWS, BUILDING HEDGES & TERRACING LAND ALL HELP TO INCREASE THE DEPTH OF SNOW & CROP YIELDS.

MELTERS

IN SOME PARTS OF AMERICA IT IS SO DIFFICULT TO FIND SUITABLE PLACES TO DUMP THE SNOW CLEARED FROM ROADS THAT IT IS TIPPED INTO VAST SNOW-MELTING MACHINES, WITH OIL-FIRED BURNERS.

HOW TO THREAD BEADS AT HIGH SPEED

STIFFEN END OF THREAD BY DIPPING IN NAIL POLISH. LINE BEADS UP ON CORRUGATED CARDBOARD WITH HOLES IN LINE & SIMPLY PUSH THREAD THROUGH.

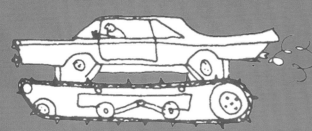

KAM SNO-BALL, 1957 – TRACKS BOLT TO ANY CAR

SKI-DOO, US – SINGLE POWERED TRACK UNDER SEAT

SNOWMOBILE BUS, US – TRAVELS AT 80KM/H

SOAP ☆ ☆

SUBSTANCE FOR REMOVING GREASE & DIRT

SOAP WAS NOT WIDELY USED IN THE CLASSICAL WORLD. THE GREEKS & ROMANS CLEANED THEMSELVES BY BATHING IN HOT WATER & SCRAPING THEIR BODIES WITH A SORT OF BLUNT KNIFE (STRIGIL). PLINY MENTIONS SOAP AS "AN INVENTION OF THE GAULS FOR GIVING A SHEEN TO THE HAIR". LATER ROMAN WRITERS RECOMMEND ITS MEDICINAL USE AS A CURE FOR ELEPHANTIASIS & SEPTIC CUTS BUT NOT FOR EVERYDAY WASHING.

GALLIC SOAP

THE SOAP TAX

UNTIL THE 1850S, THE WIDESPREAD USE OF SOAP WAS LIMITED BY THE SOAP TAX, WHICH MADE IT AN EXPENSIVE LUXURY ITEM. THE ABOLITION OF THE TAX IN GLADSTONE'S 1853 BUDGET CAME AT A TIME WHEN HYGIENE & SANITATION WERE BEING PURSUED BY PIONEERS WITH VICTORIAN ENERGY, EARNESTNESS & FANATICISM. GLADSTONE DESCRIBED THE TAX IN HIS BUDGET SPEECH AS "AN ARTICLE OF TAXATION WHICH IS MOST INJURIOUS TO BOTH THE COMFORT & HEALTH OF THE PEOPLE".

SOAP MOLECULES

SOAP IS COMPOSED OF LONG MOLECULES. ONE END OF EACH IS WATER-SOLUBLE, & THE OTHER IS INSOLUBLE IN WATER BUT SOLUBLE IN OIL & GREASE. THE MOLECULES FORM A THIN LAYER BETWEEN GREASY DIRT & WATER, & THEN "PULL" THE DIRT INTO THE WATER.

HOME-MADE SOAP

IN THE MIDDLE AGES, HOUSEWIVES OFTEN MADE THEIR OWN CRUDE SOAP BY BOILING ASHES FROM THE FIRE WITH ANIMAL FATS. FINE SOAPS WERE MADE FROM OLIVE OIL INSTEAD OF FAT, & THESE WERE IMPORTED FROM SUCH PLACES AS CASTILE IN SPAIN.

SOAP MANUFACTURE

SOAP IS MADE BY CAUSTIC SODA & FATS BOILED TOGETHER. SOAP-BOILERS TRADITIONALLY MADE THEIR SODA BY HEATING ASHES & LIME TOGETHER. THE INTRODUCTION OF SYNTHETIC SODA IN THE EARLY 1800S, ALTHOUGH AT FIRST RESISTED BY THE SOAP-BOILERS, MADE CHEAP MASS-PRODUCED SOAP AVAILABLE. ONE OF THE FIRST MEN TO UTILIZE SYNTHETIC SODA WAS JOSIAS GAMBLE, WHO OPENED A NEW WORKS IN ST HELEN'S (LANCS) IN 1828.

TRANSPARENT SOAP

TRANSPARENT SOAP WAS INTRODUCED IN 1748 BY ANDREW PEARS. IT IS MADE BY ORDINARY SOAP BEING DISSOLVED IN ALCOHOL, WHICH IS THEN DISTILLED TO LEAVE A JELLY & LEFT TO DRY IN MOULDS.

THE CLEAN BRITISH

A SWISS SOAP & DETERGENT MANUFACTURERS' SURVEY FOUND THAT THE BRITISH USE 1,163G OF SOAP PER PERSON PER YEAR – MORE THAN ANY OTHER EUROPEANS. THE BELGIANS USE THE LEAST, WITH ONLY 476G PER PERSON.

SOAP PLANTS

BEFORE THE INTRODUCTION OF SOAP, VARIOUS PLANTS WERE USED FOR WASHING. ONE SUCH WAS THE BRITISH SOAPWORT. WET LEAVES SQUEEZED BETWEEN THE HANDS CREATED A CONSIDERABLE LATHER.

SPEECH

COMMUNICATIVE HUMAN NOISES ISSUING FROM MOUTHS

VOCAL CORDS

THE VOCAL CORDS VIBRATE AT DIFFERENT SPEEDS TO GIVE A SCALE OF MUSICAL NOTES. SPEECH THAT DOES NOT USE VOCAL CORDS COMES OUT AS A WHISPER. MEN HAVE LOWER VOICES THAN WOMEN BECAUSE THEIR VOCAL CORDS ARE 50% LONGER & VIBRATE MORE SLOWLY.

VOCAL CORDS

VOWELS

THE SPACES IN FRONT OF & BEHIND THE TONGUE RESONATE AT TWO DIFFERENT FREQUENCIES ACCORDING TO THEIR SIZE (LIKE ORGAN PIPES). THESE DOUBLE RESONANCES MAKE THE COMPLICATED WAVE FORMS OF THE VOWELS.

CONSONANTS

CONSONANTS ARE MORE COMPLICATED TO SPEAK THAN VOWELS. THE NOSE IS USED FOR N, M, & NG. (EX) PLOSIVE BURSTS OF AIR ARE USED FOR P, B, T, D, K & G.

IMITATION

SCIENTISTS HAVE BEEN SURPRISED TO DISCOVER THAT THE MOUTH MOVEMENTS OF PARENTS IN SPEAKING ARE IMITATED BY ONE-DAY-OLD BABIES, ALTHOUGH THEY DO NOT LEARN TO SPEAK FOR ALMOST 2 YEARS.

FAST TALKING

THE FASTEST SPEAKING RECORDED IN BRITAIN WAS A COMMENTARY ON A GREYHOUND RACE BY RAYMOND GLENDENNING (176 WORDS IN 30 SECONDS).

SYNTHESIS

COMPUTER VOICE SYNTHESIZERS GENERATE 64 SOUNDS CALLED PHONEMES. THE MEMORY STORES WORDS AS SEQUENCES OF THESE PHONEMES.

HOTTENTOTS SPEAK WHILE INHALING, MAKING "EXPLOSIVE" CLICKING NOISES WITH THEIR TONGUES.

VISUALS V. VERBALS

ANALYSIS

MODERN COMPUTER SPEECH RECOGNITION SYSTEMS CAN TRANSCRIBE SPOKEN MATERIAL AT IMPRESSIVE SPEEDS AND WITH UP TO 99% ACCURACY. EARLY SYSTEMS OFTEN TOOK WELL OVER AN HOUR TO TRANSCRIBE A SENTENCE SPOKEN IN JUST 30 SECONDS.

98% OF ADULTS LISTENING TO THE SOUND "BA" WHILE WATCHING A VIDEO OF LIPS MOUTHING "GA" ARE CONVINCED THEY HEAR THE SOUND "DA". THIS ILLUSION WORKS WITH OTHER SOUNDS & IS THOUGHT TO BE CAUSED BY THE BRAIN MAKING A GUESS, COMPROMISING THE INFORMATION RECEIVED.

COMPETENT MALEVOLENCE

A US STUDY ON PUBLIC SPEAKING HAS FOUND THAT THE FASTER THE SPEECH, THE MORE COMPETENT BUT THE LESS BENEVOLENT THE SPEAKER IS JUDGED TO BE.

ANIMAL IGNORANCE

THE DIFFICULTY ANIMALS HAVE IN COMPREHENDING HUMAN SPEECH ARISES PARTLY BECAUSE THEY CAN HEAR MUCH HIGHER & LOWER NOTES THAN HUMANS. AS THEIR SOUND-DETECTING NERVES ARE SPREAD OVER A WIDER RANGE THERE ARE FEWER AT SPEECH FREQUENCIES. THIS MAY PREVENT THEIR HEARING THE SUBTLE DIFFERENCES BETWEEN VOWELS ETC.

HOW TO STOP YOUR NOSE GOING RED

RUB YOUR EARS VIGOROUSLY & THE BLOOD SHOULD RUSH FROM YOUR NOSE TO YOUR EARS.

SPIES

PEOPLE EMPLOYED IN COLLECTING SECRET INFORMATION

SOME SPIES IN WORLD WAR I WERE SOMEWHAT NAIVE. A NAVAL CENSOR, SUSPICIOUS OF A CABLE WHICH SAID SIMPLY "MOTHER IS DEAD", CHANGED THE WORDING TO "MOTHER IS DECEASED". WHEN HE NOTICED THE REPLY "IS MOTHER DEAD OR DECEASED?" HE WAS SURE THERE WAS SOME INTRIGUE. SHORTLY AFTERWARDS THE SENDER WAS ARRESTED & PROVED TO BE A SPY.

A COMPUTER-PROOF CODE

MOST CIPHERS CAN BE CRACKED BY CAREFUL ANALYSIS USING CIPHER COMPUTERS. HOWEVER, THE RUSSIANS ONCE USED A SERIES OF CIPHERS THAT DEFIED ALL ATTEMPTS AT ANALYSIS TILL AN AGENT WAS ARRESTED CARRYING A CODEBOOK. IT WAS FOUND THAT THE COMPUTER HAD BEEN BAFFLED BECAUSE IN COMPOSING THE CODE, WHEN ADDING OR SUBTRACTING, THE SPY HAD IGNORED ANY CARRY-OVERS OR DEDUCTIONS FROM ONE COLUMN TO ANOTHER (E.G. 689 + 576 = 155)

INCRIMINATING CABLES

J32 942 LONDON
DE WEER JANSEN DUINSTART 105 DEN
HAAG HOLLAND (+) MOTHER IS DEAD

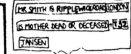

MR SMITH 16 RIPPLEWIOLROAD LONDON
IS MOTHER DEAD OR DECEASED + T.52
JANSEN

CONFIDENTIAL CONFERENCES

ELECTRONIC BUGGING DEVICES HAVE BECOME SO SMALL & SOPHISTICATED THAT SOME ARE ALMOST IMPOSSIBLE TO DETECT. HOWEVER, ONE US FIRM ONCE MARKETED A SYSTEM TO ENSURE COMPLETELY BUG-PROOF CONVERSATION. THE PARTICIPANTS WORE HEADSETS & MOUTHCUP MICROPHONES. THE MOUTHCUP PREVENTED LIP READING & HELPED TO CUT DOWN SOUND LEAKAGE. FURTHERMORE, TO BEAT ULTRA-SENSITIVE MICROPHONES, A LOUD NOISE WAS TRIGGERED EVERY TIME SOMEONE SPOKE, WHICH DROWNED ANY SPEECH NOISE. IT ALSO EMITTED RANDOM ELECTROMAGNETIC RADIATION.

SPIES DRIVING HITLER MAD

ONE OF THE MOST BIZARRE ENTERPRISES OF BRITISH MILITARY INTELLIGENCE IN WORLD WAR II WAS A MASTER PLAN TO DRIVE HITLER MAD FROM EXAMINATION OF PRE-WAR PSYCHOLOGICAL REPORTS ON THE FUHRER, PSYCHOANALYSTS DEDUCED THAT EXPOSURE TO OBSCENE LITERATURE MIGHT DRIVE HIM INSANE. A COLLECTION OF MATERIAL WAS ASSEMBLED TO BE DROPPED FROM A PLANE OVER HITLER'S HQ. THE COLONEL IN CHARGE OF THE FLIGHT VETOED THE MISSION AT THE LAST MINUTE, SAYING IT WAS TOO LUDICROUS.

THE TELEPHONE BUG

ONE OF THE MOST DIFFICULT BUGS TO DETECT WAS THE TELEPHONE BUG. THE EAVESDROPPER RANG THE VICTIM, SAID HE HAD THE WRONG NUMBER & WAITED FOR THE VICTIM TO HANG UP, SO THE LINE WAS LEFT OPEN. THE BUG, CONCEALED IN THE VICTIM'S TELEPHONE EARPIECE, WAS THEN ACTIVATED WHEN THE EAVESDROPPER BLEW A WHISTLE INTO HIS TELEPHONE. THE DEVICE WOULD THEN PICK UP ANY VOICES IN THE VICTIM'S ROOM – TRANSMITTING THEM DOWN THE TELEPHONE LINE TO ANYWHERE IN THE WORLD THAT WAS LINKED BY PHONE.

THE LASER BUG

AN INGENIOUS LASER SPYING DEVICE WAS ONCE DEVELOPED. AIMED AT A WINDOW, IT WOULD PICK UP ANY CONVERSATION INSIDE BY ANALYSING THE MINUTE VIBRATIONS OF THE GLASS. UNFORTUNATELY THE DEVICE DID NOT WORK IF THE CURTAINS WERE DRAWN.

A CAREER AS A SPY

IN THE PAST THE FRENCH COUNTER-ESPIONAGE SERVICE HAS HAD TROUBLE RECRUITING, PARTICULARLY COMPUTER & COMMUNICATIONS SPECIALISTS. "LE MONDE" ONCE REPORTED THAT THEY HAD RESORTED TO PLACING SMALL ADS IN NEWSPAPERS.

HOW TO MAKE A MATCHBOX LAND UPRIGHT

IF A MATCHBOX IS DROPPED ON ITS END FROM ABOUT 25CM IT IS ALMOST CERTAIN TO FALL OVER. HOWEVER, IF YOU FIRST HALF-PULL OUT THE DRAWER IT WILL LAND UPRIGHT.

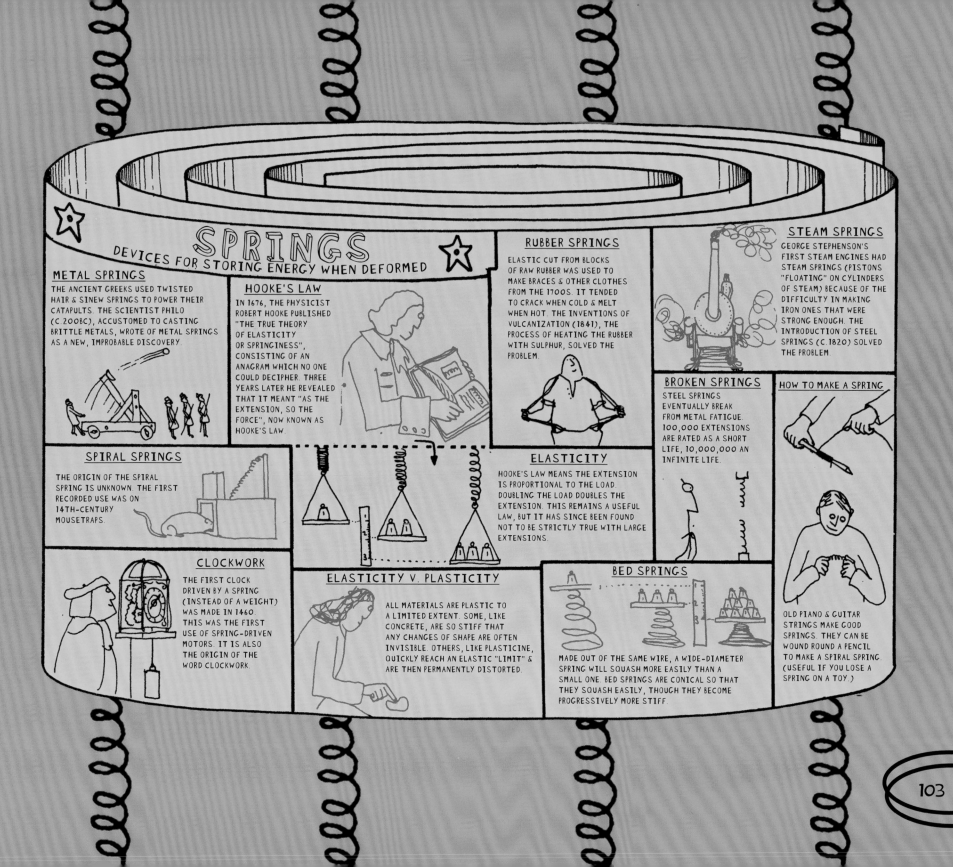

SPRINGS
DEVICES FOR STORING ENERGY WHEN DEFORMED

METAL SPRINGS

THE ANCIENT GREEKS USED TWISTED HAIR & SINEW SPRINGS TO POWER THEIR CATAPULTS. THE SCIENTIST PHILO (C.200BC), ACCUSTOMED TO CASTING BRITTLE METALS, WROTE OF METAL SPRINGS AS A NEW, IMPROBABLE DISCOVERY.

HOOKE'S LAW

IN 1676, THE PHYSICIST ROBERT HOOKE PUBLISHED "THE TRUE THEORY OF ELASTICITY OR SPRINGINESS", CONSISTING OF AN ANAGRAM WHICH NO ONE COULD DECIPHER. THREE YEARS LATER HE REVEALED THAT IT MEANT "AS THE EXTENSION, SO THE FORCE", NOW KNOWN AS HOOKE'S LAW.

RUBBER SPRINGS

ELASTIC CUT FROM BLOCKS OF RAW RUBBER WAS USED TO MAKE BRACES & OTHER CLOTHES FROM THE 1700S. IT TENDED TO CRACK WHEN COLD & MELT WHEN HOT. THE INVENTIONS OF VULCANIZATION (1841), THE PROCESS OF HEATING THE RUBBER WITH SULPHUR, SOLVED THE PROBLEM.

STEAM SPRINGS

GEORGE STEPHENSON'S FIRST STEAM ENGINES HAD STEAM SPRINGS (PISTONS "FLOATING" ON CYLINDERS OF STEAM) BECAUSE OF THE DIFFICULTY IN MAKING IRON ONES THAT WERE STRONG ENOUGH. THE INTRODUCTION OF STEEL SPRINGS (C.1820) SOLVED THE PROBLEM.

SPIRAL SPRINGS

THE ORIGIN OF THE SPIRAL SPRING IS UNKNOWN. THE FIRST RECORDED USE WAS ON 14TH-CENTURY MOUSETRAPS.

ELASTICITY

HOOKE'S LAW MEANS THE EXTENSION IS PROPORTIONAL TO THE LOAD. DOUBLING THE LOAD DOUBLES THE EXTENSION. THIS REMAINS A USEFUL LAW, BUT IT HAS SINCE BEEN FOUND NOT TO BE STRICTLY TRUE WITH LARGE EXTENSIONS.

BROKEN SPRINGS

STEEL SPRINGS EVENTUALLY BREAK FROM METAL FATIGUE. 100,000 EXTENSIONS ARE RATED AS A SHORT LIFE, 10,000,000 AN INFINITE LIFE.

HOW TO MAKE A SPRING

OLD PIANO & GUITAR STRINGS MAKE GOOD SPRINGS. THEY CAN BE WOUND ROUND A PENCIL TO MAKE A SPIRAL SPRING. (USEFUL IF YOU LOSE A SPRING ON A TOY.)

CLOCKWORK

THE FIRST CLOCK DRIVEN BY A SPRING (INSTEAD OF A WEIGHT) WAS MADE IN 1460. THIS WAS THE FIRST USE OF SPRING-DRIVEN MOTORS. IT IS ALSO THE ORIGIN OF THE WORD CLOCKWORK.

ELASTICITY V. PLASTICITY

ALL MATERIALS ARE PLASTIC TO A LIMITED EXTENT. SOME, LIKE CONCRETE, ARE SO STIFF THAT ANY CHANGES OF SHAPE ARE OFTEN INVISIBLE. OTHERS, LIKE PLASTICINE, QUICKLY REACH AN ELASTIC "LIMIT" & ARE THEN PERMANENTLY DISTORTED.

BED SPRINGS

MADE OUT OF THE SAME WIRE, A WIDE-DIAMETER SPRING WILL SQUASH MORE EASILY THAN A SMALL ONE. BED SPRINGS ARE CONICAL SO THAT THEY SQUASH EASILY, THOUGH THEY BECOME PROGRESSIVELY MORE STIFF.

SWORDS

OFFENSIVE WEAPONS WITH LONG SHARP BLADES

THE IRON AGE

THE MOST IMPORTANT APPLICATION OF IRON IN THE EARLY IRON AGE WAS FOR THE MANUFACTURE OF SWORDS. THEY HAD PREVIOUSLY BEEN MADE OF BRONZE BUT THIS WAS COMPARATIVELY SOFT & HAD TO BE WIELDED WITH CARE & RESTRAINT. THE FORCE OF A STROKE FROM AN IRON SWORD WAS LIMITED ONLY BY THE STRENGTH OF THE HUMAN ARM.

FENCING

FENCING USED TO BE CONSIDERABLY MORE TREACHEROUS THAN IT IS TODAY. "THE EXPERT SWORDSMAN'S COMPANION", PUBLISHED IN 1728, ADVISES THE READER NEVER TO SHAKE HANDS WITH AN OPPONENT WHO STILL HOLDS A SWORD LEST HE BE PULLED & IMPALED ON ITS POINT. ALSO TO BEWARE OF BEING BLINDED BY OPPONENTS CARRYING POCKETFULS OF DUST.

THE FLAMBOYANT SWORD

THE SCALLOPED EDGE ON MANY MODERN CARVING KNIVES IS NOT A RECENT INVENTION. IT FIRST APPEARED IN THE 1500S KNOWN AS A FLAMBOYANT BLADE. IT IS FOUND ON THE HEAVY 1.8M-LONG, TWO-HANDED SWORD, WHIRLED ABOVE THE HEAD TO CREATE A "FENCE" OF STEEL.

THE JAPANESE SWORD

CUT OR THRUST

THERE HAS ALWAYS BEEN HOT DISPUTE AS TO WHETHER A SWORD SHOULD BE DESIGNED PRIMARILY FOR THRUSTING (THIN & STRAIGHT) OR FOR SLASHING (WIDE & CURVED). A DETERMINED THRUST, ESPECIALLY FROM A HORSEMAN AT FULL GALLOP, WAS DIFFICULT TO PARRY &, IF DRIVEN HOME, WOULD PROBABLY KILL THE VICTIM OUTRIGHT. FROM THE TIME OF PRINCE RUPERT & CROMWELL IN THE CIVIL WAR THE BRITISH CAVALRY ATTACKED AT FULL GALLOP, USING BOTH THE THRUST & THE SLASH. THE USE OF THE POINT ONLY WAS FIRMLY LAID DOWN IN THE 20TH CENTURY.

THE JAPANESE HELD THE SWORD IN PARTICULARLY HIGH ESTEEM & SURROUNDED ITS MANUFACTURE WITH SEMI-RELIGIOUS RITUAL. THE SMITH COMMENCED THE DAY'S WORK WITH A BATH & THE WORKSHOP WAS FESTOONED WITH CHARMS & FLAGS TO HOLD EVIL INFLUENCES AT BAY. BLADES WERE MADE FROM STRIPS OF IRON REPEATEDLY HAMMERED OUT & FOLDED IN HALF. A BLADE THUS HAMMERED & FOLDED 20 TIMES CONSISTED OF NEARLY 4 MILLION LAYERS.

THE SHRINKING SWORD

UP UNTIL ABOUT 1450 SWORDS BECAME INCREASINGLY LARGE, IN ORDER TO PENETRATE THE INCREASINGLY EFFECTIVE ARMOUR. HOWEVER, BECAUSE OF THE EXTREME WEIGHT & CLUMSINESS OF BULLET-PROOF ARMOUR, THE INTRODUCTION OF FIREARMS LED TO THE ABANDONMENT OF ARMOUR & THE APPEARANCE OF SMALLER SWORDS CALLED RAPIERS IN THE 1500S. 100 YEARS LATER, SWORDS BECAME SMALLER STILL WITH THE RENAISSANCE FASHION FOR THE ROMAN SWORD. THE BRITISH INFANTRY FINALLY CEASED CARRYING SWORDS IN BATTLE IN 1768.

HOW TO MAKE YOURSELF INTO A BIRD

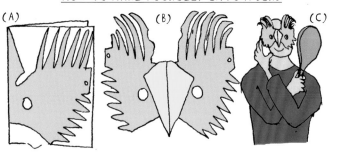

FOLD PIECE OF CARD IN HALF, THEN CUT SHAPE AS SHOWN (A). FOLD OVER NOSE & ATTACH ELASTIC (B). PUT MASK ON (C).

THERMOMETERS
INSTRUMENTS FOR MEASURING TEMPERATURE

GALEN'S DEGREES

THE PHYSICIST GALEN (AD C.150) WAS THE FIRST MAN TO ATTEMPT TO MEASURE TEMPERATURE. HE PROPOSED A SCALE OF 4 DEGREES OF COLD & 4 DEGREES OF HEAT WITH A NEUTRAL POINT (EQUAL PARTS OF BOILING & FREEZING WATER) IN BETWEEN

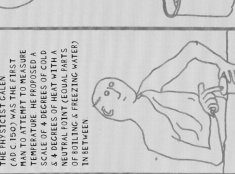

AIR THERMOMETER

THE EARLIEST THERMOMETER, WHICH APPEARED DURING THE 1550s, WORKED BY THE EXPANSION OF AIR. ITS MAIN DEFECT WAS THAT IT RESPONDED TO CHANGES IN ATMOSPHERIC PRESSURE AS WELL AS TEMPERATURE

LIQUID THERMOMETER

THE LIQUID-IN-GLASS THERMOMETER, WHICH RELIES ON THE EXPANSION OF THE LIQUID, WAS INVENTED BY FERDINAND II, GRAND DUKE OF TUSCANY, IN 1640. UNFORTUNATELY, THERE WAS NO STANDARD SCALE OF TEMPERATURE AT THE TIME, SO NO TWO THERMOMETERS AGREED.

DISCOVERIES

THE INVENTION OF THE THERMOMETER DISPELLED THE BELIEF THAT WELL-WATER WAS WARMER IN THE WINTER THAN IN THE SUMMER, ALSO THE BELIEF THAT PEOPLE WHO LIVED IN THE TROPICS HAD A HIGHER BODY TEMPERATURE

FAHRENHEIT

DANIEL FAHRENHEIT (1686–1736) WAS A GERMAN INSTRUMENT MAKER. HIS SCALE OF TEMPERATURE DIVIDES THE INTERVAL BETWEEN THE FREEZING & BOILING POINTS OF WATER INTO 180 "DEGREES". ALTHOUGH HE POPULARIZED THE SCALE, IT WAS INVENTED BY A SWEDISH PHYSICIST CALLED RÖMER IN ABOUT 1700.

POTTERY THERMOMETERS

POTTERS MEASURE THE TEMPERATURE INSIDE THEIR KILNS BY WATCHING SMALL POTTERY CONES PLACED INSIDE BEFORE FIRING. EACH IS MARKED WITH THE SPECIFIC TEMPERATURE AT WHICH IT COLLAPSES (I.E. BECOMES LIQUID).

MOVING ZERO

IN THE LATE-19TH CENTURY, IT WAS REALIZED THAT THE ZERO POINT OF GLASS-MERCURY THERMOMETERS ROSE SLIGHTLY AS THEY AGED. PHYSICISTS WERE BAFFLED UNTIL IT WAS REALIZED THAT THE MERCURY WAS SLOWLY DISSOLVING THE LEAD IN THE GLASS. ALL THERMOMETERS ARE NOW MADE OF SPECIAL "HARD GLASS".

ACCURATE TEMPERATURE

MERCURY THERMOMETERS RELY ON THE ASSUMPTION THAT EQUAL CHANGES OF VOLUME CORRESPOND TO EQUAL CHANGES IN TEMPERATURE. THIS IS NOT EXACTLY TRUE. AN EXACT DEFINITION OF A DEGREE USING THE THEORETICAL LAWS OF THERMODYNAMICS WAS WORKED OUT BY LORD KELVIN IN 1848.

CUMBERSOME TEMPERATURE

THE DISADVANTAGE OF KELVIN'S DEFINITION IS THAT IT CAN BE MEASURED DIRECTLY ONLY WITH A "CONSTANT VOLUME GAS THERMOMETER" (A LARGE COMPLEX DEVICE WHICH REQUIRES ELABORATE MATHEMATICAL CORRECTIONS BEFORE A READING CAN BE DEDUCED). IT IS NOW USED ONLY FOR CALIBRATING OTHER THERMOMETERS.

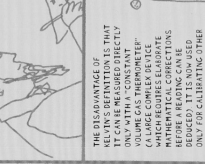

HOW TO EXTINGUISH A CANDLE WITH A WIRE

COPPER WIRE

PIN

WIND A COIL OF COPPER WIRE & HOLD IT OVER A CANDLE FLAME WITH A PIN. THE WIRE WILL ABSORB HEAT SO RAPIDLY THAT THE FLAME WILL BE EXTINGUISHED IN A FEW SECONDS

CELSIUS

THE CELSIUS (CENTIGRADE) SCALE IS MISNAMED, AS PROFESSOR CELSIUS'S SCALE ACTUALLY HAD 0° AS WATER'S BOILING POINT & 100° AS ITS FREEZING POINT

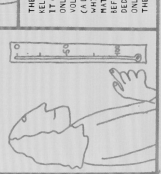

TOMATOES
SOFT, RED PULPY EDIBLE FRUIT

HISTORIC TOMATOES

TOMATOES WERE PROBABLY FIRST NOTICED BY MAN WHEN THEY APPEARED GROWING AS WEEDS IN SOUTH AMERICAN MAIZE FIELDS. CULTIVATION HAD INCREASED THE YIELD & GREATLY IMPROVED THE VARIETIES BY THE TIME THE SPANIARDS CAME, IN THE 16TH CENTURY. THE FIRST TYPE OF TOMATO TO BE INTRODUCED INTO EUROPE SEEMS TO HAVE BEEN YELLOW, HENCE THE NAME "GOLDEN APPLE" BY WHICH IT WAS FIRST KNOWN. IT WAS EATEN AS A FRUIT & WAS NOT USED AS A VEGETABLE UNTIL THE 19TH CENTURY.

ENORMOUS TOMATOES

THE LARGEST TOMATO EVER RECORDED WEIGHED 3.51KG & WAS GROWN IN 1986 IN OKLAHOMA, USA.

SEEDLESS TOMATOES

TOMATO PLANTS IN GREENHOUSES OFTEN DO NOT POLLINATE, SO THAT FEW OF THE FLOWERS GIVE RISE TO FRUIT. HOWEVER, SPRAYING THE PLANTS WITH A CHEMICAL CALLED AUXIN GIVES COMPLETE "SETTING" OF FRUIT, MOST OF WHICH IS SEEDLESS (INFERTILE). AUXINS OCCUR NATURALLY IN MANY PLANT SPECIES. THEY HAVE THE EFFECT OF STIMULATING THE GROWTH OF LATERAL BUDS & FRUIT & DEPRESSING THE GROWTH OF LENGTHENING SHOOTS. OTHER USES OF AUXINS INCLUDE DELAYING THE OPENING OF FLOWER BUDS ON FRUIT TREES SO AS TO AVOID LATE FROSTS, DEPRESSING GROWTH IN NURSERY TREES DURING TRANSPORT, & INHIBITING THE SPROUTING OF POTATOES IN STORAGE.

TOMATOES IN PIPES

IT IS POSSIBLE TO GROW TOMATOES (& CUCUMBERS) IN VERTICAL PIPES. THESE PIPES ARE FULL OF EARTH & HAVE NOTCHES CUT IN THE SIDES. SEEDLINGS ARE PLANTED IN EACH NOTCH & WATER IS CONTINUALLY FED TO THE TOP OF THE PIPES. IT IS CLAIMED THAT 10-15 PLANTS CAN THUS BE GROWN IN THE AREA NORMALLY OCCUPIED BY ONE.

POISONOUS TOMATOES

THE STEMS & LEAVES OF TOMATO PLANTS ARE TOXIC, CONTAINING POISONS CALLED SOLANINES. THESE ARE ALSO PRESENT IN THE GREEN "EYES" OF POTATOES. THEY ARE NOT DESTROYED BY BOILING OR COOKING & CAN CAUSE BURNING OF THE THROAT, HEADACHES, VOMITING, CONVULSIONS & UNCONSCIOUSNESS. HOWEVER, FATAL CASES ARE EXTREMELY RARE.

HOW TO MAKE THE SOUND OF RAIN

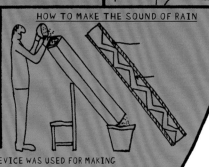

THIS DEVICE WAS USED FOR MAKING THEATRICAL RAIN EFFECTS. THE SQUARE TUBE IS MADE FROM WOODEN PLANKS NAILED TOGETHER & THE DIAGONAL PARTITIONS MADE FROM SHEET METAL SCREWED TO THE PLANKS. DRIED PEAS ARE DROPPED IN AT THE TOP. THE VIOLENCE OF THE "RAIN" DEPENDS ON THE NUMBER OF PEAS & THE SLOPE OF THE TUBE.

CLEVER TOMATOES

TOMATO JUICE CONTAINS A STRONG GERMINATION-INHIBITOR. IT PREVENTS THE SEEDS FROM GERMINATING UNTIL THE SPRING WHEN THE FRUIT HAS ROTTED. THIS GIVES SEEDLINGS A BETTER CHANCE OF SURVIVAL THAN IF THEY GERMINATE IN WINTER.

TWINS

INDIVIDUALS CONCEIVED SIMULTANEOUSLY

OMINOUS TWINS

THE IBO OF NIGERIA TRADITIONALLY SAW THE BIRTH OF TWINS AS A BAD OMEN. THEY THREW AWAY ANY FOOD, WATER & FIREWOOD LEFT FROM THE NIGHT OF THE BIRTH.

ILL-FATED TWINS

THE YUROK INDIANS OF NORTH AMERICA KILLED THE FEMALE OF A MALE-FEMALE PAIR FOR SUPERSTITIOUS REASONS.

HEAVENLY TWINS

THE COCOPAS INDIANS OF NORTH AMERICA TREATED TWINS PARTICULARLY WELL. THEY BELIEVED TWINS WERE VISITORS FROM HEAVEN & WOULD RETURN THERE IF THEY DID NOT ENJOY LIFE ON EARTH.

WILD TWINS

IN PARTS OF UGANDA TWINS WERE SEEN ALMOST AS WILD ANIMALS & HAD SUCH A REPUTATION FOR BEING FEARLESS THAT THEY WERE USED TO LEAD CHARGES IN WARS.

TWIN FATHERS

THE SALIVA TRIBE OF SOUTH AMERICA BELIEVED THAT TWINS MUST HAVE DIFFERENT FATHERS. THE MOTHER WAS OFTEN PUNISHED BY HER HUSBAND.

FRATERNAL TWINS

TWO SEPARATE EGGS ARE FERTILIZED SIMULTANEOUSLY. THEY DO NOT SHARE THE SAME GENES & CAN BE OPPOSITE SEXES.

IDENTICAL TWINS

THESE OCCUR ONCE IN ABOUT 500 BIRTHS WHEN A SINGLE EGG SPLITS IN HALF SHORTLY AFTER FERTILIZATION. THEY ARE ALWAYS THE SAME SEX & PHYSICALLY IDENTICAL BECAUSE THEY HAVE THE SAME GENES.

TWIN ARMADILLOS

MOST ANIMALS THAT HAVE MULTIPLE BIRTHS CONCEIVE BY FERTILIZING MANY EGGS SIMULTANEOUSLY. THE NINE-BANDED ARMADILLO IS AN EXCEPTION. THE MALE FERTILIZES ONE EGG WHICH LATER SPLITS – SO THE YOUNG ARE IDENTICAL TWINS.

NUTRITION

SHEEP ARE OFTEN OVERFED BEFORE MATING TO INCREASE LITTER SIZE. THE INCIDENCE OF HUMAN TWINS FELL SLIGHTLY DURING WORLD WAR II BECAUSE OF MALNUTRITION IN COUNTRIES WHERE FOOD WAS SCARCE.

AGE

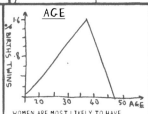

WOMEN ARE MOST LIKELY TO HAVE TWINS BETWEEN 30 & 40 BECAUSE THEY RELEASE TWO EGGS AT A TIME MORE FREQUENTLY DURING THIS PERIOD.

TESTING FOR TWINS

A TRADITIONAL METHOD OF DETECTING TWINS WAS TO HAVE 2 DOCTORS LISTENING TO & CALLING OUT THE FOETUS'S HEARTBEAT. IF THEIR CALLS DID NOT COINCIDE IT WAS ASSUMED THAT THERE WERE TWO FOETUSES.

IN THE PAST, TWINS WERE SOMETIMES DETECTED BEFORE BIRTH OWING TO A HORMONE PRESENT AT MUCH HIGHER LEVELS IN WOMEN BEARING TWINS. HOWEVER, MODERN ULTRASOUND TECHNIQUES HAVE NOW MADE DETECTION OF TWINS MUCH EASIER.

HEREDITY

SISTERS OF MOTHERS OF TWINS ARE 2.5 TIMES MORE LIKELY TO HAVE TWINS THAN OTHER WOMEN. SISTERS OF FRATERNAL TWINS ARE 4 TIMES MORE LIKELY TO HAVE TWINS.

RACE

IT IS NOT KNOWN WHY LIKELIHOOD OF FRATERNAL TWINS VARIES WITH RACE.

FREQUENCY

MORE FREQUENT SEX INCREASES THE LIKELIHOOD OF A SECOND EGG BEING FERTILIZED.

DRUGS

FERTILITY DRUGS CAN INCREASE THE CHANCE OF TWINS FROM 1 IN 100 TO 1 IN 4.

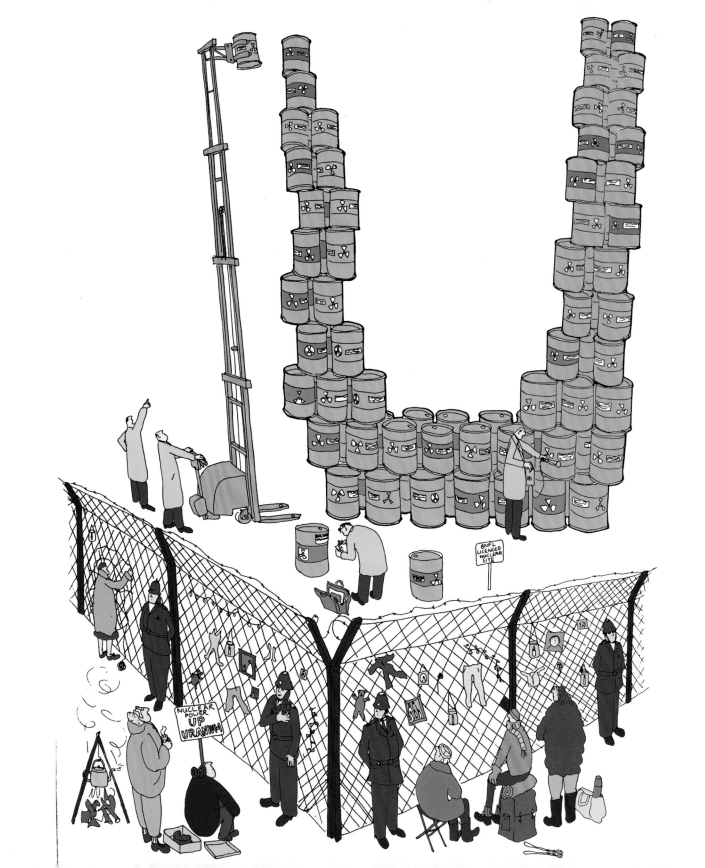

☆ UNDERGROUND TRAINS ☆

THE METROPOLITAN

THE WORLD'S FIRST UNDERGROUND LINE WAS THE LONDON METROPOLITAN FROM FARRINGDON TO PADDINGTON, WHICH OPENED IN 1863. DESIGNED FOR STEAM ENGINES, THE TUNNELS WERE SHALLOW, WITH OPEN SECTIONS AT REGULAR INTERVALS.

THE SMOKELESS ENGINE

THE METROPOLITAN LINE WAS DESIGNED TO BE USED BY A SPECIAL STEAM ENGINE WITH FIRE BRICKS UNDER THE BOILER. THE IDEA WAS TO SHUT DOWN THE FIRE INSIDE TUNNELS, RELYING ON THE HEAT OF THE BRICKS TO MAKE STEAM UNTIL THE NEXT OPEN SECTION. IT NEVER WORKED.

VENTILATION

WHILE ORDINARY STEAM ENGINES HAD TO BE USED, VENTILATION REMAINED A PROBLEM. PEOPLE FREQUENTLY FAINTED DESPITE THE ADDITION OF LARGE VENTILATION SHAFTS.

STANDING

WHEN THE METROPOLITAN LINE OPENED, IT WAS THOUGHT TO BE DANGEROUS TO REMAIN STANDING & PASSENGERS WERE PROSECUTED FOR DOING SO.

THE TUBE

THE FIRST DEEP UNDERGROUND TUBE RAILWAY WAS BUILT UNDER THE THAMES NEAR TOWER BRIDGE IN 1870. THE TRAINS WERE PULLED BY CABLES FROM ENGINES ON THE SURFACE. THE TUNNEL WAS ONLY 2M IN DIAMETER & EACH TRAIN COULD HOLD ONLY 12 PEOPLE. AFTER A YEAR IT WAS CONVERTED TO A PEDESTRIAN TUNNEL. IT NOW CARRIES WATER PIPES.

ELECTRIC TRAINS

UNDERGROUND RAILWAYS DID NOT BECOME FULLY PRACTICAL UNTIL THE INTRODUCTION OF SMOKELESS ELECTRIC TRAINS IN THE 1880S. LONDON'S FIRST ELECTRIC TUBE TRAINS WERE ALMOST WINDOWLESS & CONDUCTORS HAD TO SHOUT OUT THE NAMES OF STATIONS.

THERE ARE OVER 70,000 SQ M OF MARBLE IN MOSCOW'S TUBE STATIONS.

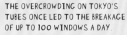
OVER 70 TONNES OF RUBBISH A DAY IS DEPOSITED ON NEW YORK'S SUBWAYS.

THE OVERCROWDING ON TOKYO'S TUBES ONCE LED TO THE BREAKAGE OF UP TO 100 WINDOWS A DAY.

WOMEN WERE NOT EMPLOYED ON THE LONDON UNDERGROUND UNTIL 1940.

RUBBER WHEELS

THE PARIS METRO HAS MANY TRAINS WITH RUBBER TYRES. THEY CAN ACCELERATE 50% FASTER & TURN TIGHTER CORNERS THAN THE CONVENTIONAL STEEL WHEELS. HOWEVER, RUBBER TYRES USE 3 TIMES AS MUCH ENERGY & THE CONCRETE TRACK SOON GETS COATED WITH A VENEER OF RUBBER WHICH REDUCES THE ACCELERATION.

CLEANING

THE PARIS METRO HAS A TUNNEL-CLEANING TRAIN WHICH IS LIKE A GIANT VACUUM CLEANER. A LARGE FAN BLOWS THE DIRT OFF THE WALLS & ANOTHER SUCKS IT UP, DUMPING IT IN THE TRUCKS BEHIND.

HUMPS

AN INGENIOUS WAY OF SAVING ENERGY USED ON SOME MODERN TUBES IS TO BUILD THE STATIONS ON "HUMPS". GRAVITY THEN ASSISTS BRAKING & ACCELERATION.

EMERGENCIES

THERE ARE 2 BARE COPPER TELEPHONE WIRES RUNNING ALONGSIDE THE TRACK ON THE LONDON UNDERGROUND. IN THE PAST, IF A TRAIN GOT STUCK THE DRIVER WOULD LEAN OUT OF HIS WINDOW & CLIP ON A TELEPHONE. DRIVERS STILL USE THESE WIRES TO CUT OFF THE ELECTRICITY TO THE RAILS BY CONNECTING THEM TOGETHER.

HOW TO FIND THE AGE OF A CARRIAGE

THE DATE OF MANUFACTURE IS USUALLY CAST ON THE FLOOR PLATES BENEATH THE SLIDING DOORS.

UNDERWEAR

BICYCLING

THE NEW FASHION FOR LADIES' BICYCLES IN THE 1890S, WHICH INTRODUCED BLOOMERS & DIVIDED SKIRTS, ALSO HAD A CONSIDERABLE EFFECT ON UNDERWEAR, MAKING RIGID CORSETS & CRINOLINES IMPRACTICAL.

TANGOING

THE VIOLENT, JERKY MOVEMENTS OF THE TANGO, WHICH CAME INTO FASHION IN 1911, WERE ALSO INCOMPATIBLE WITH "RIGID" UNDERWEAR.

BRASSIÈRES

THE BRASSIÈRE EVOLVED FROM THE EDWARDIAN CORSET. THE FRENCH WORD REFERS TO A HARNESS OR CHILD'S VEST. THE FACT THAT THE BRA WAS ORIGINALLY KNOWN AS A "BACKLESS BRASSIÈRE" MAY EXPLAIN THIS CHOICE OF WORD.

HANDKERCHIEF BRAS

THE MODERN STYLE OF BRA WAS INVENTED BY A NEW YORK DÉBUTANTE CALLED MARY PHELPS JACOB IN 1913, DESIGNED BY EXPERIMENTS WITH FOLDED HANDKERCHIEFS. IT DID NOT COME INTO FASHION FOR ANOTHER 15 YEARS.

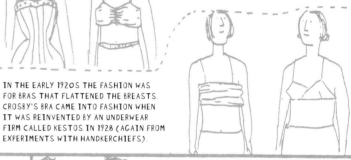

IN THE EARLY 1920S THE FASHION WAS FOR BRAS THAT FLATTENED THE BREASTS. CROSBY'S BRA CAME INTO FASHION WHEN IT WAS REINVENTED BY AN UNDERWEAR FIRM CALLED KESTOS IN 1928 (AGAIN FROM EXPERIMENTS WITH HANDKERCHIEFS).

JAEGER

IN 1878 A GERMAN, DR JAEGER, PUBLISHED A BOOK ADVOCATING WEARING WOOL NEXT TO THE SKIN. AN ENGLISH GROCER WAS SO IMPRESSED BY THIS THAT HE STARTED MANUFACTURING "DR JAEGER'S SANITARY WOOLLEN SYSTEM". THIS GREATLY INFLUENCED THE STYLE OF UNDERWEAR FOR BOTH MEN & WOMEN UNTIL THE 1950S (THIS WAS THE ORIGIN OF THE FIRM JAEGER).

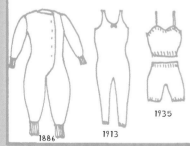

1886   1913   1935

AERTEX

THE CELLULAR COTTON MATERIAL AERTEX WAS INVENTED IN 1887 BY AN MP CALLED HASLAM, INTERESTED IN MAKING HEALTHIER UNDERWEAR. THE IDEA WAS THAT FRESH AIR SHOULD BE NOT ONLY BREATHED BUT ALSO ALLOWED IN CONTACT WITH THE SKIN.

PANTS

UNTIL 200 YEARS AGO, WOMEN DID NOT WEAR PANTS – THEIR LONG, HEAVY SKIRTS & PETTICOATS PREVENTED ANY IMMODESTY. PANTS, ORIGINALLY THOUGHT UNFEMININE, EVOLVED FROM LONG DRAWERS SHOWING BENEATH SKIRTS, WHICH CAME INTO FASHION FOR YOUNG GIRLS IN THE 1790S.

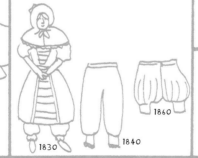

1830   1840   1860

STOCKINGS

THE EARLIEST RECORD OF STOCKINGS IS IN A PAINTING OF 1306. STOCKINGS WERE HELD UP BY GARTERS UNTIL THE INTRODUCTION OF SUSPENDERS IN THE 1880S (FIRST USED BY FRENCH MUSIC-HALL DANCERS & ONLY LATER ADOPTED AS RESPECTABLE DRESS).

TIGHTS

TIGHTS WERE FIRST WORN BY MEN IN THE 14TH–16TH CENTURIES. THEY DID NOT COME INTO FASHION FOR WOMEN UNTIL THE 1960S WHEN MINISKIRTS EXPOSED THE TOPS OF STOCKINGS.

☆ UTOPIAS ☆

REAL OR IMAGINARY SOCIETIES CONSIDERED TO BE PERFECT

SPARTA

ACCOUNTS OF THE ANCIENT GREEK MILITARY STATE OF SPARTA ARE PART MYTH & PART HISTORY. LATER WRITERS LOOKED BACK ON IT AS A FORM OF UTOPIA.

SPARTA WAS VERY AUSTERE. PERSONAL WEALTH, TRAVEL, DOMESTICITY & EVEN CRAFTSMANSHIP WERE SUPPRESSED. ADULTERY WAS ENCOURAGED BUT EACH BABY WAS INSPECTED AT BIRTH BY THE ELDERS & DROPPED DOWN A DEEP CAVE IF NOT "HEALTHY" ENOUGH.

THE MILLENARISTS

REFERENCES IN THE BIBLICAL BOOK OF REVELATIONS LED SOME EARLY CHRISTIANS (MILLENARISTS) TO BELIEVE THAT THERE WOULD EVENTUALLY BE A HEAVEN ON EARTH.

IN 1420 THE HUSSITES, A BOHEMIAN MILLENARIST SECT, CONVINCED THAT THE TIME FOR HEAVEN ON EARTH HAD COME, SEIZED THE TOWN OF TABOR (IN TODAY'S CZECH REPUBLIC). THEY LIVED BY WARFARE, KEEPING THEIR BOOTY IN A COMMUNAL PIT IN THE TOWN. THEY WERE DEFEATED IN 1434, WHEN 13,000 OF THE 18,000-STRONG ARMY WERE MASSACRED.

GOOD PLACE/NO PLACE

THE WORD "UTOPIA" WAS INVENTED BY THE ENGLISH WRITER SIR THOMAS MORE (C.1515). HE TOOK IT FROM EITHER THE GREEK EU = GOOD, OR OU = NOT (+ TOPOS = PLACE). THUS HE COULD HAVE MEANT EITHER "GOOD PLACE" OR "NO PLACE".

MORE'S UTOPIA IS A COMMUNAL ISLAND. LAWS AGAINST SEDUCTION & CORRUPTION ARE STRICT, GAMES & TRAVEL ARE RESTRICTED. ALL RELIGIONS ARE TOLERATED BUT ANYONE WHO BECOMES TOO HEATED ABOUT RELIGIOUS MATTERS IS BANISHED. TO PLACATE ANGRY CHURCHMEN, MORE CALLED THE STORYTELLER OF HIS BOOK MYTHLODAY (DISPENSER OF NONSENSE).

THE DIGGERS

THE ENCLOSURES, RESTRICTING ACCESS TO LAND BY THE POOR, CAUSED A FAMOUS ATTEMPT AT A UTOPIAN REFORM. WINSTANLEY, THE ENGLISH REFORMER, & 30 "DIGGERS" OR "TRUE LEVELLERS" OCCUPIED SOME WASTE GROUND IN SURREY IN 1649 & STARTED CULTIVATING IT.

THEIR CROPS & PROPERTY WERE ATTACKED & BURNED SEVERAL TIMES BY ANGRY LOCALS BUT EACH TIME THE DIGGERS RETURNED — UNTIL A PARSON WOODFORD LED A PARTICULARLY VIOLENT ATTACK IN 1650.

CHRISTIANIA

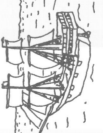 

DURING THE 1960s, MANY HIPPIES STARTED UTOPIAN COMMUNITIES TO ESCAPE FROM THE MODERN INDUSTRIAL WORLD.

ONE OF THE MOST FAMOUS IS THE TOWN OF CHRISTIANIA, DENMARK. ABANDONED ARMY BARRACKS, OCCUPIED BY SQUATTERS IN 1971, HAVE DEVELOPED INTO A TOWN OF ABOUT 1,000 PEOPLE. DESPITE CONTINUAL THREATS OF EVICTION, THEY PAY NO TAX & ORGANIZE THEIR OWN POLICING & SOCIAL SERVICES.

THE SHAKERS

BY THE MID-1700s THERE WAS ALREADY A STRONG FEELING THAT INDUSTRIAL CAPITALISM WAS UNNATURAL & CREATING INHUMAN CONDITIONS. MANY SECTS, MOSTLY RELIGIOUS, SET OFF FOR AMERICA TO FOUND THEIR UTOPIAS.

ONE SECT, THE SHAKERS, BELIEVED THEIR VILLAGES WERE EACH A SMALL PART OF THE GARDEN OF EDEN. THEIR LIFE CENTRED ON RELIGIOUS MEETINGS & ECSTATIC WHIRLING & SHAKING. THEY WERE NOT ALLOWED TO HAVE CHILDREN BUT RECRUITED MORE THAN 6,000 MEMBERS.

TOLSTOY'S COMMUNES

SEVERAL UTOPIAN "COMMUNIST" COLONIES WERE FOUNDED BY TOLSTOY'S SUPPORTERS IN BRITAIN IN THE 1890s.

FEW LASTED LONG. THE MORE COMMITTED & ENERGETIC MEMBERS DID THE WORK OF EVERYBODY ELSE. THOSE WHO LEFT DID SO WITH THE BEST CLOTHES & ANY AVAILABLE MONEY.

MEGASTRUCTURES

MANY TECHNOLOGICAL UTOPIAS HAVE BEEN PROPOSED — CULMINATING IN 1960s "MEGASTRUCTURES" WHICH WOULD CONTAIN WHOLE CITIES WITH MOVABLE "PLUG-IN" HOMES. FLOATING & WALKING CITIES WERE ALSO SUGGESTED.

ARCOSANTI (ARIZONA) IS AN EXPERIMENTAL "HIGH-TECH" UTOPIA, DESIGNED TO HOUSE 3,000 PEOPLE IN CLOSE PROXIMITY. ITS FOUNDER, SOLERI, BELIEVES THAT THE AWESOMNESS OF THE STRUCTURE & THE COMPLEXITY OF ITS CONSTRUCTION ARE POSITIVE ALTERNATIVES TO WAR, SQUALOR & SOCIAL STRIFE.

VACUUM CLEANERS

MACHINES FOR REMOVING DIRT BY SUCTION

NOISY SERPENTS

BOOTH'S FIRST MACHINES (NICKNAMED "NOISY SERPENTS") WERE HORSE-DRAWN & WERE CONNECTED BY HOSE TO ROOMS IN THE HOUSE.

SUCKING NOT BLOWING

THE VACUUM CLEANER WAS INVENTED IN 1902 IN BRITAIN BY A BRIDGE BUILDER CALLED HUBERT BOOTH AFTER WATCHING A NOT VERY SUCCESSFUL DEMONSTRATION OF A RAILWAY CARRIAGE CLEANER WHICH BLEW THE DUST OUT. HE REALIZED THAT SUCKING IT IN WOULD WORK BETTER.

BEATING

BEFORE THE INVENTION OF VACUUM CLEANERS, CARPETS & UPHOLSTERY WERE TAKEN OUTSIDE ONCE A YEAR & BEATEN TO GET THE DUST OUT. THIS WAS THE ORIGIN OF "SPRING CLEANING".

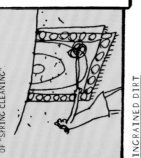

INGRAINED DIRT

MANY PLACES HAD NEVER BEEN PROPERLY CLEANED BEFORE THE INTRODUCTION OF THE VACUUM CLEANER. ONE PARISIAN THEATRE RECORDED THAT 217KG OF DUST WAS REMOVED FROM ITS SEATS.

HOOVER'S CLEANER

W. H. HOOVER WAS A HARNESS-MAKER WHOSE BUSINESS WAS HIT BY THE ADVENT OF THE CAR. IN 1907 HE BOUGHT THE RIGHTS TO MANUFACTURE THE FIRST PORTABLE VACUUM CLEANER FROM HIS WIFE'S COUSIN, THE CARETAKER OF A US DEPARTMENT STORE, WHO HAD PATENTED IT.

EARLY MACHINES

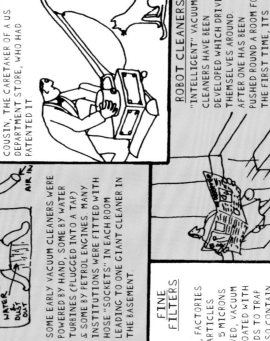

WATER & DUST OUT

AIR IN

SOME EARLY VACUUM CLEANERS WERE POWERED BY HAND, SOME BY WATER TURBINES (PLUGGED INTO A TAP) & SOME BY PETROL ENGINES. MANY INSTITUTIONS WERE FITTED WITH HOSE "SOCKETS" IN EACH ROOM LEADING TO ONE GIANT CLEANER IN THE BASEMENT.

FILTERS

THE CLOTH FILTERS INSIDE VACUUM CLEANERS TRAP PARTICLES BIGGER THAN ABOUT 5 MICRONS (5/1,000MM). EVERYTHING SMALLER (UP TO 15% OF HOUSE DUST) PASSES STRAIGHT THROUGH THE MACHINE & COMES OUT WITH THE EXHAUST AIR.

FINE FILTERS

IN HOSPITALS, FACTORIES ETC., WHERE PARTICLES SMALLER THAN 5 MICRONS MUST BE REMOVED, VACUUM FILTERS ARE COATED WITH STICKY LIQUIDS TO TRAP BITS. THEY ALSO CONTAIN "ACTIVATED" CARBON WHICH CAN ABSORB CHEMICALS.

ROBOT CLEANERS

"INTELLIGENT" VACUUM CLEANERS HAVE BEEN DEVELOPED WHICH DRIVE THEMSELVES AROUND. AFTER ONE HAS BEEN PUSHED ROUND A ROOM FOR THE FIRST TIME, ITS MEMORY STORES THE PATH & REPEATS IT, AVOIDING OBSTACLES WHERE NECESSARY.

HOW TO DETERMINE THE SEX OF AN EARWIG

MALE
CURVED SHORT PINCERS

FEMALE
LONG STRAIGHT PINCERS

BIN-TYPE CLEANERS

BIN-TYPE VACUUM CLEANERS HAVE THE ADVANTAGE OF PICKING UP WOOD SHAVINGS & OTHER LARGE BITS & PIECES. HOWEVER, THEY ARE MORE NOISY, MORE BULKY & NO BETTER AT SUCKING DUST THAN ORDINARY CLEANERS (ACCORDING TO "WHICH" MAGAZINE).

UPRIGHT CLEANER

UPRIGHT VACUUM CLEANERS ARE BETTER AT CLEANING CARPETS THAN OTHER TYPES BECAUSE THE ROTATING BRUSH DISLODGES THE DIRT. THEY ARE SEVERAL TIMES MORE POPULAR IN BRITAIN THAN IN ANY OTHER COUNTRY.

☆ VIOLINS ☆

ORIGINS

THE VIOLIN APPEARED IN ABOUT 1550, DERIVED FROM VARIOUS EARLIER INSTRUMENTS, NOTABLY THE REBEC & THE FIDDLE. SINCE THE LIFETIME OF STRADIVARI (1644–1737), VIOLIN DESIGN HAS CHANGED VERY LITTLE.

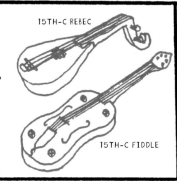

15TH-C REBEC

15TH-C FIDDLE

MECHANICS

(1) THE VIBRATION OF THE STRINGS ROCKS THE BRIDGE UP & DOWN, PIVOTING ON THE SOUNDPOST.

(2) THE SOUND BAR TRANSMITS THE MOVEMENT OF THE BRIDGE TO BOTH ENDS OF THE SOUNDBOARD.

(3) THE F-HOLES ALLOW THE BRIDGE TO ROCK MORE FREELY.

(4) THE VIBRATION OF THE SOUNDBOARD PUMPS AIR VIBRATIONS OUT OF THE F-HOLES, CREATING THE SOUND.

SOUND BAR · SOUND POST · BRIDGE · SOUND BOARD

STRADIVARIUS

WOOD IS COMPOSED OF TUBULAR CELLS NORMALLY CLOSED AT BOTH ENDS. RECENT ANALYSIS OF STRADIVARIUS VIOLINS UNDER A MICROSCOPE HAS REVEALED THAT THE ENDS OF THE CELLS ARE OPEN. THIS IS BELIEVED TO BE THE REASON FOR THE INSTRUMENTS' EXCEPTIONAL SOUND.

IT IS NOT KNOWN WHETHER THE CELL ENDS WERE OPENED BY SECRET PRE-TREATMENT & VARNISHING TECHNIQUES OR WHETHER THEY SIMPLY FELL OUT AS THE INSTRUMENTS AGED.

BOWING

WHEN HORSEHAIR IS RUBBED WITH ROSIN (RESIN EXUDED BY TREES), MINUTE RIGID SAW TEETH STAND UP. THESE PULL AT THE STRINGS & MAKE THEM VIBRATE.

BOW TENSION

CONVEX

CONCAVE

EARLY BOWS WERE CONVEX & COULD NOT BE HIGHLY TENSIONED. THE LOWER THE TENSION OF THE BOW, THE FASTER IT HAS TO BE PULLED ACROSS THE STRINGS TO MAKE A NOISE. THUS, LONG EVEN NOTES WERE ALMOST IMPOSSIBLE WITH EARLY BOWS.

SQUEAKS

THE VIOLIN IS DESIGNED NOT TO SQUEAK. HIGHER OVERTONES ARE DAMPED DOWN BY THE SLIM BRIDGE & THE POSITION OF THE SOUNDPOST (A SMALL DISTANCE FROM THE BRIDGE, NOT DIRECTLY UNDER IT).

STRINGS

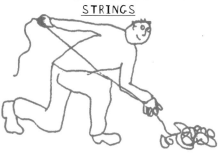

VIOLIN STRINGS WERE TRADITIONALLY MADE OF GUT. A YOUNG SHEEP'S GUT WAS PULLED INSIDE OUT, SCRAPED & CLEANED, THEN TWISTED, STRETCHED & LEFT TO DRY. THERE IS SOME EVIDENCE THAT RAMS' GUTS WERE STRONGER THAN EWES'.

VARNISH

THE VARNISH USED ON VIOLINS GREATLY AFFECTS THE SOUND. MODERN VARNISHES ARE CONSIDERED TO BE TOO RUBBERY, DAMPENING THE SOUND.

VOLCANOES ☆

STRUCTURES FORMED BY HOLES IN THE EARTH'S CRUST

THE OLYMPUS MONS

SO MUCH LAVA HAS BEEN EJECTED THAT THE WHOLE VOLCANO HAS LOST ITS SUPPORT & HAS SUBSIDED, LEAVING AN OUTSIDE RING 600KM ACROSS. THE REMAINS OF THE VENT ARE VISIBLE IN THE MIDDLE.

VOLCANOES & WEATHER

AFTER A LARGE ERUPTION THE WEATHER ALL OVER THE WORLD TENDS TO BECOME COOLER THAN USUAL & THEN MORE WINDY. THIS IS THOUGHT TO BE CAUSED BY THE DUST SENT INTO THE STRATOSPHERE WHERE IT SPREADS OVER THE WHOLE GLOBE IN A FEW MONTHS, REDUCING THE AMOUNT OF SOLAR ENERGY REACHING THE SURFACE. AFTER ABOUT A YEAR THE DUST TENDS TO BE SWEPT AWAY FROM THE EQUATOR & TO SETTLE ABOVE THE POLES. THIS INCREASES THE DIFFERENCE IN HEATING BETWEEN EQUATOR & POLES, WHICH LEADS TO MORE VIGOROUS ATMOSPHERIC CIRCULATION.

NOISY GODS

SOME ERUPTIONS IN HAWAII ARE PRECEDED BY A PECULIAR LOW-PITCHED HUMMING OR ROARING. ITS NATURE & ORIGIN ARE STILL A MYSTERY TO SCIENTISTS BUT THE HAWAIIANS SAY IT IS MADE BY PELE (THE GODDESS OF VOLCANOES).

NOISY LAVA

WHEN A VOLCANO EJECTS A FIERY FOUNTAIN OF RED-HOT LAVA, THE FRAGMENTS COOL VERY RAPIDLY WHILE IN THE AIR, FORMING A SORT OF GLASS. THIS RESULTS IN A NOISE MADE BY THE FALLING FRAGMENTS, SAID TO RESEMBLE THE CONTINUOUS SMASHING OF CROCKERY.

PUMICE ISLANDS

PUMICE IS A LIGHT FOAM OF SOLIDIFIED FROTHY LAVA DURING THE ERUPTION OF KRAKATOA IN 1883, SO MUCH PUMICE WAS FORMED THAT HUGE FLOATING ISLANDS WERE CREATED & FORMED A SERIOUS SHIPPING HAZARD FOR A YEAR.

ATLANTIS

AN ENORMOUS ERUPTION ON THE MEDITERRANEAN ISLAND OF THERA, IN ABOUT 1470 BC, WRECKED CRETE'S MINOAN CIVILIZATION & CAUSED THERA TO DISAPPEAR BENEATH THE SEA. THIS IS PROBABLY THE ORIGIN OF THE LEGEND OF ATLANTIS. IN 590 BC, THE GREEK TRAVELLER SOLON LEARNT FROM EGYPTIAN HISTORIANS HOW DISASTER HAD IN ANCIENT TIMES STRUCK THE PEOPLE "FAR FROM THE WEST", CUTTING OFF THEIR TRADE. THE IDEA OF A LOST ISLAND WAS BORN & PLATO, FROM ABOUT 380 BC, WOVE SOLON'S STORY INTO THE EPIC SAGA OF ATLANTIS.

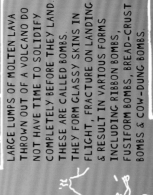

VOLCANIC BOMBS

LARGE LUMPS OF MOLTEN LAVA THROWN OUT OF A VOLCANO DO NOT HAVE TIME TO SOLIDIFY COMPLETELY BEFORE THEY LAND. THESE ARE CALLED BOMBS. THEY FORM GLASSY SKINS IN FLIGHT, FRACTURE ON LANDING & RESULT IN VARIOUS FORMS INCLUDING RIBBON BOMBS, FUSIFORM BOMBS, BREAD-CRUST BOMBS & COW-DUNG BOMBS.

UNFAIR DIVERSION?

LAVA FLOWS CAN BE DIVERTED BY USING WATER HOSES TO BUILD A WALL OF SOLIDIFIED LAVA. HOWEVER, IN SICILY THIS HAS BEEN THOUGHT TO BE UNFAIR TO ONE'S NEIGHBOURS.

HOW TO MAKE YOURSELF INTO A PIG

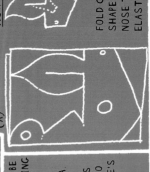
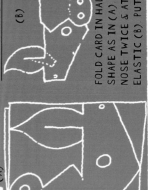
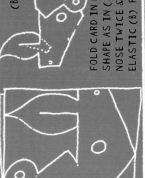
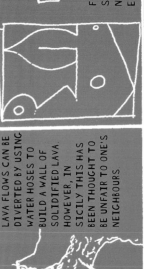

FOLD CARD IN HALF & CUT SHAPE AS IN (A). FOLD OVER NOSE TWICE & ATTACH ELASTIC (B). PUT MASK ON (C).

WATCHES
SMALL TIMEPIECES WORN BY PEOPLE

EGGS

THE EARLIEST PORTABLE CLOCKS (C.1550) ARE KNOWN AS NUREMBURG EGGS. THEY WERE DESIGNED TO BE HUNG FROM THE NECK, LIKE THE SCENT BOTTLES OF THE PERIOD.

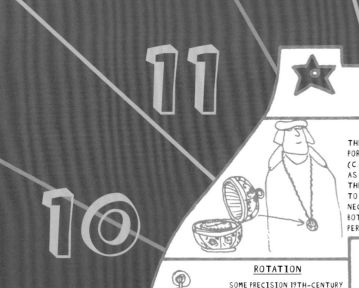

HAIRSPRINGS

MINUTES

THE HAIRSPRING IMPROVED THE ACCURACY OF WATCHES SO MUCH THAT A MINUTE HAND BECAME USABLE. AT FIRST TWIN HANDS WERE THOUGHT TO BE CONFUSING & MINUTES WERE SHOWN ON A SEPARATE DIAL.

THE HAIRSPRING WAS INTRODUCED BY THE DUTCH SCIENTIST HUYGENS IN 1675. THIS PERFORMS THE SAME FUNCTION AS GRAVITY ON A PENDULUM, GIVING THE WHEEL A "NATURAL" CONSTANT FREQUENCY.

ROTATION

SOME PRECISION 19TH-CENTURY WATCHES HAD MOVEMENTS WHICH SLOWLY ROTATED IN THE CASE. THIS EVENED OUT ANY IMBALANCE & FRICTION. AS WATCHES IMPROVED THIS WAS NO LONGER FOUND NECESSARY.

JEWELS

JEWELS WERE FIRST USED IN 1671 TO REDUCE THE FRICTION IN BEARINGS. THE METHOD OF DRILLING HOLES THROUGH THE JEWELS (DRILL BITS COATED IN POWDERED DIAMOND) REMAINED THE SECRET OF A FEW ENGLISH WATCHMAKERS FOR 100 YEARS.

WRIST WATCHES

WRIST WATCHES ARE SURPRISINGLY RECENT, FIRST GAINING POPULARITY WITH ARTILLERY OFFICERS IN WORLD WAR I.

GEARS

ENLARGED TO THE SAME SCALE, THE GEARS ON WATCHES ARE NO MORE ACCURATE THAN THE BIG WOODEN GEARS ON OLD WINDMILLS.

OIL

OIL IS THE BANE OF ALL MECHANICAL WATCHES. AFTER A TIME IT FORMS, EITHER A "GRINDING PASTE" WITH QUARTZ DUST FROM THE AIR OR A HARD COAT LIKE VARNISH.

QUARTZ

QUARTZ WATCHES HAVE A TINY PIECE OF QUARTZ WHICH VIBRATES (LIKE A TUNING FORK). IT IS MOUNTED IN A MINUTE VACUUM CHAMBER. THE ELECTRONICS KEEP THE QUARTZ VIBRATING & COUNT THE VIBRATIONS.

SPEAKING WATCHES

HITACHI ONCE PATENTED A FLAT TRANSPARENT LOUDSPEAKER WHICH COULD BE MOUNTED IN A LIQUID-CRYSTAL WATCH DISPLAY. THE LOUDSPEAKER ALSO ACTED AS A MICROPHONE, MAKING WRISTWATCH WALKIE-TALKIES A POSSIBILITY.

HOW TO MAKE A COMPASS FROM A WATCH

SOUTH

HOLD WATCH LEVEL & TURN IT SO HOUR HAND FACES SUN. HALF-WAY BETWEEN 12 O'CLOCK & HOUR HAND WILL THEN POINT ROUGHLY SOUTH.

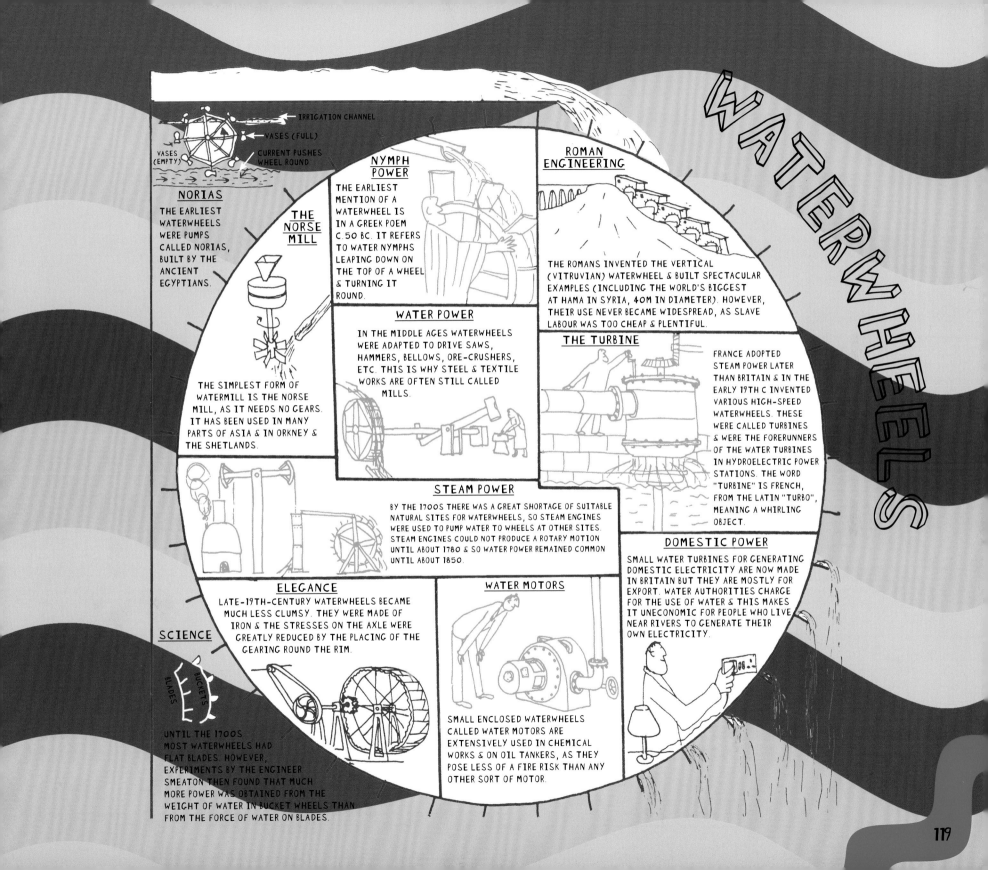

WATERWHEELS

NORIAS

THE EARLIEST WATERWHEELS WERE PUMPS CALLED NORIAS, BUILT BY THE ANCIENT EGYPTIANS.

- IRRIGATION CHANNEL
- VASES (FULL)
- VASES (EMPTY)
- CURRENT PUSHES WHEEL ROUND

THE NORSE MILL

THE SIMPLEST FORM OF WATERMILL IS THE NORSE MILL, AS IT NEEDS NO GEARS. IT HAS BEEN USED IN MANY PARTS OF ASIA & IN ORKNEY & THE SHETLANDS.

NYMPH POWER

THE EARLIEST MENTION OF A WATERWHEEL IS IN A GREEK POEM C 50 BC. IT REFERS TO WATER NYMPHS LEAPING DOWN ON THE TOP OF A WHEEL & TURNING IT ROUND.

WATER POWER

IN THE MIDDLE AGES WATERWHEELS WERE ADAPTED TO DRIVE SAWS, HAMMERS, BELLOWS, ORE-CRUSHERS, ETC. THIS IS WHY STEEL & TEXTILE WORKS ARE OFTEN STILL CALLED MILLS.

ROMAN ENGINEERING

THE ROMANS INVENTED THE VERTICAL (VITRUVIAN) WATERWHEEL & BUILT SPECTACULAR EXAMPLES (INCLUDING THE WORLD'S BIGGEST AT HAMA IN SYRIA, 40M IN DIAMETER). HOWEVER, THEIR USE NEVER BECAME WIDESPREAD, AS SLAVE LABOUR WAS TOO CHEAP & PLENTIFUL.

THE TURBINE

FRANCE ADOPTED STEAM POWER LATER THAN BRITAIN & IN THE EARLY 19TH C INVENTED VARIOUS HIGH-SPEED WATERWHEELS. THESE WERE CALLED TURBINES & WERE THE FORERUNNERS OF THE WATER TURBINES IN HYDROELECTRIC POWER STATIONS. THE WORD "TURBINE" IS FRENCH, FROM THE LATIN "TURBO", MEANING A WHIRLING OBJECT.

STEAM POWER

BY THE 1700S THERE WAS A GREAT SHORTAGE OF SUITABLE NATURAL SITES FOR WATERWHEELS, SO STEAM ENGINES WERE USED TO PUMP WATER TO WHEELS AT OTHER SITES. STEAM ENGINES COULD NOT PRODUCE A ROTARY MOTION UNTIL ABOUT 1780 & SO WATER POWER REMAINED COMMON UNTIL ABOUT 1850.

DOMESTIC POWER

SMALL WATER TURBINES FOR GENERATING DOMESTIC ELECTRICITY ARE NOW MADE IN BRITAIN BUT THEY ARE MOSTLY FOR EXPORT. WATER AUTHORITIES CHARGE FOR THE USE OF WATER & THIS MAKES IT UNECONOMIC FOR PEOPLE WHO LIVE NEAR RIVERS TO GENERATE THEIR OWN ELECTRICITY.

ELEGANCE

LATE-19TH-CENTURY WATERWHEELS BECAME MUCH LESS CLUMSY. THEY WERE MADE OF IRON & THE STRESSES ON THE AXLE WERE GREATLY REDUCED BY THE PLACING OF THE GEARING ROUND THE RIM.

WATER MOTORS

SMALL ENCLOSED WATERWHEELS CALLED WATER MOTORS ARE EXTENSIVELY USED IN CHEMICAL WORKS & ON OIL TANKERS, AS THEY POSE LESS OF A FIRE RISK THAN ANY OTHER SORT OF MOTOR.

SCIENCE

- BUCKETS
- BLADES

UNTIL THE 1700S MOST WATERWHEELS HAD FLAT BLADES. HOWEVER, EXPERIMENTS BY THE ENGINEER SMEATON THEN FOUND THAT MUCH MORE POWER WAS OBTAINED FROM THE WEIGHT OF WATER IN BUCKET WHEELS THAN FROM THE FORCE OF WATER ON BLADES.

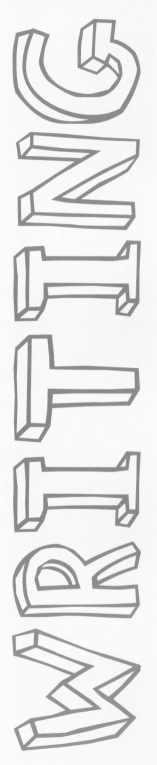

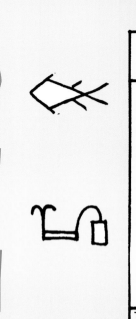

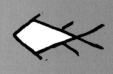

☆ WRITING ☆
SYSTEMS OF PERPETUATING VOCAL COMMUNICATION

ALPHA & BETA

HOW ALPHABETS STARTED
THE FIRST "WRITING" WAS BASED ON PICTURES OF OBJECTS (PICTOGRAMS).

(EGYPTIAN)   (MESOPOTAMIAN)   (CHINESE)

IDEAS & ACTIONS WERE SOMETIMES REPRESENTED BY COMBINATIONS OF OBJECTS (IDEOGRAMS).

(EGYPTIAN)   (CHINESE)   (EGYPTIAN)
EYE + TEARS   RECTANGLE (MOUTH)   SPLIT REED +
= WEEP   + VAPOUR = SPEECH   VIAL = WRITING

THE SUMERIANS DEVELOPED A SYSTEM OF USING THE SAME OBJECT FOR ALL THE WORDS THAT SOUNDED ROUGHLY THE SAME (HIEROGLYPHICS). THIS WAS LATER SIMPLIFIED BY THE PHOENICIANS WHO USED ONE OBJECT TO REPRESENT EACH HARD SOUND (AN ALPHABET LACKING VOWELS).

THE LETTER "A" COMES FROM THE PHOENICIAN PICTOGRAM FOR ALEPH, ⟍, AN OX.

THE GREEKS ADOPTED THE SYMBOL, TURNED ON ITS SIDE, TO SIGNIFY THE SOUND OF "A", & FORGOT IT WAS A PICTURE OF AN OX'S HEAD. "B" HAS ALSO BEEN TURNED ON ITS SIDE. IT CAME FROM BETH, ⟁, THE PHOENICIAN PICTOGRAM FOR A HOUSE.

THE 65 VARIETIES

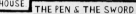

THERE ARE NOW 65 ALPHABETS IN USE. ROTOKAS IS THE SHORTEST (11 LETTERS) & CAMBODIAN IS THE LONGEST (74 LETTERS).

THE ROMANS WROTE ON WAXED PLATES USING METAL STYLUS PENS. THESE HAD THE ADVANTAGE OF ALSO SERVING AS WEAPONS. SOME BELIEVE THE CONSPIRATORS KILLED JULIUS CAESAR WITH THEIR PENS.

THE PEN & THE SWORD

THE FIRST PAPER

THE DEVELOPMENT OF PAPER IS SAID TO OWE MUCH TO CAI LUN IN AD 100. HE ATTEMPTED TO IMITATE A MATERIAL USED BY CERTAIN WASPS TO CONSTRUCT THEIR HIVES. HE BOILED, BEAT & WASHED PIECES OF BARK, LINEN RAGS & OLD FISHING NETS & PRODUCED A SOFT TOUGH WHITE SHEET, GREATLY SUPERIOR TO THE SQUASHED REEDS (PAPYRUS) USED BY THE EGYPTIANS.

THE LARGEST LETTERS IN THE WORLD ARE 180M HIGH ON A HILLSIDE SIGN IN NULLARBOR, WESTERN AUSTRALIA.

THE SMALLEST WRITING TO DATE HAS BEEN ACHIEVED AT OSAKA UNIVERSITY, WHERE AN ATOMIC PEN HAS MADE LETTERS 40,000 TIMES NARROWER THAN A HUMAN HAIR.

HOW TO MAKE A TEDDY BEAR VANISH

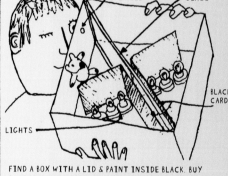

EYE HOLE   GLASS

BLACK CARD

LIGHTS

FIND A BOX WITH A LID & PAINT INSIDE BLACK. BUY GLASS TO FIT ACROSS DIAGONAL & POLISH IT. ALSO BUY 6 BULBS (6V), SOCKETS & BATTERIES. STICK EVERYTHING INSIDE BOX. PUNCH SMALL EYE HOLE; CONNECT BULBS & PUT ON LID (OMITTED IN DRAWING).

THE INVENTION OF PRINTING WITH MOVABLE TYPE WAS FIRST MADE BY PI CHENG IN AD 1040 USING PICTOGRAMS CARVED INTO A BLOCK OF CLAY. UNFORTUNATELY THE CHINESE WRITTEN LANGUAGE HAD 40,000 CHARACTERS & THE METHOD DID NOT PROVE POPULAR. THIS CAUSED A LACK OF CHEAPLY ACCESSIBLE KNOWLEDGE WHICH IS THOUGHT TO BE PARTLY RESPONSIBLE FOR CHINA'S LATENESS IN DEVELOPING OF A TECHNOLOGICAL SOCIETY.

CHINESE PRINTING

BEAR VISIBLE

BEAR INVISIBLE

X-RAYS

WAVES CAPABLE OF PENETRATING MATTER OPAQUE TO LIGHT

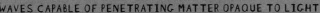

MYSTERIOUS RAYS

RONTGEN DISCOVERED X-RAYS IN 1895. WHILE EXPERIMENTING WITH A GAS DISCHARGE TUBE, HE NOTICED THAT SOME CRYSTALS NEAR THE TUBE STARTED TO GLOW. HE COATED A GLASS PLATE WITH THE CRYSTALS, & THIS PLATE GLOWED ALL OVER BUT ANY DENSE SOLID OBJECT BETWEEN TUBE & PLATE CAST A SHADOW ON THE PLATE.

IF TWO WIRES ARE SEALED INTO A GLASS TUBE IN A VACUUM & A SUFFICIENTLY HIGH VOLTAGE IS APPLIED BETWEEN THEM, THE TUBE WILL BEGIN TO GLOW. THIS WAS DISCOVERED IN ABOUT 1850 & WAS BELIEVED TO BE CAUSED BY SOMETHING RADIATING FROM THE NEGATIVE WIRE OR CATHODE. MANY SCIENTISTS STUDIED THESE "CATHODE RAYS" & WHILE CERTAIN INEXPLICABLE EFFECTS WERE OBSERVED, IT WAS NOT TILL 1894 THAT RONTGEN PUT FORWARD THE IDEA THAT THE CATHODE WAS EMITTING A SECOND MYSTERIOUS RAY - THE X-RAY.

DANGEROUS RAYS

NO ONE APPRECIATED THE DANGERS OF X-RAYS AT FIRST. ONE OF THE FIRST MEDICAL CASES WAS A PATIENT WITH A BULLET LODGED IN HIS HEAD. AFTER AN X-RAY THE BULLET WAS LOCATED, BUT ALSO HIS HAIR ALL FELL OUT. FORTUNATELY THE EARLY X-RAY SOURCES WERE NOT VERY STRONG & THERE WERE FEW CASES OF SERIOUS IRRADIATION.

EXTRAVAGANT CLAIMS

RÖNTGEN'S FIRST PAPER ON X-RAYS INCLUDED A PHOTOGRAPH OF HIS HAND, ILLUMINATED THROUGH X-RAYS, CLEARLY REVEALING ITS BONES. THIS CAUGHT THE PUBLIC IMAGINATION & THE NEWSPAPERS REPORTED THE DISCOVERY WITH ZEST. WILD CLAIMS WERE MADE: AN OHIO FARMER WAS REPORTED TO HAVE TURNED METAL TO GOLD, ANIMAL LOVERS BELIEVED THAT IT WOULD MAKE VIVISECTION OBSOLETE, & SOME PEOPLE THOUGHT IT WOULD BOOST THE CAUSE OF TEMPERANCE (BY SHOWING DRUNKARDS WHAT THEY WERE DOING TO THEIR SYSTEM). A NEW YORK PAPER ANNOUNCED THAT THE COLLEGE OF PHYSICIANS WERE USING X-RAYS "TO REFLECT ANATOMICAL DRAWINGS DIRECTLY INTO THE BRAINS OF THEIR STUDENTS".

X-RAYS & POTATOES

X-RAYS PENETRATE THROUGH POTATOES MORE EASILY THAN THROUGH STONES OR EARTH. ONE TYPE OF HARVESTER PASSES THE MATERIAL IT HAS PICKED UP THROUGH A BEAM OF X-RAYS & A MECHANISM AUTOMATICALLY SEPARATES OUT THE POTATOES.

X-RAY LASERS

AN X-RAY LASER IS BEING DEVELOPED BY US RESEARCHERS. IT IS HOPED THAT IT WILL PROVIDE SUFFICIENTLY HIGH ENERGIES TO MAKE NUCLEAR FUSION PRACTICAL. THE X-RAY LASER'S BEAM DOES NOT DEVIATE BY MORE THAN ABOUT 5 MICROMETRES PER METRE – AN AMAZING DEGREE OF ACCURACY.

X-RAY CRAWLERS

THE GAS BOARD USES X-RAYS TO INSPECT THE WELDING ON ITS PIPELINES. THE WELDER FIXES A STRIP OF X-RAY-SENSITIVE PAPER ROUND EACH WELD WITH A SMALL RADIOACTIVE ISOTOPE. A BATTERY-POWERED X-RAY CRAWLER THEN MOVES SLOWLY ALONG THE INSIDE OF THE PIPE & RELEASES A BURST OF X-RAYS EACH TIME IT DETECTS AN ISOTOPE.

HOW TO MAKE A COIN CLICK MYSTERIOUSLY

PUT COIN OVER TOP OF COLD, EMPTY, SOFT-DRINK BOTTLE. DIP A FINGER IN WATER & LET ONE OR TWO DROPS FALL ROUND THE EDGE OF THE COIN TO SEAL THE OPENING. PLACE BOTH HANDS ROUND THE BOTTLE & HOLD FIRMLY FOR ABOUT 15 SECONDS. THE COIN WILL START TO CLICK UP & DOWN MYSTERIOUSLY. IT WILL CONTINUE TO CLICK EVEN WHEN YOU REMOVE YOUR HANDS.

YEAST

SINGLE-CELL FUNGI CAPABLE OF FERMENTING SUGARS

REPRODUCTION

YEASTS HAVE SEXES BUT, UNLIKE ANIMALS, DO NOT NEED TO MATE FOR REPRODUCTION. INSTEAD DAUGHTER CELLS GROW OUT OF AN ADULT & BREAK FREE – A PROCESS CALLED BUDDING.

SEX

WHEN YEAST CELLS MATE, THEY FUSE TO FORM A SINGLE CELL. THIS REPRODUCES BY BUDDING – JUST LIKE UNMATED CELLS – BUT CAN ALSO PRODUCE SPORES, LIKE FUNGI, FROM WHICH NEW YEASTS CAN GROW.

HUMAN YEAST

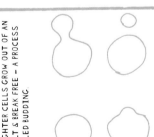

MOST PEOPLE HAVE A STRAIN OF YEAST CALLED MALASSEZIA FURFUR ON THE HAIR & FATTY PARTS OF THE SKIN, LIKE THE SCALP & THE NOSE. THE POPULATION CAN REACH 500,000 PER SQ CM. DANDRUFF IS BELIEVED TO BE CAUSED BY AN OVERGROWTH OF YEAST.

BREAD

YEAST IS ADDED TO FLOUR TO MAKE BREAD BECAUSE IT GIVES OFF CARBON-DIOXIDE GAS AS IT FERMENTS. THE GAS MAKES THE BREAD RISE.

BEER

YEASTS USED TO MAKE BEER ARE SELECTED FOR THEIR FLAVOUR & TOLERANCE OF ALCOHOL (ALL YEAST IS KILLED OFF ABOVE ABOUT 12% ALCOHOL).

BEETLE YEAST

THE WOOD-EATING BEETLE SITODREPA PANICEA DEPENDS FOR ITS SURVIVAL ON A YEAST WHICH LIVES IN ITS GUT. THE YEAST FEEDS ON THE BEETLES' FOOD (WOOD) & CONVERTS IT TO 11 PROTEINS & 8 VITAMINS.

GENETICALLY ENGINEERED

YEASTS ARE COMMONLY USED FOR GENETIC ENGINEERING BECAUSE THEIR STRUCTURE IS RELATIVELY SIMPLE. THE DRUG INTERFERON HAS RECENTLY BEEN ENGINEERED WITH A YEAST.

WINE

GRAPES ARE FERMENTED INTO WINE WITH WILD YEASTS – EITHER FROM THE GRAPE SKINS OR FROM THE WINE VATS.

HOME-MADE WINE

HOME-MADE WINES SOMETIMES HAVE A KNOCKOUT EFFECT BECAUSE SOME WILD YEASTS GENERATE MILDLY TOXIC BY-PRODUCTS.

CHAMPAGNE

CHAMPAGNE STAYS FIZZY MUCH LONGER THAN CARBONATED SOFT DRINKS. THE BUBBLES IN CHAMPAGNE COME FROM THE FERMENTATION OF A "CHAMPAGNE YEAST", PLACED IN EACH BOTTLE & REMOVED WHILE THE DRINK MATURES.

SHERRY

SHERRY IS MADE FROM WINE PASSED SLOWLY THROUGH A SERIES OF CASKS (OVER SEVERAL YEARS). EACH CASK DEVELOPS ITS OWN SCUM OF YEASTS WHICH HELP TO ADD FLAVOUR. FINALLY, THE SHERRY IS REINFORCED WITH BRANDY.

FUEL

THE CANADIAN PAPER INDUSTRY IS USING GENETIC ENGINEERING TO DEVELOP A YEAST WHICH WILL CONVERT CELLULOSE TO SUGARS. THE AIM IS TO PRODUCE ALCOHOL FUEL (FERMENTED FROM THE SUGARS) USING THE MASSIVE AMOUNTS OF WOOD PULP WHICH GO TO WASTE.

FOOD

YEASTS DEVELOPED BY BP TO REMOVE WAXES FROM CRUDE OIL HAVE LED TO YEASTS THAT CAN CONVERT OIL TO EDIBLE PROTEINS. THEY ARE NOW USED AS ANIMAL FEED BUT NOT YET FOR HUMANS.

HOW TO SHOW THE ACTIVITY OF YEAST

MIX SOME DRIED BAKER'S YEAST WITH A SUGAR SOLUTION (SEE INSTRUCTIONS ON YEAST PACKET). POUR YEAST INTO BOTTLE & PUT BALLOON OVER NECK. SEE HOW MUCH THE BALLOON INFLATES.

☆ ZINC ☆

DISCOVERY

ZINC WAS NOT DISCOVERED UNTIL COMPARATIVELY RECENTLY BECAUSE OF ITS LOW BOILING POINT (906°C). WHEN ORES OF COPPER, LEAD, TIN & IRON ARE HEATED IN A WOOD FIRE, THEY REACT WITH THE CARBON AND LEAVE A PUDDLE OF PURE METAL IN THE ASHES.

ZINC ORES REACT WITH CARBON IN THE SAME WAY, BUT IN A HOT FIRE THE METAL WOULD SIMPLY BOIL AWAY, LEAVING NO TRACE.

COPPER & ZINC

BRASS, AN ALLOY MAINLY OF COPPER & ZINC, WAS KNOWN ABOUT BEFORE PURE ZINC. IT WAS MADE BY COPPER & ZINC ORES BEING HEATED TOGETHER. ZINC ORE WAS CALLED "COUNTERFEIT" BECAUSE IT TRANSFORMS COPPER TO A GOLDEN METAL.

INDIAN ZINC

METALLIC ZINC WAS FIRST SMELTED IN INDIA IN THE 14TH CENTURY. TRAVELLERS BROUGHT BACK SAMPLES TO EUROPE WHERE IT WAS REGARDED AS A USELESS CURIOSITY.

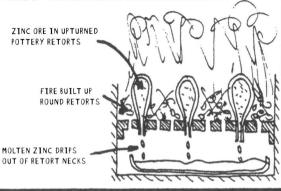

ZINC ORE IN UPTURNED POTTERY RETORTS

FIRE BUILT UP ROUND RETORTS

MOLTEN ZINC DRIPS OUT OF RETORT NECKS

BRISTOL ZINC

ZINC WAS NOT PRODUCED IN EUROPE UNTIL THE 18TH CENTURY (FIRST PRODUCED IN BRISTOL BY WILLIAM CHAMPION).

MODERN ZINC

TODAY MOST ZINC IS MADE BY TREATMENT OF THE ORE WITH SULPHURIC ACID TO MAKE ZINC SULPHATE. THIS IS PURIFIED & PUT IN A TANK WITH ALUMINIUM & LEAD ELECTRODES. WHEN ELECTRICITY IS PASSED THROUGH THE TANK, ZINC ACCUMULATES ON THE ALUMINIUM.

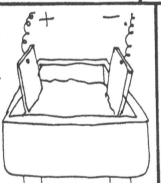

GALVANIZING

COATING STEEL IN ZINC (GALVANIZING) CAUSES AIR & WATER TO ATTACK THE ZINC INSTEAD OF THE STEEL. THE ZINC NEED NOT COMPLETELY COVER THE STEEL. SHIPS' HULLS & OIL-RIG LEGS SIMPLY HAVE INGOTS OF ZINC BOLTED ON TO THEM.

EATING ZINC

BRUNEL UNIVERSITY BIOCHEMISTRY DEPT HAS A THEORY THAT SUGGESTS WE SHOULD BE EATING MORE ZINC. MANY DISEASES INCLUDING RHEUMATISM, MULTIPLE SCLEROSIS & CANCER COULD BE CAUSED BY AN EXCESS OF IRON. EATING MORE ZINC CAN REDUCE OUR BODIES' IRON REQUIREMENT.

DIE CASTING

ZINC IS USED FOR DIE CASTING (CASTING IN STEEL DIES) PARTLY BECAUSE OF ITS LOW MELTING POINT. HIGHER TEMPERATURES REDUCE THE ACCURACY & LIFE OF THE DIES. DIE-CASTING ZINC HAS TO BE 99.99% PURE OR CASTINGS GET BRITTLE WITH AGE. HOWEVER, PURE MOLTEN ZINC DISSOLVES STEEL, SO 4% ALUMINIUM IS ADDED TO PREVENT THIS.

Index of Experiments

B

Baffle with dominoes, 54
Bleach flowers, 64
Break a finger in two without damaging it, 8

C

Calculate a friend's age & the change in
    their pocket, 34
Collect oxygen from ivy, 95
Cut a card without cutting a ribbon round it,
    15

D

Determine the sex of an earwig, 114
Do a coin trick, 10
Do a simple card trick, 80

E

Escape from a bee when cycling, 16
Extinguish a candle with a wire, 106

F

Feel a dead hand, 66
Find the age of a tube carriage, 110
Find the height of a church spire, 76
Find your walking speed, 44
Find water in a desert, 26
Float a boater, 79

G

Get an enemy's feet wet, 12

H

Hypnotize a trout, 52

I

Improve your ears with two umbrellas, 14

K

Keep cut flowers fresh, 9

L

Levitate, 79
Levitate yourself, 22
Look for lice, 68

M

Magic an orange into an apple, 36
Make your arms rise, 6
Make a candle last longer, 78
Make a cat spark, 67
Make clear ice cubes, 86
Make a coin click mysteriously, 122
Make a compass from a watch, 118
Make custard pies, 74
Make a double bass, 58
Make an E.T. finger, 23
Make a matchbox land upright, 102
Make a microscope, 29
Make a neon light up, 40
Make newspaper logs, 84
Make a paper ladder, 233
Make a pencil change colour, 21
Make a ping-pong ball float in the middle of a
    glass of water, 84
Make a quill pen, 88
Make a race track for marbles, 94
Make Rice Krispies jump, 90
Make a set of chimes, 73
Make a screwdriver magnetic, 70
Make the sound of rain, 107
Make a spaceship powered by a balloon, 42

Make a spinning-card puzzle, 60
Make a spring, 103
Make the sound of applause, 95
Make structures from peas & toothpicks, 38
Make a teddy bear vanish, 120
Make yourself into a bird, 104
Make yourself into a clown, 62
Make yourself into a pig, 116
Mind-read, 75

P

Pull a string right through your neck, 30

R

Remove scratches from plastic sunglasses, 51
Re-thread a damaged bolt, 71

S

Separate people tied together, 96
Show the activity of yeast, 124
Solve an equestrian puzzle, 45
Stop your nose going red, 101

T

Tell if you are left-eyed, 65
Test if a number divides by 13, 59
Test your visual memory, 72
Thread beads at high speed, 99
Thread a needle 12 times, 87
Turn yourself into a flexible giant, 49

W

Write with a calculator, 7

Subject Index

A
Anaesthetics, 6
Animal eyes, 7
Armour, 8
Aspirin, 9
Athletics, 10

B
Beasts, 12
Beds, 13
Body, 14
Bone, 15
Bumble-bees, 16

C
Cannibalism, 18
Carbon dating, 19
Cats, 20
Cellulose, 21
Chocolate, 22
Clock, 23
Cloud, 23
Compass, 24
Crane, 25
Crocodile, 26

D
Diving, 28
Dolphins, 29
Dragons, 30

E
Elephants, 32
Escalators, 33
Evolution, 34

F
Faces, 36
Feet, 37
Fire engines, 38
Flags, 39
Furniture, 40

G
Gears, 42
Giant pandas, 43
Goats, 44
Gorillas, 45
Guitars, 46

H
Hearts, 48
Herons, 49
Hibernation, 50
Human eyes, 51
Hypnosis, 52

I
Ice, 54
Inflatable boats, 55
Inventions, 56

J
Jellyfish, 58
Jet engines, 59
Jungles, 60

K
Kangaroos, 62

L
Leaves, 64
Left-handedness, 65
Lenses, 66
Libraries, 67
Lice, 68

M
Magnetism, 70
Malaria, 71
Memory, 72
Mosques, 73
Movies, 74
Mummies, 75
Music, 76

N
Neon, 78
Nerves, 79
Nickel, 79
Nylon, 80

O
Obesity, 82
Olympics, 83
Oranges, 84
Orchids, 84

P
Parasites, 86
Penicillin, 87
Pens, 88
Perpetual motion, 89
PVC, 90

Q
Quartz, 92

R
Radar, 94
Railways, 95
Rain, 95
Rubber, 96

S
Satellites, 98
Snow, 99
Soap, 100
Speech, 101
Spies, 102
Springs, 103
Swords, 104

T
Thermometers, 106
Tomatoes, 107
Twins, 108

U
Underground trains, 110
Underwear, 111
Utopias, 112

V
Vacuum cleaners, 114
Violins, 115
Volcanoes, 116

W
Watches, 118
Waterwheels, 119
Writing, 120

X
X-rays, 122

Y
Yeast, 124

Z
Zinc, 126